Diane J. Goodman

Promoting
Diversity and
Social Justice

Educating

People From

Privileged

Groups

WINTER ROUNDTABLE SERIES

Sage Publications, Inc.
International Educational and Professional Publisher
Thousand Oaks ▪ London ▪ New Delhi

For information:

>Sage Publications, Inc.
>2455 Teller Road
>Thousand Oaks, California 91320
>E-mail: order@sagepub.com

>Sage Publications Ltd.
>6 Bonhill Street
>London EC2A 4PU
>United Kingdom

>Sage Publications India Pvt. Ltd.
>M-32 Market
>Greater Kailash I
>New Delhi 110 048 India

Printed in the United States of America

Library of Congress Cataloging-in-Publication Data

Goodman, Diane J.
 Promoting diversity and social justice: Educating people from privileged groups / by Diane J. Goodman.
  p. cm. — (Winter roundtable series; 2)
 Includes bibliographical references and index.
  ISBN 0-7619-1079-4 (cloth: alk. paper)
  ISBN 0-7619-1080-8 (pbk.: alk. paper)
  1. Social justice. 2. Multiculturalism. 3. Upper class—Attitudes. 4. Social conflict. 5. Conflict management. 6. Social psychology. I. Title. II. Series.
 HM671 .G66 2000
 303.3'72—dc21   00-009061

01 02 03 10 9 8 7 6 5 4 3 2 1

Acquiring Editor: Nancy S. Hale
Editorial Assistant: Heidi Van Middlesworth
Production Editor: Diana E. Axelsen
Editorial Assistant: Victoria Cheng
Typesetter/Designer: Barbara Burkholder
Indexer: Mary Mortensen
Cover Designer: Michelle Lee

Contents

Acknowledgments

This book grows out of years of learning and experience. There are many, many people from whose work I have benefited; some of them are referenced throughout the book. I want to thank the students and workshop participants who provided feedback as I presented some of this material. They challenged and stimulated my thinking and motivated me to complete the book.

A big thank you to the people who read parts of the manuscript for their support and feedback. They include Lee Bell, Robert Carter, Nan Frane, Pat Griffin, Ricki Mazella, Tema Okun, Nancy Schniedewind, Glen Weinbaum, and Charmaine Wijeyesinghe. I also appreciate Robert Carter's initial encouragement and suggestion that I write a book when all I was envisioning was a chapter.

I am particularly indebted and grateful to Rob Koegel, who read the whole manuscript (at least once). It was a gift to feel that I could send first drafts and know that I would get thoughtful, honest, insightful, and detailed feedback. He consistently did so with such open-hearted generosity. There is no doubt that this book is better written because of him. And, I thank Rob for helping me learn how to "sing."

Finally, to Glen, whose love and support gave me the privilege of having time to focus on writing and helped make completing this book possible.

To Halle and her generation, so that they might grow up in a more caring and just world.

1

Introduction

In graduate school, my dissertation advisor told me, "People usually do research on the issues they're trying to work out in their own lives." That was true about me then, and it still is now.

Since the early 1980s, I have been doing what feels like my life's work: educating about diversity and social justice. I have done so in a range of contexts—universities, nonprofit agencies, schools, women's organizations, and community groups; in different roles—as a professor, trainer, consultant, facilitator, and affirmative action officer; and with various groups of people—students (of all ages), teachers, counselors, administrators, managers, staff members, board members, police, local citizens, and activists.

This has been an ongoing learning experience, both personally and professionally. Issues of oppression and multiculturalism have complex histories and continually evolve. New concerns and manifestations of inequality emerge as social, political, and economic changes occur in our country and throughout the world. Demographics shift, and social dynamics become increasingly complex. Personally, I am continually faced with trying to stay abreast of current issues, working on raising my own consciousness, and exploring the significance of my own social identities. Professionally, as the social climate changes, so does the way we need to educate for social justice. People's attitudes about different groups shift, as do their ways of explaining inequalities. Different concerns become more prominent and evoke new sets of feelings and reactions. One of the most challenging aspects of social justice education is working with people from privileged or dominant groups—those who are in the more powerful position in a particular type of oppression. At times, I have been impressed and humbled by their degree of openness, courage, and risk taking. At other times, I have been frustrated, angered, and stymied by their unwillingness to consider new information, rethink assumptions, or express concern for others. It is in the latter situations that I, and many of my colleagues, have struggled the most.

It is critical that we are able to engage people from privileged groups in social justice issues. From a simple educational perspective, most educators will have a mix of people in their classes or groups, including those from dominant groups. For sessions to run smoothly and for learning to be maximized, ideally, all participants should be productively involved. From a social change perspective, people from privileged groups perpetuate oppression through individual acts, as well as through institutional and cultural practices. They have access to resources, information, and power that can either block or help facilitate change. People from privileged groups who are allies can influence decision making, allocate funds, share needed skills and knowledge, and be role models for other dominant group members to support equity. It also helps to have people from privileged groups as part of the change effort. Even though more people from oppressed groups are likely to push for greater social justice, as people from privileged groups join in the struggle, it increases the critical mass needed to effect change. Furthermore, if we care about liberation, we need to care about liberating all people. As I'll discuss further, oppression diminishes all human beings.

My experiences, both positive and negative, and my commitment to justice led me to write this book. In part, I was involved in a quest to more effectively understand and work with people from dominant groups on social justice issues. I wanted to be a better educator and change agent. I also wanted to share with others what I have learned and found useful. As I have presented some of this material at conferences, workshops, and classes, I have found people hungry for ways to think about and address diversity issues, especially with people from privileged groups. My choice to focus on working with people from dominant groups in no way implies that this is more important than working with people from oppressed groups. It is a response to my own experiences and to what I perceived as a need in the field.

I am extremely fortunate to have had graduate training in a program focused on diversity and social justice training at the University of Massachusetts in Amherst. The courses on oppression theory, workshop design, psychological education, group dynamics, and developmental theories and the workshops on racism, sexism, heterosexism, classism, ableism, and anti-Semitism were invaluable. And although they were not my only source of education, I am indebted to the faculty and students there who provided me with such rich learning opportunities (and who continue to be valued colleagues).

Many people educating about social justice do so with very little training in how to do this type of education. Often, people are well versed in content areas but less trained or skilled in issues of pedagogy or process. Generally, people rely on their natural talent, intuition, and trial and error. These are indispensable. Yet I find I am most effective when I can also draw on other theories and frameworks. These allow me to better make sense of what is occurring, and they inform my responses. This background helps me plan my approaches and anticipate reactions.

In this book, I share some of the theories, perspectives, and strategies I have found most useful when working with adults from privileged groups on diversity and social justice issues. It is written for practitioners who already have a commitment to these issues. I am not trying to convince readers of the existence of oppression or of the need to value differences and promote equity. My hope is that these theoretical tools will allow educators to be more reflective and intentional in their work, helping them to consider who they're working with, what they're doing, why they're doing it, and how to educate more effectively. The fields of education and psychology are heavily drawn upon. Yet in doing so, I attempt to continually consider the individual in social context, to embed a psychological analysis within a structural analysis. I want to recognize the interplay between the external and the internal, how the sociopolitical context affects individual attitudes and behaviors and, thus, our classroom dynamics.

Some general principles and practices are reviewed that are helpful in most educational situations, but they are discussed in relation to working with people from dominant groups. This is not a how-to book, providing detailed activities and exercises; nor is it a cookbook that promises that if you follow this simple recipe, you'll have a perfect educational experience. I offer educational and psychological perspectives to inform one's practice and increase one's options in addressing situations. I'll suggest approaches, but I will not supply easy answers. There are none. I try not to be prescriptive, but in an effort to be concrete, examples and specific suggestions are offered. I encourage readers to take and adapt what is useful. This is not everything you need to know to teach about diversity and social justice. Readers are referred to the appendix for some additional resources, especially for ideas for particular activities. An explanation of the title will further clarify the focus of the book.

About the Title

Promoting Diversity and Social Justice

The term *diversity* has become a buzzword with a variety of connotations and synonyms. Schools are addressing "multiculturalism," businesses are learning to "value diversity," and our society is grappling with "cultural pluralism." These efforts usually promote the understanding, acceptance, and appreciation of cultural differences. For people to live together in a caring and just world, this is important work. Consciousness-raising can increase an awareness of self and others. It allows people to challenge stereotypes, overcome prejudices, and develop relationships with different kinds of people. It can help individuals enlarge their narrow worldview and recognize that there are other legitimate ways of thinking, being, and doing. At times, diversity training allows people to work and live together more productively and peacefully.

Unfortunately, most diversity work stops here. It tends to focus on individuals and interpersonal dynamics. I add the words *social justice* to indicate that I advocate going farther. Social justice also involves addressing issues of equity, power relations, and institutionalized oppression. It seeks to establish a more equitable distribution of power and resources so that all people can live with dignity, self-determination, and physical and psychological safety. It creates opportunities for people to reach their full potential within a mutually responsible, interdependent society. Working toward social justice requires changing unjust institutional structures, policies, and practices and challenging the dominant ideology. Social justice educators seek to create the conditions required for a true democracy, one that includes the full and equal participation of all groups in the society.

Educating

I use the term *educating* in the broadest sense. I do not limit education to classrooms or to teacher-student relationships. Whenever we help people learn, think, and grow, we are involved in education. Educating involves increasing knowledge, developing skills, raising consciousness, and enhancing critical thinking. Social justice education takes many forms in many contexts, from lectures in formal classroom settings to conversations over the kitchen table to policy presentations in conference rooms.

This book is intended for anyone who educates others about diversity and equity. Although the primary focus is on professors, teachers, and trainers in classrooms and workshops, others who are involved in social change—such as counselors, organizers, student affairs personnel, community educators, advocates, and group facilitators—may find this information relevant. The principles and perspectives discussed can be applied to a range of situations and audiences. Therefore, I will use a variety of terms to reflect different contexts and relationships: *teacher, facilitator, educator, trainer,* as well as *student* and *participant.* I hope the language (i.e., teacher and student) will not interfere with translating and applying the concepts and strategies to other situations.

The people we encounter in our classes, workshops, and meetings are often starting from different places in the educational process. They come with varying knowledge, attitudes, experiences, predispositions, prejudices, and expectations about diversity and social justice issues. On one end of this continuum may be people who are highly resistant to exploring multicultural issues. They may be very defensive and closed-minded. Others may be cautiously open to new information and perspectives. They are guarded but willing to consider some alternative views. Some may be eager to explore these issues and to find ways to make change. They embrace the opportunity to grapple with diversity issues and to expand their awareness. Occasionally, on the other end of the continuum, we get people who are already committed to social justice and are anxious to further their growth and take positive action. Ultimately, I would like people from privileged groups to be committed to being allies and to be able to act in solidarity with people from oppressed groups (and others from privileged groups) to promote equity. Social justice education is about facilitating movement along this continuum.

As I will discuss at length, when people are resistant, they are unwilling to learn. Our first step is to reduce resistance and create an openness to the educational process. Once people are in a more neutral state, we can consider how to challenge apathy and spark interest. As concern and commitment grow, we need to nurture this development and foster ways to act on their convictions. In this book, I focus on a few of the places on this continuum between resistance and alliance. The first is on resistance—how to understand the reasons for resistance and find ways to prevent and address it. The second is on motivating support for social justice—exploring why people from privileged groups support equity and developing ways to appeal to and encourage this in our educational work.

People From Privileged Groups

The term *people from privileged groups* implies that there are people from nonprivileged groups. Systems of oppression are characterized by dominant-subordinate relations. There are unequal power relationships that allow one group to benefit at the expense of another group. The various ways people name the two sides of this dynamic reflect these qualities: *oppressor* and *oppressed*, *advantaged* and *disadvantaged*, *dominant* and *subordinate*, *agent* and *target*, *privileged* and *marginalized*, *dominator* and *dominated*, *majority* and *minority*. Although I am not fully comfortable with any of the existing language, I will use a variety of terms to refer to groups in the more and less powerful roles. I chose the term *privileged group* for the title because it is the term that people seem most familiar with. Yet I also use the term *dominant group* because it reflects the fact that this group not only gets privileges and has greater social power but also sets the norms. Its values, images, and experiences are most pervasive in and representative of the culture—in other words, dominant. In using such language, I in no way imply that there are any inherent qualities that make either group deserving of its status. These are socially constructed and reproduced social dynamics.

Membership in a dominant or subordinate group is ascribed to us simply on the basis of our social identity or how we are socially categorized. The categories and language used to refer to different groups of people are imperfect and problematic for a variety of reasons. People often do not fit neatly into these boxes. Dividing people into dominant and subordinate groups tends to promote dualistic and dichotomous thinking. It implies that people can easily be classified into one group or the other (i.e., either White or a person of color, either able-bodied or disabled; Rosenblum & Travis, 1996, pp. 14-25). Yet there are degrees, gradations, and variations within and between social groups, and our individual social identities are not distinct from each other. One component of our identity is not completely separate from other aspects of ourselves. However, oppression operates on the basis of how society (the privileged group) views and names individuals, not necessarily on the basis of how people define themselves. Moreover, the ways in which identities are socially constructed and valued change. For example, with the Americans with Disabilities Act, we are continually redefining what makes someone "disabled." When the Irish first came to this country, they were not considered White by the dominant group (White Anglo-Saxon Protestants), but they were granted that status to prevent them from aligning with African Americans (Ignatiev, 1995). People in positions of power have used the categorizing and naming of groups for the purposes of control and domination. Even though there are numerous problems with trying to classify people in this way, I think it is helpful in order to discuss power relationships and dynamics of oppression.

The chart below (Table 1.1) outlines various types of oppression and the corresponding dominant and subordinate groups for some of the most common forms of social injustice in the United States. Although these forms of oppression occur globally, my focus will be on how they operate within the United States. This is not an exhaustive list; I could include several others as well, such as ethnocentrism (oppression based in ethnicity), other types of religious oppression, anti-Arab oppression, linguicism (oppression based on language), and sizism or fat oppression (oppression based on physical size or weight). Their lack of inclusion in the chart does not mean to imply that these types of oppression are less important or less harmful. I encourage readers to apply what is relevant to other forms of social injustice.

Table 1.1 Oppression Chart

Types of Oppression	Dominant Group	Subordinate Group
Sexism	Males	Females
Racism	Whites (People of European descent)	People of color (People of African, Asian, Latin American, Native American descent); biracial/ multiracial people
Heterosexism	Heterosexuals	Gays, lesbians, bisexuals, transgendered people
Classism	Middle and upper classes	Poor and working classes
Ageism	People in early and middle adulthood	Children and elders
Ableism	Able-bodied/ nondisabled people	People with disabilities
Anti-Semitism	Christian	Jews

We all have multiple social identities that, depending on the social category, may place us in either a dominant or subordinate group, on different sides of the power dynamic. I, like most others, am part of both advantaged and disadvantaged groups. For example, I am a woman and a Jew and therefore am part of the subordinate group in sexism and anti-Semitism. Yet I am also White, heterosexual, able-bodied, middle-class, and in my middle-adult years, which makes me a member of several dominant groups as well. Our particular constellation of social identities shapes our experiences and our sense of self.

Throughout the book, I refer to individuals from privileged groups and, in doing so, imply that there are some shared experiences for members from different privileged groups as well as for people from the same privileged group. However, I recognize that people have other identities that make up who they are and that affect each one's experience and identity as a dominant-group member (i.e., being middle-class, female, and Jewish affects my experience of being White). Even as I focus on a single dominant identity, it is important to remember that all aspects of our social identities are interrelated and interact. Obviously, in reality, one's dominant-group identity cannot be isolated from one's other social identities. Yet to explore the meaning of being part of a privileged group, I have found it helpful to temporarily narrow the lens to focus on this dimension of one's experience. Even though I try to continually keep present the fact that other social positions do make a difference and that all dominant groups are not the same, for the purpose of clarity and simplicity, I speak in more general terms. Frameworks that seek to simplify and make accessible complicated dynamics never capture the full complexity of the situation or issue. These models and concepts and this language can be useful as pedagogical tools, ways to help people understand social dynamics and their role in them. Please keep in mind that the map is not the territory. I hope educators will be able to highlight the variations and intricacies as they work with these topics in their particular settings.

As I wrote about people from privileged groups, I struggled with whether to use the term *they* or *we* because, depending on what identity I thought of, I could be one of "them" or not. For the most part, I refer to people from privileged groups with the less personal term *they* because I am not part of the dominant group in all cases. (I use the term *we* to refer to other educators.) When I refer to people from dominant groups, I am not referring to people who are part of the dominant group in all forms of oppression—White, heterosexual, Christian, middle-aged, able-bodied, middle- to upper-class men. I am referring only to people who, within a particular type of oppression, are part of the advantaged group.

Benefits and Limitations of
Discussing Privileged Groups in General

Instead of choosing to focus on educating Whites about racism or men about sexism or heterosexuals about heterosexism, I have chosen to focus on educating people from privileged groups in general. In using this approach, I hope to highlight the common roots and the interlocking nature of systems of domination. I have found that there are many similar dynamics, patterns, and themes across different forms of oppression (Adair, 1993; Adair & Howell, 1988). Many of the same issues are encountered when working with people from privileged groups, regardless of the particular ism. Because I, along with many others, educate about multiple forms of oppression, I thought this book would be more useful if it was kept broader, instead of being narrowed to only one type of oppression.

However, this does not mean that I think all forms of oppression are the same or that there are no differences in educating people from different dominant groups. Each type of oppression has particular characteristics and dynamics. For example, with sexism and racism, one's identity and dominant or subordinate status are fairly fixed. However, with ageism, it is natural that these change, and with classism and ableism, it is possible that they will. With sexism and ageism, there are usually close, even intimate, relationships between members of the dominant and subordinate groups, whereas with racism and heterosexism, it is possible for people from the dominant groups to avoid close relationships with members of the subordinate groups. There are also different attitudes toward the disadvantaged group. In racism, there is often fear; in ableism, pity; in heterosexism, revulsion; and in ageism, condescension. With some forms of oppression, it is easier for some members of the oppressed group to "pass," such as with heterosexism, anti-Semitism, and classism, yet this is more difficult or nearly impossible for other people from subordinate groups, such as in the cases of sexism, racism, or ableism (if the person has an obvious disability). There are also different histories and social functions of the oppression (i.e., the particular use and treatment of African Americans in the United States). Young (1990) identifies five "faces of oppression," which include exploitation, marginalization, powerlessness, cultural imperialism, and violence. A social group may be considered oppressed if its members experience one or more of these conditions. Therefore, the type and degree of oppressive actions enacted and experienced may vary as well.

All these differences warrant attention when educating about social justice. They also have implications for educating privileged-group members about different forms of oppression. Even though there are many common responses and generally effective strategies, we are likely to encounter specific types of reactions when educating about certain types of oppression. For example, when addressing heterosexism, we are likely to find resistance based on moral and religious beliefs, which is unlikely to occur with other isms. With classism, I have found that critiques of capitalism and our classist system can quickly evoke defensiveness and distorted views of other economic systems. People feel that their desire for upward mobility is being threatened or criticized and that the only alternative is some version of repressive communism. Red-baiting may also occur.

There are clearly some limitations or dangers in choosing this broad, inclusive approach. Some of the nuances and distinctiveness of particular forms of oppression are sacrificed. What is gained in generalizability is lost in specificity. My intention is not to deny or obscure differences among various forms of oppression, though some of this occurs when speaking more generally. Using an inclusive framework does not eliminate the need to provide a more in-depth treatment of particular topics and isms. This broader approach also means that I will not be able to adequately deal with issues that are unique to educating about specific forms of oppression. Given these various constraints, I strongly urge readers to use the resources listed in the appendix and available elsewhere to gain the needed information to address these concerns.

Overview of the Book

In this chapter, I lay out the purpose, rationale, and parameters of the book. The concepts of privileged groups and social identities are clarified. Chapter 2 focuses on describing privileged groups to develop a better understanding of the people we are working with. I highlight key characteristics of dominant groups and dominant-group members, discuss how multiple identities affect the experience of privilege, and explore the resistance to seeing oneself as privileged. Chapter 3 reviews several theories of individual development and change. These perspectives aid in creating environments and approaches that meet the needs of different individuals and that facilitate the learning process. In Chapter 4, I define and explore the various sociopolitical and psychological reasons for resistance from people from dominant groups. Why we are likely to receive the most resistance from White men is also considered. By understanding some of the sources of the resistance, we can better address it. This is the focus of Chapter 5, in which I suggest a range of strategies to prevent and address the resistance we may encounter when working with dominant-group members. Chapter 6 presents a host of psychological, social, intellectual, moral or spiritual, and material costs of oppression to people from privileged groups. This challenges the win-lose framework that assumes that people from dominant groups solely receive benefits from injustice and would only lose out if there were greater equity. Chapter 7 then moves to the question of why people from privileged groups would support social justice. I discuss how empathy, moral and spiritual values, and self-interest are key sources of motivation. Chapter 8 explores how to build on these elements to develop and enlist support for change. I demonstrate the importance of meeting people where they are and addressing their needs and concerns. Chapter 9 turns to issues for social justice educators. I consider how our own social identity development affects our work, factors that affect our educational efficacy, and ways to enhance our effectiveness as educators and change agents. The final chapter explores how to sustain a sense of hope and possibility that we can create a more just and caring world. I discuss the need to shift our current dominant paradigm, the importance of having an alternative vision, and hopeful signs that people from privileged groups can embrace more equitable relations and social systems. I include the potential benefits of social justice to people from privileged groups and the need for both individual and systemic change.

Educating about diversity and social justice is a challenging yet rewarding endeavor. It is a never-ending process and an ongoing opportunity to learn. Many of the ideas in the book are works in progress, and I offer them as contributions to the growing field of people struggling with how to best educate for social justice. I hope that these ideas will advance our efforts to work with people from privileged groups and, as a result, strengthen our collective ability to make this world one that values and nourishes our full humanity. I welcome your thoughts and feedback. You can reach me through the publisher or at dianejgood@aol.com.

2

About Privileged Groups

In any educational context, it is helpful to know your audience to understand with whom you're working. Being a member of a privileged group affects one's worldview, assumptions, and behavior. In this chapter, I'll explore what it means to be part of a privileged group and the significance of this for our educational efforts. Specifically, I'll discuss some common characteristics of dominant groups and dominant-group members, multiple identities and the experience of privilege, and the resistance to acknowledging one's privilege.

Characteristics of Privileged Groups

There are several key attributes of privileged groups. The first part of the discussion will focus on what characterizes a dominant group.[1] I will then consider the implications of these qualities for members of privileged groups. Although I will focus on what is generally true for dominant groups, I recognize that there are important variations among forms of oppression and among individuals.

Cultural and Institutional Domination

Oppression entails domination, the ability for one social group to systematically control, manipulate, and use other people for its own ends. Domination is created and maintained through interpersonal, cultural, and institutional forces. The privileged group creates systems and structures that reflect its values, embody its characteristics, and advance its interests. Unequal power systems are sustained by shaping people's worldviews, controlling resources, and constraining opportunities. Because domination has both ideological and structural dimensions, it can take many forms. At times, the domination is blatant and coercive, and the advantages to the privileged group are clear, such as with Jim Crow laws or forced (uninformed) sterilization. Often, however, it is more subtle and insidious, with less obvious benefits to the privileged group, such as media images that portray women as sex objects or economic policies that maintain some unemployment to ensure a pool of cheap, surplus labor.

Privileged groups define the mainstream culture—behavior patterns, symbols, institutions, values, and other human-made components of society (Banks, 1991). They determine what is acceptable and unacceptable, what is valued and ignored. Other groups are relegated to being subcultures. For example, the dominant cultural norms are reflected in our standards of beauty. The image of a beautiful woman is someone who is young, extremely thin, tall, and light-skinned, has Anglo features and finely textured hair, and often is blond and blue-eyed. White (European) culture, as expressed in music, art, dance, and literature, is considered more sophisticated than and superior to the culture of other racial/ethnic groups. According to mainstream time norms, people should be ruled by the clock. People are expected to be prompt and to end meetings according to prearranged times. Other cultural groups are more relaxed about time and begin and complete activities when they feel ready to do so. Often, this is seen as lazy and undisciplined.

Advantaged groups also establish the dominant ideology—a pervasive set of ideas and ways of looking at reality. The dominant ideology shapes individual consciousness and both justifies and conceals domination (Kreisberg, 1992, p. 15). Privileged groups are able to impose their conception of reality on subordinate groups. As Jean Baker Miller (1976) explains,

> A dominant group has the greatest influence in determining a culture's overall outlook—its philosophy, morality, social theory and even its science. The dominant group, thus, legitimizes the unequal relationship and incorporates it into society's guiding concepts. (p. 8)

This dominant ideology, which I discuss in more depth in Chapter 4, is embedded in institutional structures and practices that shape our consciousness and experiences. What we learn (and don't learn) in school, what we see (and don't see) in the media, how we are expected to act at work, how our economy is structured, what individuals are held up as role models, and what research gets funded and validated reflect and reinforce the dominant ideology. This informs our sense of what is important, true, and real about ourselves, others, and the world.

Institutional power also allows for the control of subordinate groups. As of 1997, the top 10% of the population controls approximately 73% of the wealth in this country (Wolff, 1998), there are only two women CEOs in the Fortune 500 companies (seven in the Fortune 1,000),[2] and women and people of color are still grossly underrepresented in Congress. Privileged groups use this power to establish policies and procedures that can provide, deny, or limit opportunities and access to resources and power. They exercise control over access to health care, housing, education, employment, political representation, fair judicial treatment, and legal rights.

Dominant groups also define acceptable roles for people in subordinate groups. These roles usually involve providing services that people from advantaged groups don't want to do or don't highly value. This social manipulation impedes human dignity and self-determination. Conversely, people from privileged groups can provide benefits to others from their own social group—by sharing information, providing jobs, creating laws and policies, contributing money, making appointments to boards and committees, and facilitating social and political connections.

The control of the dominant belief system and major institutions results in psychological domination as well. People from both privileged and marginalized groups often begin to accept the messages from the dominant culture about dominant-group superiority and subordinate-group inferiority. For people from oppressed groups, this *internalized oppression*—the belief in their own inferiority—undermines their self-esteem, sense of empowerment, and intragroup solidarity. It encourages unhealthy, dysfunctional behavior. In addition, people from oppressed groups are encouraged to develop personal and psychological characteristics that are pleasing to the privileged group—to be submissive, dependent, and docile (Miller, 1976). As long as people believe that they are inferior or deserve their plight, consider their treatment fair or for their own benefit, or are constrained in their self-development, they will not effectively challenge the current system.

Because the dominant ideology is embedded in our institutional practices and individual consciousness, for oppression to continue, we just need to act as usual, to go along with the status quo. It does not require malice or bad intentions to perpetuate systems of domination. We have been conditioned to see our social systems as normal and natural, even if some societal inequities are recognized.

Because only privileged groups have institutional power and the ability to systematically enforce their views, only they may be oppressive (e.g., racist, sexist, ableist, etc.). Certainly, people from all social groups (advantaged and disadvantaged) have prejudices and may act in discriminatory ways. Women may stereotype men, gays may deride heterosexuals, and Latinos may favor other Latinos for jobs. However, I, like many others, make the distinction between oppression and other terms such as prejudice, bigotry, or bias. None of the oppressed groups have the societal power to systematically disadvantage the corresponding privileged group. Consequently, from this line of thinking, there is no "reverse racism," even though people of color can act in hurtful, unfair ways toward White people. The shorthand definition "prejudice + social power = oppression" is useful to capture this distinction.

Normalcy

The dominant culture and societal norms are based on the characteristics of the privileged group (Wildman, 1996). The dominant group becomes the point of reference against which other groups are judged. It becomes normal. This standard of normalcy is also used to define what is good and right. These cultural norms become institutionalized and establish policy and practice. Catherine MacKinnon (1989) illustrates how this is true about men.

Men's physiology defines most sports, their health needs largely define insurance coverage, their socially designed biographies define workplace expectations and successful career patterns, their perspectives and concerns define quality in scholarship, their experiences and obsessions define merit, their military service defines citizenship, their presence defines family, their inability to get

> along with each other—their wars and rulerships—defines history, their image defines god, and their genitals define sex. (p. 224)

White (Christian), middle-class, heterosexual norms pervade our culture. Schools are one place where this is evident. The communication patterns and cultural styles used in most educational settings are more typical of White, upper middle-class families. There is an emphasis on individualistic learning, competition, and quiet and controlled classrooms, as opposed to collectivist values, oral traditions, and more active behavior, which are more common in other cultural groups (Delpit, 1995; Greenfield & Cocking, 1996; Viadro, 1996). The structure and content of standardized tests have been based on White, middle-class males, giving rise to concerns about gender and cultural bias (Sadker & Sadker, 1994). The conformity, or lack thereof, to these norms has significant impact on educational success and achievement.

This is also true in the workplace. Consider the style of speech and dress required for success in the business world. "Proper" English, suits or other "professional" attire, and a refined interpersonal style are the accepted standards. Domhoff and Zweigenhaft (1998a) found in a study of the experiences of women, Jews, African Americans, Asians, Latinos, and gay men and lesbians in positions of corporate leadership that although the faces may be more diverse, the behaviors and values remain the same. To be successful, members of these groups must conform to the norms and expectations of the dominant group. "Hedging against traditional stereotypes, Jewish and Black executives must be properly reserved, Asian executives properly assertive, gay executives traditionally masculine, and lesbian executives traditionally feminine" (Domhoff & Zweigenhaft, 1998b, p. 44). People must not be "too Jewish," "too Black," or "too gay."

The image of a "good family" (still) consists of a mother who is home raising children and a father who is earning the money. When I recently bought a house, I got a strong dose of these cultural norms. Over the past several months, I have made many calls about hiring someone to do work in the house, saying only that I recently bought it and giving my full name (first and last). With few exceptions, people referred to me as Mrs. Goodman and assumed that I had a "handy husband" and that I would be home during the day. The possibility that I might be single or a lesbian was not part of most people's thinking.

Other cultural norms are also widespread. Christian holidays are officially recognized and celebrated. Although everyone has the day off for major Christian holidays, people from other religious groups must take personal or vacation days to observe their holidays. I became painfully aware that I was not part of the norm when I attended a huge educational conference in a major hotel in San Francisco during the week of Passover and there was not a matzoh in sight. Look in most mainstream greeting card stores, and notice how often you see a person with a disability, a person of color, or a gay couple on the front, unless the card is targeted to that particular population.

We often become aware of the norms when we are exposed to the reverse or an exception. Try switching to all-female pronouns when reading something that uses the generic *he*. When I visited Atlanta, I was struck the first time I saw brown mannequins throughout a department store, despite having lived around New York City and other urban areas of the Northeast. Guided fantasies that reverse the norms, such as ones where homosexuality is the most common and accepted form of sexual orientation (e.g., Thompson et al., 1990), also illustrate what we take for granted as standard and appropriate.

Moreover, we tend to indicate the identity of an individual only when he or she is not what we consider the norm; otherwise, his or her social identity is assumed and unnamed. People are likely to refer to the "woman doctor," "Black leader," "Latino businessman," "lesbian teacher," or "disabled lawyer," even when the individual's social identity is not significant to the story. Yet how often would someone use the terms *male, White, able-bodied,* or *heterosexual* to refer to individuals in similar positions? More specifically, I've never heard Bill Gates referred to as the "White businessman" or Bill Clinton as the "male president." Sometimes only through exposure to difference can we begin to see what we have become accustomed to and take to be normal.

Superiority

This sense of normalcy also leads to a sense of superiority: Not only is it normal, it's better. Differences get converted into "better" or "worse," with the attributes of the dominant group being the winners.

In a study of mental health, Broverman, Broverman, Clarkson, Rosencrantz, and Vogel (1970) asked clinicians to describe a "healthy man," a "healthy woman," and a "healthy adult." A healthy woman was described as emotional, dependent, and submissive. The description of a healthy man was largely the same as that of a healthy adult—rational, independent, ambitious, and active. Not only was *man* the standard for *adult*, but a healthy woman could not be a healthy adult. (This study has been replicated many times since, with inconsistent results.) Furthermore, not only is Standard English more socially accepted, it is considered "better" than other cultural dialects. And heterosexual nuclear families are more common than gay or lesbian families, but they also are considered the "best" family structure.

Even the same traits may be named and valued differently depending on whether they are associated with a privileged or an oppressed group. Christians are "thrifty," whereas Jews are "cheap"; heterosexual men are "studs," whereas gay men are "promiscuous"; men are "leaders," whereas women are "bitches"; Whites are "shrewd," whereas Asians are "sneaky." Privileged groups uphold their own attributes as preferable while distorting and disparaging the qualities of others.

Superiority is not always conveyed in blatant and intentional ways. In reference to racism, bell hooks (1989) calls this type of superiority "White supremacy." She defines it as the unconscious, internalized values and attitudes that maintain domination, even when people do not support or display overt discrimination or prejudice (p. 113). It is the expectation (often unconscious) that people of color should assimilate to White norms to be acceptable and accepted. A similar process occurs when women are expected to adopt "male" styles of leadership and communication to be viewed as competent and effective in the workplace (though they can't be too "masculine" either). Trying to get people from disadvantaged groups to be "more like us" is usually a sign of supremacy at work, carrying the implicit message that "our way" is better.

This sense of superiority extends from the characteristics and culture of the dominant group to the individuals themselves. Oppression is commonly defined, in part, as the belief in the inherent superiority of one group over another. This influences how people are viewed and treated. People in professional positions are considered worthier of respect than are people in working-class jobs. There is usually more public outcry when a White woman is raped or a White child is killed than when this occurs to a woman or child of color. People with developmental disabilities have been seen as appropriate guinea pigs for dangerous medical experiments.

People from disadvantaged groups are generally labeled as substandard or aberrant. They are assumed to be less capable because of innate defects or deficiencies (Miller, 1976). For example, women are too emotional, Blacks are less intelligent, gays are morally deviant, and people with disabilities are defective. Not only are people from subordinate groups somehow inferior, but by logical extension, people from dominant groups are superior. This reasoning allows privileged groups to rationalize the systematic unfair treatment of people from oppressed groups and to feel entitled to power and privilege.

Privilege

Oppression involves both systematic disadvantage and advantage. Most discussions of social injustice focus on the subjugation of oppressed groups—the ways in which they are discriminated against, marginalized, exploited, manipulated, demeaned, and physically and emotionally attacked. Less attention is given to the other part of the dynamic—the privileging of the dominant group. This "system of advantage" (Wellman, 1977) bestows on people from privileged groups greater access to power, resources, and opportunities that are denied to others and usually gained at their expense.

Social oppression creates privilege systems—benefits or unearned advantages systematically afforded people from dominant groups simply because of their social group membership. "What makes something a privilege is the unequal way in which it is distributed and the effect it has on elevating some people over others" (Johnson, 1997, p. 175). It includes what we are able to take for granted or do not have to think about simply because we are part of an advantaged group; people from disadvantaged groups cannot make the same assumptions. Peggy McIntosh (1988) describes White privilege as "an invisible weightless knapsack of special provisions, maps, passports, codebooks, visas, clothes, tools and blank checks" (p. 71). Privileges do not need to be desired—we get them whether we want them or not and whether we are aware of them or not. Privileges can be both material and psychological. They can include concrete benefits as well as psychological freedoms; often, these are interrelated.

McIntosh (1998) lists numerous privileges for Whites that reflect these two interconnected dimensions. She writes,

> I can go home from most meetings of the organizations I belong to feeling somewhat tied in, rather than isolated, out-of-place, outnumbered, unheard, feared or hated; I can arrange to protect my children most of the time from people who might not like them; I can go into a supermarket and find the food I grew up with, into a hairdresser's shop and find someone who can deal with my hair; I can be pretty sure that if I ask to talk to "the person in charge" I will be facing a person of my race; I can be pretty sure that my children will be given curricular materials that testify to the existence of their race; I can take a job with an affirmative action employer without having co-workers on the job suspect that I got it because of my race; I can do well in a challenging situation without being called a credit to my race; I can swear, or dress in second hand clothes, or not answer letters, or be late to meetings without having people attribute these behaviors to the bad morals, the poverty, or the illiteracy of my race; I can think over many options, social, political, imaginative or professional, without asking whether a person of my race would be accepted or allowed to do what I want to do. (pp. 5-9)

Male privilege is evident in an exercise I do with groups of university men and women.[3] I ask them to describe what they do on a daily basis to ensure their safety. The men have a hard time coming up with a list. On the other hand, the women quickly cite numerous efforts: locking doors, walking with buddies, getting rides, avoiding certain areas, checking their cars, staying inside during late hours. Men have the privilege of being able to move about with less thought, worry, and constraint. (For men facing other forms of oppression—racism, classism, heterosexism, or ableism—the privilege of safety may be significantly limited.)

People with class privilege have access to the best medical care; to leisure and vacations; to good housing, food, and clothing; and to governmental financial advantages (e.g., tax breaks, write-offs for mortgages). They feel entitled to be treated respectfully, to be taken seriously, and to have opportunities to use their talents. They can choose work that may be meaningful, though not well compensated, knowing they have a safety net—other marketable skills, opportunities for education, or financial resources. They can use connections to get jobs or to be admitted to college. It's interesting to note that when opportunities are gained because of connections, there is not the outcry about merit. On the other hand, affirmative action is constantly attacked.[4]

Able-bodied people do not have to think about access to buildings—for education, cultural events, employment, or socializing; about travel—around one's own town, vacation areas, or conference sites; or about needing assistance to do basic daily tasks. They do not fear that people will assume them to be less intelligent or less productive solely because of a (possibly irrelevant) disability.

Heterosexuals can freely display public affection, talk openly about their partner, have their relationship publicly acknowledged and celebrated, and be protected from discrimination. They don't need to worry whether it's all right to bring their partner to events (and then whether they can dance together); whether they'll lose their job if they're out; whether they'll be accepted by their neighbors, or whether their partner will be considered as family under hospital guidelines and thus be able to visit or make medical decisions.

I became aware of another aspect of heterosexual privilege when I worked on a committee against homophobia on a university campus. When I was hired to do human relations education, it was clear that few people on campus were willing to publicly deal with issues of homophobia, despite the often-stated need and some very active (though essentially closeted) gay and lesbian faculty and staff. I quickly formed a committee (open to everyone) to address gay, lesbian, and bisexual issues on campus. There was a lot of interest and a strong representation of lesbians, gay men, and bisexuals. Although we worked very collaboratively, I was the chair and contact person, regularly sending out notices of our meetings and events and being called by the student newspaper to report on our activities. On a campus that felt unsafe to most gays, I realized that as a heterosexual, I had more freedom to be public about working against homophobia than my lesbian and gay colleagues. I had the safety of not being "found out," despite assumptions that I was a lesbian. It felt like a privilege to be able to be visible around this issue. (This is not to deny the fact that people from privileged groups do face risks when being allies.)

Michelle Fine (1997) notes how the creation and reproduction of privilege relies on the interdependence between dominant and subordinate groups. The privileged group is only privileged in relation to the targeted group. In many cases, a sense of privilege is gained through the deprecation and deprivation of the disadvantaged group. She observes this dynamic at work in a school in a low-inome community in the South. In a context where no one is receiving a good education, it is only because the White students are receiving more opportunities relative to the Black students and can align themselves with Whiteness (i.e., with a superior identity) that they can consider themselves privileged.

Promoting identification with superiority and privilege also helps to prevent people from an advantaged group from allying with people from one of their disadvantaged groups. White, poor, working-class men have often used (and have been encouraged to use) their "whiteness" to feel privileged while rejecting alliances with men of color in similar class positions (Roediger, 1991). They rely on racism and their sense of White privilege to create separation, instead of forging a common struggle against classism and economic exploitation.

Moreover, oppression is maintained not just by taking actions against disadvantaged groups but also by increasing privileges for advantaged groups. Instead of, or in addition to, active hostile actions taken against people of color, there may be a resurgence of pro-White policies and practices (Gaertner et al., 1997). According to Fine (1997),

> Where we look for evidence of discrimination and prejudice will have to move to the cumulative benefits of being White, rather than the (exclusive) tracking of blatant racism against, in this case, Blacks. Documenting racism *against*, as if separable from racism *for*, may be a diversionary strategy by which our eyes have been averted from the real prize. (p. 60)

Because oppression creates not only disadvantages for subordinate groups but also advantages for the dominant group, we need to examine both parts of the dynamic. White women and people of color may not be actively denied jobs, but unless they are included in the informal social network, mentored, encouraged to take on new responsibilities, and provided opportunities for professional development, the net effect is that they will not advance at the same rate as White men. White men are being privileged, even though White women and people of color may not be facing overt discrimination.

McIntosh (1998) also makes distinctions among privileges. She suggests that some are advantages that everyone is entitled to and that these should be a right; these need to be extended to all. Examples include having your neighbors be decent to you, not having your race work against you in employment, or not being followed or harassed in stores. Other privileges confer dominance and reinforce our present hierarchies, such as being able to ignore less powerful people, to manipulate our legal system to avoid punishment, to withhold information or resources, or to advance our interests to the detriment of others. These need to be rejected and eliminated. Therefore, as we examine privilege systems, we need to consider how privileges are constructed, how they are used to further systemic and structural inequality, and how to ensure that everyone has access to the privileges that should be human rights.

Individuals From Privileged Groups

Individuals are affected by being part of a privileged group and the dominant culture. Their experiences and perspectives are shaped by their social position. The effects of being dominant group members are reflected in people's attitudes, thinking, and behavior. I'll discuss several of the most common traits.

Lack of Consciousness

People from privileged groups tend to have little awareness of their own dominant identity, of the privileges it affords them, of the oppression suffered by the corresponding disadvantaged group, and of how they perpetuate it. In the first place, people from privileged groups generally do not think about their dominant group identity.

I conduct a couple of activities that highlight this point. At the beginning of a class or workshop, I'll ask each person to introduce herself or himself by choosing words to describe who she or he is. People of color will virtually always refer to their racial/cultural identity, whereas someone who is White rarely will. (Tatum, 1997, and Wildman, 1996, report similar findings.)

In another activity, I list common social categories—race, sex, religion, sexual orientation, ability or disability, class, age, and ethnicity— and I ask people to choose the two or three that are most important to who they are, to their sense of identity. I later ask them to choose the three that feel least important. Again, most people include in their three most important identities subordinate ones (though depending on the group, people are less likely to reveal their sexual orientation if they are gay, lesbian, or bisexual). The three least important are dominant identities. The one consistent exception is gender; both females and males often include it in their top three. This is not surprising because gender is such a salient and referenced social category.

When these results are pointed out to people in the class, I ask them why they think this occurs and why they chose the identities they did. People who choose a subordinate identity as most important talk about feeling very aware of that identity—it makes them feel different, others make them aware of it, it has created obstacles to overcome, or it is where they get mistreated. On the other hand, they recognize that their dominant identity is something to which they generally do not need to pay attention.[5] Even though we are most exposed to information about privileged groups, people from these groups tend to have the least self-awareness about that aspect of their identity and its social significance. This absence of consciousness about their social identity seems to, in part, reflect unequal power relationships. Miller (1976) maintains that people from dominant groups are deprived of feedback about their behavior because people from subordinate groups feel it's unsafe to give such feedback for fear of negative repercussions. Therefore, people from privileged groups don't learn about their impact on others. Nor do mainstream institutions (media, schools) provide this kind of perspective. (I also think that most people from privileged groups are not interested in or are afraid of knowing anyway, a point discussed later.) Nonetheless, people from advantaged groups are allowed to, and in fact encouraged to, remain unaware. In contrast, people from disadvantaged groups become highly attuned to and knowledgeable about the dominant group because their survival depends on it.

This lack of awareness relates to being the norm and therefore not needing to think about one's social identity. It's like being a fish in water—when one is surrounded by water as part of one's natural environment, it's hard to be aware of it. And this water has been filtered through the dominant ideology. People from privileged groups are surrounded by their culture and, therefore, they don't notice it. This allows them to see themselves as individuals, not as part of a group that has social power and privilege. Although members of other social groups may be lumped together, obliterating individual and intragroup differences, people from privileged groups tend to see themselves as unique individuals who succeed or fail on the basis of their own merit.

Moreover, this fish-in-water phenomenon contributes to the lack of awareness that people from dominant groups have about their privileges. Because the norm or reality is perceived as including these benefits, the privileges are not visible to members of the dominant group (Wildman, 1996). As I stated earlier, because privileges are things we usually take for granted and assume to exist, they therefore tend to be invisible. Frequently, we do not realize that something is a privilege until we compare it with the experience of the disadvantaged group. Several examples illustrate this occurrence.

One Sunday morning, I was in New York City saying good-bye to my then-boyfriend. As we stood on the curb next to my car, kissing, I heard some people clapping, down the block behind me. We stopped, and as I slowly turned around, I saw four men sitting on the back of a truck, laughing and applauding. I felt mortified. As I was recounting this episode to a lesbian friend of mine, it suddenly occurred to me how this was about heterosexual privilege. I could blithely and obliviously kiss on the street and then be applauded for my action. I doubt that my gay or lesbian friends would so unconsciously kiss their lovers in public or that they would be likely to get such a positive reaction for doing so. I had the luxury of just worrying about being embarrassed.

I am usually unaware of my privilege as an able-bodied person until I am with a person who is disabled. For several days of a conference I was attending, I wandered about the large hotels looking for the sessions, joined friends for meals, and explored the city. I then met a colleague who used a wheelchair. She generally limited herself to the sessions that were being held in one hotel because navigating it was difficult enough. Trying to get out of the hotel, cross the streets, and move about other hotels was too time-consuming and exhausting. Finding an accessible place to have dinner became another issue. After spending most of the day together, we arrived back at our hotel and found that the elevator in the lobby that stopped at our floor was closed for the evening. Because the suggested alternative was up an escalator (which was impossible to do in a wheelchair), we ended up taking the freight elevator. Technically, the hotel and the conference were wheelchair accessible. However, it made me realize how much I take my mobility, and what it affords me, for granted.

In the above examples, the privilege is clear if we try to become conscious of it. In other cases, the privilege is more hidden. In an effort to explore sex discrimination, the television show *Prime Time* matched a White man and a White woman on all variables except sex (e.g., overall appearance, education, etc.).[6] The two individuals went out separately to look for jobs, buy a car, and do other tasks. Both applied for a job as a territory manager for a landscape business that was advertised in the newspaper. Even though, on the basis of their resumes, the woman was better qualified for the job, when the man was interviewed, he took an aptitude test and was told about managerial possibilities; when the woman was interviewed, she took a typing test and was asked about her secretarial skills.

The staff at *Prime Time* conducted a similar experiment with a White man and a Black man to examine racism.[7] In one situation, both men responded to an ad for an apartment to rent. The Black man was told that the apartment was rented, whereas the White man, who went in later, was told that the apartment was still available. In both of these situations, not only did the White man receive better treatment and more opportunities than the White woman or Black man, but those options and advancements were gained at their expense. The White man had these chances because others were denied the same opportunity. If there had not been hidden cameras, the White man never would have known that the White woman and Black man were not treated as he was—he was just being treated nicely. Unfortunately, this kind of treatment becomes a privilege, an unearned advantage. Dominant-group members may be unaware that they are the recipients of privileged treatment and that this is at the expense of others. They therefore believe that their achievements are based on their own merit, not on systematic advantage. (See Chapter 2 of Hawkesworth, 1993, for a review of the research that documents how sexist bias privileges men at women's expense.)

Last, because the privileges are sometimes hidden and the discrimination is subtle, people from privileged groups don't realize the pervasiveness of oppression. They assume their experiences and treatment are normal. This assumption, coupled with little knowledge of the injustices that people from disadvantaged groups face, allows them to remain unconscious of other experiences. People from advantaged groups are taught to notice neither inequalities nor privileges. They are "privileged to remain innocent" (Lazarre, 1996).

This lack of consciousness allows for the unintentional perpetuation of injustice. People do not realize that what they are doing is biased or discriminatory. There are innumerable examples of this, yet one recent situation in particular captures this well. A photo in a local newspaper featured a White boy and an African American boy, with the White boy in the foreground. The title announced the winner of the geography bee. The caption began with the name of the White boy and the fact that he finished in second place. It then explained that the other boy was the winner and gave the other boy's name. Even when the African American deserved the spotlight, from looking at the photo (and the order of the information in the caption), it appeared that the White boy was the winner. A positive image of an African American male was diminished there, yet newspapers have no difficulty highlighting African American males when they are involved in illegal activity. Although some people may intentionally promote racist or other oppressive images, I doubt whether the photographer or the editor of the newspaper intended to convey such a distorted and implicitly racist message. Yet they colluded with institutional racism. Because people do not have to act in overtly discriminatory ways but have only to behave normally or unconsciously to perpetuate oppression, it is easy for members of dominant groups to remain unaware of the impact of their own actions or of their institution's practices. They are less likely to realize how business as usual could still cause injustice.

Denial and Avoidance of Oppression

There is a fine line between recognizing that some privileges may be less obvious and therefore easy to overlook and choosing not to see or look for those privileges. Similarly, there is a difference between lacking an awareness of the extent of social injustice and deciding not to acknowledge it. People from privileged groups have the options to deny the existence of oppression and to avoid dealing with it. Lazarre (1996) refers to this as "willful innocence" (p. 49).[8] For the reasons cited above, people from privileged groups tend to be less conscious of oppression and more likely to deny that it exists. In their reality, they are generally unhampered by their social identity and ignorant of the mistreatment of others. Along with a sense of superiority, it becomes easy for them to proclaim that if it is not an issue from their perspective, then it's not an issue. Because their lives can proceed rather well under the current circumstances, they do not need to bother to explore or listen to the complaints of others. They can ignore claims of discrimination and label those who raise issues as oversensitive or troublemakers. Denying that there is oppression also allows the system of domination to remain in place and be justified.

This is exacerbated by the fact that people from advantaged and disadvantaged groups tend to define oppression differently. In the case of racism, Whites are more likely to see racism as "individual acts of meanness" (McIntosh, 1988, p. 18), as individual acts of prejudice and discrimination, or as extreme actions that are the exception rather than the norm. Blacks are more likely to see it also as a series of daily indignities and as a system of institutionalized practices and policies that works to their disadvantage (Duke, 1992; Shipler, 1997). Therefore, if people only recognize injustice when it is blatantly expressed by individuals, they will never understand the depth and breadth of social oppression.

Admitting that there is oppression and that one participates in it opens up the possibility of personal discomfort. As Allan Johnson (1997) explains, people from privileged groups feel they should be exempt from such an experience:

> Dominant groups typically show the least tolerance for allowing themselves to feel guilt and shame. Privilege, after all, should exempt one from having to feel such things. They experience reminders of their potential for feeling guilt as an affront that infringes on their sense of entitlement to a life unplagued by concern for how their privilege affects other people. The right to deny that privilege exists is an integral part of privilege itself. So men can be quick to complain about "being made to feel guilty" without actually *feeling* guilty. (p. 62)

This privilege is sometimes referred to as "the right to comfort." This was expressed very directly at a training I conducted with a group of university students. The first several activities highlighted the group's diversity and clearly made the point that we need to value our differences and create equality for all groups. After participating in an exercise that physically demonstrated White privilege and institutional racism, a White male said that he didn't like the activity because it made him feel uncomfortable and bad about being White. He understood that the point of the activity was to demonstrate inequities and knew that the purpose was not to make White people feel guilty. Nevertheless, he still insisted that his discomfort made him not want to engage and, therefore, that the activity was counterproductive. He felt entitled to the privilege of not having to be uncomfortable and therefore had the privilege of choosing not to confront issues of racism.

People from privileged groups can also choose to remain silent when they are aware of injustice. The impact on people from disadvantaged groups is usually more profound and immediate and, thus, more likely to elicit a greater need to respond. Because people from privileged groups are usually less directly affected, they can decide not to take action. In fact, there is incentive not to do so. First, people from advantaged groups who point out inequities and challenge the status quo often put themselves at risk. They may face retaliation at work or school, ostracism, harassment, or violence. Second, pointing out inequities and challenging the status quo disrupts a system that largely works to their benefit. People from privileged groups tend to have more to lose, at least in the short run, if they make waves. (However, in Chapter 5, I'll discuss the extensive costs of oppression to people from dominant groups as well.)

Sense of Superiority and Entitlement

Being part of the norm, a member of the dominant group, and the beneficiary of (invisible) privileges often leads to a sense of superiority and entitlement, or *internalized supremacy*. Even though this sense of identity is false and unearned, people from dominant groups come to expect certain treatment and opportunities. They feel that they deserve the privileges that they have come to assume will be theirs. This attitude is beyond a healthy sense of self-respect or pride in one's cultural group; it can be arrogance and snobbery.

iduals not only expect their needs to get met but often be-
their needs should supersede others' needs.

People with class privilege (money or status) expect their phone calls to be returned promptly and their work to receive priority. I notice that students who are upper middle-class, especially males, feel more entitled to my time and attention as a professor. They expect individual attention and accommodations to meet their needs. In general, men expect their wants and desires to take precedence over a woman's. Sometimes, people have a clear sense of entitlement and consciously believe that they deserve special treatment. Many times, people who are acting entitled rarely see their behavior in this light. They are just doing what they think anyone would or should do.

This sense of superiority often becomes evident when people from an advantaged group encounter someone from a disadvantaged group who is in a position of expertise or authority over them. Men may balk at having a woman boss, or Whites may be uncomfortable with a person of color as the doctor or consultant. People from privileged groups are often suspect of the ability, knowledge, or right to such status of people from oppressed groups. This may reflect more than just stereotypes and bias. This arrangement calls into question the implicit superiority of people from the dominant group and what they assume is the appropriate social order.

Multiple Identities and the Experience of Privilege

In my description of common characteristics of people from privileged groups, I have narrowly focused on a single aspect of one's identity. However, that is only one strand of a whole tapestry. Individuals' other social identities color their experience of that dominant identity and, more broadly, affect their overall experience of both privilege and oppression. Not everyone benefits equally; one's privileges are mediated by one's other social positions. Other social statuses affect the degree to which one experiences the advantages of privilege.

Privileges gained through a dominant identity may be mitigated or reduced because of a subordinate identity. Class privilege certainly provides many advantages, yet it may be limited by racism, sexism, or heterosexism. Even middle and upper-class Black men get stopped by police and are suspected of criminal activity; in fact, being in an affluent neighborhood or driving an expensive car will often bring on this suspicion. Women in high-level positions still do not command the same respect or influence as men in similar positions. Openly gay men do not have the same access to corporate or political power (or membership in the old-boy network) as heterosexual men. (As described earlier in this chapter, people from various oppressed groups rarely have the same access to high-level institutional power, and when they do, it is at a cost.)

Nor does privilege in one area prevent subordination in another. Wealthy women are still subject to sexual violence, even though they have greater opportunities to protect their safety. Being able-bodied, heterosexual, and White does not exempt a working-class person from class oppression. A White man in his 30s who has the benefits of race, sex, and age may still face employment discrimination because he has a disability.

On the other hand, the experience of oppression in one aspect generally does not eradicate the experience of privilege in another. Some feminists feel that because they are all women and experience sexism, their experiences are similar. White women, able-bodied women, or heterosexual women often ignore the way they have privileges in other parts of their lives. Some Jews may be subject to anti-Semitism yet still have White-skin privilege. Men of color confront racism yet still benefit from sexism and patriarchy. However, in extreme cases, other dominant identities or privilege are irrelevant. No aspect of privilege could protect the Japanese from internment, the Native Americans from removal, or the Jews from extermination.

Though not absolute, our particular mix of identities does shape our experiences. Privilege can help alleviate experiences of oppression. The more dominant identities one has, the more one can draw on those privileges to deal with the discrimination and disempowerment faced in one's subordinate roles. The more subordinate identities one has, the more likely that the privilege one does have is eroded. However, this is not simply an additive game; our social identities are not a balance sheet in which one can just compare the number of identities on the dominant side and the number on the subordinate side and know how much power, privilege, or freedom one has. Individuals and the dynamics of oppression are much more complicated than that. Some people argue that certain oppressions are worse than others or have greater impact. As noted in the previous chapter, Young (1990) points out there may be different "faces" or manifestations of oppression that are experienced to greater or lesser degrees by different oppressed groups. Oppressions may be linked but not comparable. As Audre Lorde (1983) asserts, "there is no hierarchy of oppressions."

Resistance to Seeing Oneself as Privileged

Many people have reactions to considering themselves privileged or dominant. Some people have difficulty thinking in those terms about themselves; others can do it but just don't like the idea. There are several reasons for these types of responses.

First, being *privileged, dominant,* or an *oppressor* has negative connotations. People assume it means that people willfully discriminate against or mistreat others. It seems to refer to the "bad guys." Most people don't see themselves or want to see themselves in that light. They consider themselves nice people who try to treat people fairly.

Second, most people do not even realize that they are privileged or part of groups with greater social power. As I have described, most people from dominant groups don't think about that identity; they see themselves simply as normal. They also do not realize the extent of systemic inequalities and the ways in which they are advantaged. It is hard to accept being privileged when you are unaware of your privileges or feel you have earned them.

Even if people from dominant groups are aware of their social status, they don't feel privileged or powerful. Most people are struggling to live their lives. They worry about their jobs, their families, their health. They personally don't have access to great amounts of resources or make decisions that affect the nation. More people feel controlled, rather than in control. Given the individualistic and competitive nature of our society, few people feel secure. The fact that most people think of themselves as individuals, rather than as members of a social group, exacerbates the difficulty they have with seeing themselves as privileged. Because individuals alone do not themselves create and maintain dominant ideologies and oppressive structures, it is understandable that an individual would not feel that he or she had much of a role in societal oppression. Because individuals personally don't feel advantaged, it is difficult to acknowledge that they are part of a group that is. A White woman expresses this realization: "I never thought about it before, but there are many privileges to being White. In my personal life, I cannot say that I have ever felt that I had the advantage over a Black person, but I am aware that my race has the advantage" (Tatum, 1997, p. 102). Alternatively, some people from dominant groups feel that they are the ones at a disadvantage. This is particularly true for Whites who feel that people of color are now the ones getting the benefits, especially in the job market. However, when taking part in exercises in which White people are asked if they would rather be a person of color, virtually no Whites indicate that they would like to switch.

Moreover, the sense of privilege is relative. First, Johnson (1997) contends that people tend to assess their relative standing in comparison to people like themselves (looking sideways) or to people more advantaged than themselves (looking up). Rarely do we judge ourselves in relation to people worse off than ourselves (downward). Therefore, if our peers or those above us seem better off than we do, it is of little comfort or consequence that others are in worse positions. Therefore, people are usually quite aware of their relative deprivation but refuse to acknowledge their relative privilege.

Second, not all people in a particular advantaged group are similarly situated. Certainly, the experience of class privilege of someone in the top 1% of wealth in the United States is quite different from that of someone who is comfortably middle-class. Third, other subordinate identities erode one's sense of privilege. Some people from a targeted group claim that their oppression undermines any privileges they may receive from their dominant identity. Rather, I would say that other social positions affect the degree to which someone is advantaged in one's dominant identity. An individual can recognize privileges due to one's dominant identities while also acknowledging how those identities are affected by his or her other targeted identities. Privilege and oppression are not mutually exclusive, even if there is a dynamic between them.

As noted before, people tend to focus on their subordinate identities. For people who are part of a privileged group, their targeted identity or identities will usually have greater significance than their dominant identity or identities. This makes it more difficult for them to identify themselves as someone from a privileged group and to acknowledge that status. Most people will tend to see themselves as someone from a disadvantaged group, ignoring their privileges in other aspects of their lives. In the models of social identity development that I will describe in the following chapter, there is a stage in which people are very invested in their subordinate identity. At that point, it is particularly challenging for individuals to examine their privilege from a dominant identity.

Conclusion

This chapter broadly describes privileged groups and offers perspectives to appreciate how they might see themselves and the world. The dominant culture both overtly and covertly promotes the normalcy and superiority of the advantaged group and that group's right to domination and privilege. People from advantaged groups therefore tend to be less aware and less sensitive to oppression and feel entitled to privileges (which they don't see and believe are deserved). There is generally little opportunity, support, or incentive for people from privileged groups to explore their identity and examine its social implications. Thus, this provides a social imperative and challenge for social justice educators. In the following chapter, I will discuss ways to approach facilitating an educational process toward awareness and change.

Notes

1. The writings of Jean Baker Miller (1976) and the growing body of work on "Whiteness" (e.g., Fine, Weis, Powell, & Mun Wong, 1997; Frankenberg, 1993; McIntosh, 1988) are particularly helpful in describing the experiences of dominant groups.

2. 1997 Catalyst Census of Women Corporate Officers. This statistic is from the Top Earners category.

3. I first saw this exercise done by Jackson Katz at the University of Rhode Island in 1993.

4. John Larew (1996) explores this issue in his article, "Why Are Droves of Unqualified, Unprepared Kids Getting into Our Top Colleges? Because Their Dads Are Alumni."

5. Gallagher (1997) has challenged this presumption in his research with White college students. He found that instead of it being an invisible identity, "being White was an explicit, meaningful part of how students constructed their social identities" (p. 28). Students felt that their "Whiteness" intruded on most of their everyday activities. He raises interesting questions as to the construction and meaning of whiteness in the 1990s, given a variety of social and political factors.

6. A video of this segment, "The Fairer Sex" (a segment of a *Prime Time ABC News* program) is available from Core Vision Media, 1359 Barclay Blvd., Buffalo Grove, IL 60089, (800) 537-3130.

7. A video of this segment, "True Colors" (a segment of *Prime Time ABC News*), is available from Prime Time ABC News, P.O. Box 2284, South Burlington, VT 05407, (800) 913-3434.

8. See Kivel (1996, pp. 40-46) for a discussion of the ways in which Whites retain benefits and avoid responsibility for racism.

3

Perspectives on Individual Change and Development

Education, especially social justice education, is about change. The hope is to transform or broaden attitudes, beliefs, and behaviors. We may use a variety of strategies: cognitive strategies that offer new information or analyses, behavioral strategies that foster interpersonal contact or participation in new experiences, or emotional strategies that encourage empathy and personal insight. However, an educator cannot make someone change. Rather, we can provide the context, content, and process that allow an individual to grow.

There are many things that affect whether there will be shifts in someone's views or actions, including one's psychological state, personality structure, previous experiences, moment in one's life, and relationship with the educator and colleagues or classmates. These all have an impact on a person's openness to learning and change. Just as we cannot control the experience of each individual, we cannot control many of the other factors that influence one's growth. In the time that we work with someone, they may not be able or willing to engage in a process of reflection and change. We can just do our best to understand the people we are working with and to provide the ingredients that we believe will most facilitate their education.

In this chapter, several theoretical frameworks that I find helpful in designing and facilitating educational experiences and in understanding the perspectives and behaviors of people from privileged groups will be discussed. They will be addressed in relation to
diversity and social justice education, though their relevance extends to other contexts. I will primarily focus on developmental perspectives as related to personal growth in general, and to intellectual
development and social identity development in particular.

Addressing the Emotions and the Intellect

Good education involves addressing emotional (affective) and
intellectual (cognitive) dimensions (Rogers, 1980). Learning is more
stimulating and meaningful when both the intellect and feelings are
attended to. To effectively educate about diversity and social justice,
we must deal with both.

Anyone who has done social justice education knows that it is
more than an intellectual activity. Of course, we need to expose people to new perspectives, facts, theories, and analyses. They need to
acquire more accurate and complex information about issues that
the mainstream media often ignore, simplify, or distort. Yet even
when enlightening facts and theories are provided, people may still
be unmoved and remain uninvolved.

Addressing the affective aspect is important in two respects.
First, it is a key component of the learning process and central to a
sound social justice pedagogy. Fostering self-awareness and the
concern for others, two aspects of social justice education, require
dealing in the realm of feelings. People need to emotionally connect
with and care about other people and situations. The promotion of
empathy, an important educational approach, requires that people be
able to relate to the feelings of another. (See Chapters 7 and 8 for
more about empathy.) Considering one's own feelings in various circumstances provides helpful bridges to understanding the experiences
of others. Without an emotional investment, there is less incentive to
explore social justice issues or to engage in personal or social change.

Second, feelings arise in the process of learning about diversity
and justice. Students are more likely to stay engaged with the material and the process when we help them deal with their feelings. In
educating for social justice, we ask people to question their fundamental belief systems and assumptions about how the world operates. On the one hand, challenging people's self-concepts and

worldviews is threatening because they often feel anxious, fearful, confused, angry, guilty, and resentful. Different stages of social identity development, described below, are often accompanied by particular emotions. Thus, as people examine deeply rooted beliefs, we can expect emotional reactions. In addition, conflicts, with corresponding emotions, often occur among participants as issues are discussed. The learning and growth process will be impeded unless these feelings and dynamics are addressed. (This will be discussed in more detail in Chapters 4 and 5, in which resistance is discussed.)

Rose (1996) describes why dealing with emotions is critical for people from dominant groups if we expect them to be allies. In reference to racism, she explains,

> If White people only confront these issues [feelings of guilt and betrayal] on a cognitive basis, they will wind up as hostages to political correctness. They will be careful about what they say, but their actions will be rigid and self-conscious. When the process is emotional as well as cognitive, the state of being an ally becomes a matter of reclaiming one's own humanity. (pp. 41-42)

As people work through limiting and oppressive attitudes and behaviors, they can experience feelings of joy, liberation, release, and excitement.

Most educators are more comfortable staying at an intellectual level. However, students often do not allow this to occur. Whether wanted or not, invited or not, their feelings intrude. Meaningful social justice education is inherently an emotion-laden process. For students to be connected to the content, there needs to be an emotional link. Likewise, to help them stay engaged in a process of growth and change, we need to help them work through their feelings. We can intentionally structure into the class or workshop opportunities for people to appropriately deal with their emotions (e.g., journaling, sharing with peers, support groups). In any case, dealing with both the cognitive and the affective is part of the educational agenda.

Developmental Perspectives

A developmental perspective suggests that change occurs through particular sequences. As one's current perspective or way of being becomes inadequate, this creates a sense of disequilibrum and the impetus to move to new ways of seeing and being. There are common, though individualized, patterns and processes to one's growth.

I have found psychosocial and cognitive developmental theories helpful in assessing people's frames of reference or ways of understanding. It is an educational truism that we need to meet people where they are. And even though we would often like our students to be somewhere else, we are ineffective when we appeal to them at the wrong level. As Paulo Freire (1994) says, "You never get *there* by starting *there,* you get *there* from starting from some *here*" (p. 58). But how do we know where "here" is?

Developmental theories are one way that we can figure out how best to approach particular students. Like other theories, they provide a framework from which to understand people and to develop ways to respond that can facilitate their learning and growth. I can better sense where they've been, where they are, and where they may be headed. It makes it easier to anticipate certain types of reactions and interactions. Instead of the educational process feeling like random events, in which we hope for the best, developmental theories can help the process seem more coherent and help us be more proactive.

Some developmental stage theories may sound overdetermined and hierarchical. I find it most helpful to think about stages as the predominant lenses or perspectives that people use to guide their ways of perceiving and acting. Although people may exhibit thinking and behavior from various stages, they will usually have a predominant stage and are unable to fully understand or consistently act from higher stages (especially if those higher stages are more than one stage beyond their predominant stage). Likewise, even though some stage theories suggest linear, one-directional movement, I find it more useful to consider that some people may move back and forth between stages and that their development may be more like a spiral—they continue to grow but revisit similar issues in new ways. I offer these theories as I use them—as guides, not as absolute truths for each individual. They are not intended as a way to label people but as an aid in understanding different perspectives and in developing educational strategies.

Confirmation, Contradiction, Continuity

Robert Kegan (1982) has suggested a theory of human development that describes the changing ways in which people make meaning of themselves, others, and the world. He describes a process that facilitates growth to new stages of development. This process can be applied to social justice education as well. He maintains that growth unfolds through alternating periods of dynamic stability, instability, and temporary rebalance. Individuals need a sense of *confirmation,* an environment of support, before moving on to situations of *contra-diction,* conditions that challenge current meaning-making systems. They then need a context for *continuity* that allows for transforma-tion and re-equilibration. A sequence of confirmation, contradiction, and continuity can provide a framework for designing and respond-ing to issues in social justice education. I will explore each of these phases in more depth.

Confirmation

By its very nature, social justice education creates discomfort. As noted above, we are asking people to do something quite diffi-cult—to question core values and beliefs about themselves and the world. We therefore need to offer enough safety so that people can engage, but enough challenge so that people can change. When peo-ple feel too threatened, the fight-or-flight response is activated, and the likelihood of learning is diminished. Confirmation is concerned with providing a context that creates enough safety and support for people to take emotional, social, psychological, and intellectual risks. Even though this is the beginning step, as people get scared or defensive, it continually needs to be revisited so that safety can be re-established. At this point, some key aspects of the confirmation phase will be reviewed. Creating a confirming environment in the context of preventing and addressing resistance is discussed in Chapter 5.

One aspect of confirmation is establishing trust and rapport be-tween the educator and the student. Other psychological and educa-tional theorists have highlighted the importance of establishing this relationship. In counseling and family therapy, psychologists refer to this as *joining.* The therapist must be able to form a partnership with the client or family, creating a bond of trust and common purpose.

> Joining a family is more an attitude than a technique and it is the umbrella under which all therapeutic transactions occur. Joining is letting the family know that the therapist understands them and is working with and for them. Only under his [sic] protection can the family have the security to explore alternatives, try the unusual, and change. (Minuchen & Fishman, 1981, p. 32)

As this brief quote highlights, it is the stance and expression of acceptance that is central, not the particular behaviors or techniques an individual teacher uses. This is echoed by Rogers (1980), who identifies acceptance (or unconditional positive regard), genuineness, and empathic understanding as the critical conditions of any growth-promoting relationship, including those in the classroom. Educators need to respect and value people and to affirm their fundamental integrity, dignity, and self-worth. Students must be able to trust the educator before they will be willing to allow themselves to be vulnerable. The need for students to feel heard, understood, and cared about is paramount.

There are numerous ways in which educators can create a safe environment that communicates care and respect to students. It is critical to listen attentively, both verbally and nonverbally, and acknowledge students' experiences and feelings. Develop class or workshop guidelines with the participants for classroom interactions, and ensure that these agreements are upheld. Self-disclose about our own backgrounds, our experiences with different forms of injustice, and our efforts to unlearn oppression. Name or have students share the fears and concerns people often have when dealing with these issues. Reassure students that this is a learning environment by encouraging "stupid" questions and stressing that critical thinking, not the presumed party line, is what is expected. (In some contexts, we may need to acknowledge that even if people don't agree, they may be expected to uphold certain standards of behavior.) We can build on what students already know, validating their current expertise and experience. Soliciting students' input about class rules, topics to be covered, assignments, or class activities also communicates respect. Creating comfort among students or participants is also important. Icebreakers and work in pairs or small groups that allow people to get to know each other are helpful. Low-risk personal sharing and self-disclosure activities help to build trust. Encouraging people to notice their commonalities—similar experiences, likes, interests—also increases rapport. For people to feel able to let down their guards and grapple with challenges to their belief systems, there needs to be a safe and supportive environment that includes trust of the educator as well as peers.

Contradiction

Once a sense of confirmation has been established, the goal is not to overprotect students or to have them avoid uncomfortable feelings. Safety does not equal comfort. The aim is not to allow people to remain in their often-limited worldview but to help them construct new and more complex understandings of themselves and society. Significant growth often occurs when people are out of their comfort zone or are at their "learning edge." During contradiction, by creating disequilibrium, we foster the conditions that promote growth. The bulk of diversity education tends to focus on this phase. However, without first establishing trust and safety, we are less likely to be successful. In social justice education, the phase of contradiction corresponds with what is considered to be developing critical consciousness (Freire, 1970). According to Freire (1970), *conscientization* is development of critical social and political awareness. It is "learning to perceive social, political and economic contradictions, and to take action against oppressive elements of reality" (p. 19). It places the status quo in question and supports the transformation of individual and social consciousness.

Although critical thinking, in general, does not always encompass such social and political critiques, it can have elements in common with developing critical consciousness. In describing the components of critical thinking, Brookfield (1987) includes the following: identifying and challenging assumptions, becoming aware of how context shapes what is considered normal and natural ways of thinking and living, and imagining and exploring alternative ways of thinking and living (pp. 7-8). He also warns educators about this process.

> Trying to force people to analyze critically the assumptions under which they have been thinking and living is likely to serve no function other than intimidating them to the point where resistance builds up against this process. We can however, try to awaken, prompt, nurture, and encourage this process without making people feel threatened or patronized. (p. 11)

Overall, the contradiction phase engages people in reflection and analysis. As educators, we can provide opportunities for people to become aware of their unquestioned beliefs and attitudes and to then evaluate the validity of those beliefs and attitudes. We can ask them to compare their currently held views with other versions of reality; present various analyses of how and why oppression operates; help students move from basing opinions on emotional reactions to utilizing critical analysis; have them consider how the dominant ideology shapes individual consciousness, institutional structures and practices, and cultural norms; and assist them in understanding how our ideas and behaviors are culturally and historically specific and socially constructed. We can encourage people to explore how the personal is political and how individual problems often are reflective of larger social issues; we can help them to examine their privilege and to consider how oppression hurts the dominant group. Finally, we can suggest alternatives to our current system and to participants' present behaviors. For example, some people look at a woman in an abusive relationship with a man as an isolated occurrence. They may see her behavior simply as a personal weakness or an individual psychological problem. They do not consider how sexism has contributed to this relationship: how women are socialized to be submissive to men, to take care of others before themselves, and to feel incomplete without a relationship. There are cultural messages that the woman is somehow to blame for the abuse and economic realities that make it hard for women to be financially independent, especially if they have children to support. Men also have been conditioned to be dominant, aggressive, and in control and to see women as possessions. We can help students to consider a broader social analysis that then leads to different ways to thinking about how to address the issue of violence in relationships.

Educators engage people in these tasks in many ways. The specific content and activities in the contradiction phase will vary greatly depending on the group, the context, and the goals. People can be exposed to new information and analyses through readings, videos, speakers, and sharing among participants. They can actively investigate issues through research, interviews, observations, fieldwork, and participation in events. Case studies, role plays, debates, simulations, and guided imageries promote the consideration of other perspectives and alternative possibilities. In general, experiential activities are particularly effective in helping people gain new insights in fun and unexpected ways. There need to be opportunities for self-reflection and adequate processing (discussion and debriefing) of activities and experiences so that participants can gain the most from them. (For other ideas for activities, see Chapters 5, 7, and 8 and the resources in the appendix.)

The contradiction phase is also the time to expand on data generated during the confirmation phase. By building on what people have said about their own feelings and experiences, we can help them to understand their experiences in a larger social, political, and historical context. People need to expand their individualistic framework to include a more structural analysis. They often want to see everything on an individual basis and ignore the treatment of groups of people and institutionalized practices. When a person of color is denied a promotion, it may be attributed to that individual's qualifications. Yet if students review the data on the hiring and promotion of people of color, they may see a pattern of racial discrimination in that company and in other organizations. In addition, people from privileged groups may use their own personal experiences to generalize or incorrectly assume that there is pervasive discrimination against people from their group, while minimizing the discrimination faced by people from oppressed groups. A White person may also feel that he or she has been unfairly denied a job. It is necessary to help people make the distinction between behavior directed at an individual in a specific situation and actions taken systematically against groups of people over time.

People need to understand the differences in access to social power as well as the extent to which people may face discrimination or unfair treatment. In systems of oppression, despite the stereotypes and mistreatment some people may face, privileged groups still have greater opportunities, choices, access to resources, and power to define normalcy than dominated groups. A range of information (including statistics, historical perspective, and data about institutional and cultural oppression) can help people broaden their understanding of their own and others' experiences and gain a clearer picture of social reality. People need accurate information to correct misperceptions, to challenge faulty assumptions, and to fill in gaps in knowledge. They need a basis from which to question the myth of meritocracy and to recognize that the playing field is still unequally sloped and rocky.

During the contradiction phase, we try to promote questioning, generate discussion, offer alternative viewpoints, encourage risk taking, and provide resources. As disequilibrium is created, we need to be mindful of students' reactions. If too much dissonance is created, they may become fearful and defensive. They may retreat from the educational process if it feels too scary and overwhelming. We have to respect people's pace and ability to handle threatening material. Reemphasizing some of the aspects of confirmation—ensuring a safe and supportive environment and reaffirming a sense of trust and rapport—helps keeps students engaged.

As participants begin to reevaluate their beliefs and develop new understandings of themselves, others, and social reality, they need ways to integrate these new perspectives. After experiencing a sense of disequilibrium, they seek to reestablish a sense of balance, incorporating their new consciousness. This leads to the next phase, which assists them with this transition.

Continuity

In the continuity phase, our goal is to help students integrate and apply their new knowledge and awareness; they are seeking to recreate a sense of equilibrium. If a class or training is ending, it is also the time to establish closure. In the natural course of human development, this process of confirmation, contradiction, and continuity proceeds according to its own timing. In the context of a course, people may still feel in the midst of contradiction as the class is ending. Therefore, students may need to consider how to use the awareness gained so far and how to continue this process outside of the class setting.

During the continuity phase, it is useful for people to develop plans for taking action and applying what they have learned. Discuss where they may have an impact and a range of actions they can take (including those of lower and higher risk and those that target individual, institutional, and cultural oppression). Encourage people to develop a sense of empowerment and possibility, as opposed to becoming overwhelmed with the magnitude of the problems. It is especially important for people to identify ways they can get support for their newfound consciousness and commitment. Because their friends and family most likely have not shared this experience, they often do not provide the kind of support or understanding that participants need at this point. In addition to providing support, help students explore how they can continue their own education through workshops, classes, groups, or community or campus activities. (See Chapter 8 for more discussion of actions for allies.)

The model of confirmation, contradiction, and continuity provides an overarching framework from which to design educational experiences. As I'll discuss further in Chapter 5, the importance of confirmation cannot be underestimated and often is shortchanged. Establishing and reestablishing a supportive climate allows for disequilibrium and re-equilibrium to occur. This framework, which is applicable to both individuals and the class overall, provides a broad understanding of the process of change. In the next sections, I will describe two models that illustrate specific aspects of individual development: intellectual and social identity development.

Intellectual Development

During the contradiction phase, we expect people to engage in critical thinking by examining assumptions, exploring various viewpoints, analyzing positions, engaging in self-reflection, and developing their own perspectives. Their stage of intellectual development greatly influences both their competence in and their approach to these activities. It affects people's epistemological beliefs—their assumptions about knowledge and knowing. As educators, frameworks of intellectual development aid us in understanding the varied reactions to the structure and content of the class or training. These perspectives help us to create learning experiences that more effectively match the intellectual needs and abilities of our students. Moreover, they allow us to see that students' responses are often developmentally related, that students are not just being stubborn or narrow. This, in turn, helps us to be more empathic and less judgmental.

Theoretical Framework

I will briefly describe the model of intellectual development developed by William Perry (1968) and expanded upon by Belenky, Clinchy, Goldberger, and Tarule (1986). Perry's research focused on White, elite, college men, whereas that of Belenky et al. included women from various backgrounds and settings. Integrating the findings from these two studies, I will review the fundamental characteristics of each stage and then consider their educational implications. For a more complete and thorough discussion of these theories, I encourage readers to explore the original works, as well as the many other writings that have been sparked by their research that address both theory and practice. (See, for example, Baxter, 1992; Capossela, 1993; Goldberger, Clinchy, Belenky, & Tarule, 1998; Kloss, 1994; Kurfiss, 1988. Also see King & Kitchener, 1994, for a related model of the development of reflective judgment.)

Belenky et al. (1986) identified a position before the first stage in Perry's (1968) scheme. They labeled this *silence*. These women felt

mindless and voiceless, passive and powerless. They were dependent on external sources for knowledge and often feared male authority. They were the youngest and the most socially, economically, and
educationally deprived of all the women interviewed by these re-
searchers; no college women were represented in this group.

In *dualism/received knowledge* (the first stage in Perry's scheme),
people see knowledge as a collection of facts and look to the authority as the source of all knowledge. Knowledge is received, not created (for women, especially, it is gained through listening). This
phase is characterized by dualistic or dichotomous thinking—right-wrong, good-bad, either-or, us-them. People in this stage
are intolerant of ambiguity, whether in the content or the structure of
the class. As a result, they often feel confused, angry, or frustrated
when the educator does not give them the "right" answer. Such individuals frequently strive to figure out what the teacher "really
wants." Teachers may feel frustrated when these students take simplistic or narrow views on complex issues.

Students in this dualism and received-knowledge stage struggle
with considering multiple perspectives or analyses. They are unable
to see more than one view as legitimate and often have difficulty empathizing with others, especially when they don't agree. For example, suppose students were asked to consider the immigration policy in the United States in terms of whether or not there should be
more restrictions on immigrants. People in the dualism stage would
likely hold a clear position, often based on what they have heard
from a respected authority, such as a parent, politician, professor, or
social scientist. They might insist that immigrants unfairly take jobs
away from U.S. citizens, put undue strain on public schools, and are
a burden on our system, even though the dualistic person lacks a full
understanding of the issue. They would likely dismiss or be confused by someone who makes a contradictory argument, for example, by outlining ways immigrants contribute to our economy and
quality of life.

Ongoing exposure to multiple interpretations, different experiences, and varied opinions helps challenge these individuals' faith
in authorities and in finding the right answer. In the stage of *multiplicity and subjective knowledge,* people begin to recognize that some
things are unknown and that there is no definitive truth. Knowledge
is seen as a matter of opinion and is gained through first-hand experience. All opinions are valued and seen as equally valid. Individuals begin to trust their inner voice as a source of knowledge. There

is little interest in or respect for authority; women, particularly, tend to turn inward away from external (male) authorities.

Even though they now recognize some level of complexity, people in the multiplicity and subjective-knowledge stage lack the ability to assess different viewpoints. Instead, they rely on intuition, feelings, or common sense. In the immigration policy example provided above, people in this stage would come to an opinion on the basis of their gut feeling or on the basis of what they personally have seen, heard about, or experienced. They would respect each person's opinion and claim that people are entitled to feel as they do, without thinking that there is one generally right answer. However, they would tend to align with those who shared their view.

When educators expect and challenge these individuals to support their opinions (verbally or in written assignments), it will often be experienced by these individuals as a personal attack or as a result of unclear criteria for judgment. Individuals at this stage may feel that they were graded unfairly because they didn't agree with the teacher. However, as they repeatedly experience the need to provide evidence and encounter it in the materials they read, they may begin to move into the next stage.

With progress into the stage of *relativism and procedural knowledge* comes the ability to evaluate knowledge. People realize that opinions differ in quality and need to be supported with reasons. This stage is sometimes referred to as *contextualism* or *contextual relativism* because people begin to understand that knowledge is relative and contextual, that what one considers to be true depends on one's experience, perspective, and methods of reasoning—on one's standpoint. Authorities are now valued for their expertise but are not seen as the arbiters of truth.

At this stage, people begin to learn and to apply the methods (procedures) within a discipline to evaluate different positions. They use a systematic approach for answering questions and finding solutions. Belenky et al. (1986) identified two types of procedural knowers: *separate knowers* and *connected knowers*. Separate knowers tend to use objective analysis and argument to support and justify opinions. Connected knowers actively try to understand divergent views by putting themselves in the other's head to explain and clarify the other's position. Relativist/procedural knowers might approach the immigration policy situation by systematically examining studies that explore the impact of immigrants on different sectors of our society. They would be concerned with the quality of the studies—the methodologies used and who did them. They might consider how one's social position and history informs one's view. Connected knowers would be particularly interested in understanding from the other person's perspective why that person held a specific opinion—what has led the other person to a particular belief. Such knowers might now understand that immigration issues are not clear-cut, articulate the various benefits and challenges immigrants bring, and be able to make a reasonable case for a particular position. However, they may be reluctant to take a personal stand on immigration policy. As people more fully understand complexities, they recognize that they must make choices and commitments, thus ushering them into the next phase.

In the stage of *commitment in relativism/constructed knowledge*, people integrate both inner and outer knowledge, blending the inner truth with knowledge gained from others. In the process, knowers construct a personal worldview. Despite disparities and the lack of absolute surety, they make a stand or take a position. They appreciate historical and cultural contexts and recognize that the knower and the known are intertwined; that there is no objective truth. They engage in abstract thinking and meta-analysis. Constructed knowers have gained moral depth and sensitivity that guides their reasoning and action. In the immigration policy situation, people at this stage would decide what immigration policies to support on the basis of their sense of empathy and morality and on thoughtful reasoning about the information gathered.

Educational Implications

The two most challenging stages for educators tend to be those of dualism or received knowledge and multiplicity or subjective knowledge. In these stages, it is most difficult for people to engage in critical thinking and a systematic evaluation of knowledge. Critical thinking challenges these students' fundamental epistemological beliefs—that things are either right or wrong and that everyone is entitled to his or her own opinion, all of which are equally accurate and valid. What may be seen as resistance at these stages may in fact be a reflection of the level of cognitive development.

People in the stage of dualism/received knowledge are attached to their views and don't know how to deal with the complexity of issues. We can introduce a moderate degree of diversity (two or three different perspectives on the issue) as we try to challenge simplistic conceptions and open up alternatives. We can help these individuals to develop basic analytic and critical-thinking skills to make this task less overwhelming, and we can encourage personal reflection and empathy. These individuals need lots of opportunities to practice these skills. People in the stage of dualism or received knowledge benefit from concrete (not abstract), experiential learning in which the concepts or issues are made real—through examples, role plays, simulations, debates, or case studies. Activities, requirements, and assignments should be highly structured (this creates safety and eliminates some ambiguity). As people struggle with complexity, they need validation and support for their efforts from the instructor and their peers. It is unsettling to be shaken from feeling certain about an issue and to be asked to think in a way to which one is unaccustomed. Even though they may resist valuing other students as legitimate sources of knowledge, discussion with peers helps create the safety to explore new ideas and exposes them to varied experiences and opinions.

People at the multiplicity or subjective-knowledge stage appreciate cooperative, peer-oriented classrooms where they get to share their perspectives and experiences. They also need tools that help them to evaluate different views, weigh evidence, distinguish between strong and weak support, and consider counterarguments. People can be expected to provide evidence for opinions and substantiate how they reached their conclusions. Clear criteria for assessment are helpful, as are models of what a good argument looks like. To help students understand that requirements for support are not personal criticism, we can explain that to be credible to others, they need to be able to defend their views in a convincing way. In graded classes, it is helpful for students at all levels if we provide clear (and appropriate) criteria for how they will be evaluated, review examples of sample papers or answers that meet different levels of the criteria, and provide students with ample opportunity and support to meet our standards.

People in the multiplicity or subjective-knowledge stage need to be taught various reasoning strategies that value both separate and connected knowing. Not only can people be expected to critique a position according to particular methods, but they may also be expected to "feel into" a position to understand why someone reached a particular conclusion. Because they view knowledge as contextual and relative, they may find it difficult to commit to a position. We can help such people to see that disciplinary methods can complement one's inner voice, rather than supplant it. We can encourage them to use both these sources of knowledge to make a personal commitment to a perspective, to develop courage and integrity.

Most students enter college at dualism/received knowledge and move into the stages of multiplicity/subjective knowledge or relativism/procedural knowledge by the end of their college years. I frequently have adult students in graduate school who are still in the early stages. If a group is predominantly in one stage, then the class can be geared toward helping people progress through that stage and into the next. Often in classes, and especially in doing training in organizations, we can expect to find a range of developmental perspectives. As always, it is a challenge to accommodate the varying levels and needs. Here, as elsewhere, providing a variety of experiences and opportunities is most useful. I have found that a mix of both presentation and experiential activities tends to span these differences. People appreciate hearing factual information and analyses and participating in active learning. Individuals can engage in and process the activities in ways that fit their developmental level. Everyone can learn from reflecting on their own experiences, hearing different reactions, and being exposed to various connections and conclusions.

For example, I do an activity that addresses stereotypes and assumptions that tends to be effective with a range of people. Students are asked to anonymously write down two things they have felt, heard, or believed about a particular group (I'll ask them to consider several groups). They switch papers and read out what has been written. When the responses are recorded on newsprint for all to view, they consider which ones they personally feel are true or have questions about. In processing this activity, we explore stereotypes, compare similarities and differences among groups, look for patterns within groups, and consider the historical and cultural context. This activity tends to be concrete enough for dualistic thinkers but complex enough to allow for varying levels of self-examination and social analysis.

As people struggle with the process of developmental change, it is helpful to remember that what is at stake is generally more than just an intellectual perspective. As Belenky et al. (1986) well demonstrate, epistemological assumptions are usually related to one's sense of self and morality. One's way of being is often intertwined with one's way of knowing. Therefore, this process can be quite emotional as well as cognitive. This can explain some of the intensity we encounter, such as the strong investment in a particular view at the dualism/received knowledge stage or the hurt or anger as one's opinion is challenged when one is in the multiplicity/subjective knowledge stage. As people shift from one cognitive developmental stage to the next, they also shift how they see themselves—from a person incapable of creating knowledge; to someone who has inner wisdom, his or her own opinion, or both; to someone who can think reflectively and analytically; to someone who can construct his or her own sense of truth. This affects how they relate to others and how they see the world. This process can be both scary and exciting, both disconcerting and empowering.

Moreover, intellectual development is occurring within a social and political context. Our culture supports simplistic, dualistic thinking. Rarely are people exposed to complex, analytical perspectives on issues, especially as news continues to get reduced to sound bites and political slogans. A real range of viewpoints and alternative perspectives is hard to obtain in the mainstream media. Hierarchical structures reinforce received knowledge. They encourage people to listen to what the authority says and to figure out what she or he wants. This constrains opportunities for critical thinking. Furthermore, because inner knowing is not publicly valued, it is harder for people to develop this aspect of knowing and then to integrate it with external sources of knowledge. This presumably individual intellectual process is emotionally and culturally charged.

Social Identity Development

Although theories of intellectual development help us understand how people approach knowledge and knowing, models of social identity development give us insight into how people make meaning of their social identities and social reality. Social identity development theory describes a psychosocial process of change in the ways that people think about their own social-group membership, other social groups, and social oppression. It allows us to anticipate and make sense of students' responses and classroom interactions and to formulate educational approaches.

Theoretical Framework

I will first discuss the theory developed by Hardiman and Jackson (1997) that grew out of their research on Black and White racial identity development. They have expanded it to include social identity development in general for people in dominant, as well as subordinate, groups. In this chapter, I will just describe the process for people from privileged groups (in Chapter 9, I review the stages for people in subordinate groups as well). I will also present a model of White racial identity development developed by Janet Helms (1990, 1992, 1995) that is particularly useful in understanding the process of racial awareness for White people.

Both of these models suggest that people from privileged groups begin with an acceptance (conscious or unconscious) of the dominant culture's ideology that justifies the dominance of their own group. They tend to be ignorant about institutionalized oppression and privilege. Some individuals then move to questioning and resisting this worldview and structure of social relations. They begin to explore and act against oppressive attitudes and practices. Some people develop the need to create a new sense of their dominant identity that affirms their own as well as others' cultural groups. Finally, this new sense of self and social reality is internalized.

The social identity development model created by Hardiman and Jackson (1997) suggests five stages that people in the advantaged groups go through in sequential order. Each stage reflects a particular way of viewing the world and oneself as a member of a social group. Although people can act from more than one stage, they will have a predominant worldview. Moreover, for some of the stages, there are active (conscious) and passive (unconscious) manifestations. This model applies to different forms of oppression and social identities, though there are differences and variations depending on the social group. In addition, people may be at very different places in their identity development depending on which aspect of their identity is being considered (i.e., my White identity and racism or my middle-class identity and classism).

In the first stage, *naive,* there is little or no awareness of social identities and systematic inequality. This is usually the case only for young children. Although young children may be aware of differences, they do not initially attribute meaning or judgment to them in the way that they will as they get older. Yet children are very receptive to messages from their parents and their environment and move fairly quickly into the second stage.

This second stage, *acceptance,* is characterized by the acceptance of and participation in the value system and social arrangements of an unjust society. People have internalized the dominant belief system. This includes the stereotypes and messages about the superiority of their own group and the inferiority of the disadvantaged group. People in privileged groups commonly deny that there is a problem and are angry at having to deal with it or be implicated in it. They are unaware of their privileges and tend to see assimilation as the way for people from the oppressed group to behave and be successful. They often blame the victim.

In *active acceptance,* people consciously and overtly express an oppressive perspective. They tend to rationalize inequalities, attributing them to innate deficiencies. They may claim that people on welfare are just lazy and could find good work if they wanted to or that African Americans don't do as well in school because they're genetically less intelligent. In the most extreme, people in active acceptance may join supremacist organizations.

People from privileged groups who are in *passive acceptance* unintentionally and covertly perpetuate systems of inequality. From the passive (unconscious) perspective, people often deny differences, injustices, or their own collusion. *Color blindness* is one way to avoid acknowledging systematic inequities in power and privilege. These individuals may insist on treating everyone the same, regardless of background (ignoring cultural differences or experiences with oppression) or wonder why someone can't just act more "White" or "less gay" so they could fit in better. They will also maintain a sense of superiority, assuming that they need to help the disadvantaged group because its members are unable to take care of themselves or cannot make appropriate decisions. By simply accepting the dominant ideology, people in the passive acceptance stage unconsciously maintain injustice.

After people have been confronted with some experiences and information that contradict and challenge their worldview and beliefs, they may move into the third stage, *resistance.* (The term *resistance* in this model is used differently from the way I am using it in other parts of this book to refer to the unwillingness to engage in critical thinking about social justice.) They begin to question the oppressive ideology and seek to uncover the ways in which inequality is manifested individually, institutionally, and culturally. People in the dominant group begin to acknowledge their own discriminatory behaviors and examine ways in which they have been complicit in supporting and perpetuating inequality. They shift from blaming the victim to realizing the role of privileged groups in maintaining oppression. They gain an understanding of privilege systems and structural inequality. This is often accompanied by feelings of shame, guilt, and anger. Sometimes they will want to disassociate themselves from other oppressors, to be the special or "good" one, and to try to overidentify and affiliate with people in the disadvantaged group (i.e., Whites associating only with people of color, or middle- and upper-class people hanging out only with poor or working-class people). People in the stage of *active resistance* will confront discriminatory attitudes and practices, often in vocal and visible ways, such as writing letters, interrupting stereotypical comments, and changing organizational policy. People in the *passive-resistance* stage may be aware of injustice but engage in little behavioral change, avoid taking public stands or actions that entail risk, or decide to distance themselves from mainstream society.

The *resistance* stage is primarily concerned with "who I am not" and with reacting to the unjust society. The focus has been on the injustice faced by the disadvantaged group, not on the individual's own identity or culture. With this new consciousness, people from the dominant group may need to begin to answer the question, "who am I?" After feeling guilty or ashamed of their dominant identity, they may need to develop a social identity that is positive and affirming. For example, they need to consider what it means to be an antiracist White or a profeminist man. This may move them to develop a new sense of identity that characterizes the next stage.

The fourth stage is *redefinition*, in which people try to find new ways of defining themselves and their social group. In conjunction with others in the same social group, this process of identification leads people to new ways of naming themselves. Their awareness of this one form of oppression also allows them to reconsider their other social identities and forms of inequality. This can result in a more complex sense of themselves and a better understanding of the interrelatedness of different oppressions.

The final stage is *internalization*. Once people become comfortable with their new sense of identity, they are able to internalize it and apply it in different parts of their lives. To sustain this new identity in a hostile world that socializes and pressures people to maintain the current social order, it must be nurtured and supported by others. People at this stage need peers or organizations where there are people who share their perspective and can affirm this sense of identity.

The model by Janet Helms is similar to the Hardiman and Jackson model but focuses specifically on White racial identity development. Her model further elaborates the transition from racist to antiracist consciousness. In her six-stage theory, the first three perspectives, or statuses, are racist identities, whereas the last three are antiracist. Using the works of Helms (1990, 1992, 1995), Jones and Carter (1996), and Tatum (1997), I will briefly describe this model.

The first status is *contact*. It is characterized by innocence and ignorance about race and racial issues. Little attention or significance is given to race. Attitudes and stereotypes about people of color are uncritically absorbed from the dominant culture. People may acknowledge individual acts of prejudice but not institutionalized racism and White privilege. As far as they are concerned, White is just normal. Although individuals may be racist without knowing it, they do not see themselves as prejudiced.

In the next level, *disintegration,* people start to notice the social significance of race and to develop an awareness of racism and White privilege. They become conscious of their own prejudices. This gives rise to anxiety, guilt, shame, and anger. They experience some confusion and conflict about what to do with this new perspective that causes them discomfort.

This leads to *reintegration.* The individuals' feelings of guilt or denial are transformed into fear and anger at people of color. As a self-protection strategy, they will blame the victim. They seek to justify Whites' positions of advantage and superiority by devaluing people of color and idealizing Whites. People may do this in active and conscious ways or in passive and subconscious ways. It is their attempt to regain some psychological equilibrium.

During the next phase of development, Whites begin to achieve an anti-racist identity. As people gain a more complex understanding of the dynamics of racism or have experiences that sufficiently challenge their ability to rationalize racial inequality, they may move to *pseudo-independence.* This stage is characterized by the guilty White liberal. People may be self-conscious and ashamed of their Whiteness and prefer to associate with people of color. They may focus on helping people of color become equal to Whites by encouraging assimilation. Individuals may have an intellectual awareness of race and racism but have not consciously dealt with Whites' (and their own) responsibility for maintaining a system of racial injustice.

In *immersion-emersion,* people begin to assume personal responsibility for racism and actively explore racism and White culture. As they seek to understand Whiteness and develop a more positive White identity, they seek out other Whites engaged in a similar struggle for support or who can be role models. People in immersion-emersion also actively confront racism and look for both same-race and cross-race experiences.

Finally, in *autonomy,* people internalize a new meaning for Whiteness in which race is a valued part of their identity though that identity is not based on a sense of racial superiority. Because they have a complex, respectful, and sophisticated racial worldview, they are comfortable and effective cross-racially. Confronting racism and oppression is part of their daily life. Even though they have achieved this level of racial identity, they continue to be open to new information and new ways of thinking.

Educational Implications

These theories of social identity development help us appreciate the different and changing worldviews of our students. These stages can help explain individual responses as well as interpersonal dynamics. In the Hardiman and Jackson model (1997), individuals in the acceptance stage, particularly the active acceptance stage, are most likely to be resistant to social justice issues because they are most entrenched in a worldview that supports the status quo. People in the resistance stage will likely be receptive, though they may be prone to avoidance if they begin to feel too guilty and uncomfortable.

People will tend to align with others at a similar stage. Tensions often arise between and among students at different points in the process. For example, people in resistance will usually have little tolerance for someone in acceptance. People in redefinition or internalization may find it easier to be an educator or a coalition builder. However, they may be seen by some people in the resistance stage as too mainstream and by others as a role model. The above framework can also be useful in understanding our own responses to particular issues and people as well. I will address this in Chapter 8.

We can also use these models to provide educational experiences that would be most appropriate. Obviously, students can be at various levels, though most people tend to be in the acceptance or resistance stage (and occasionally at the redefinition stage). Individuals in acceptance particularly need to be exposed to material that challenges the dominant ideology and their stereotypes about different groups. They especially gain from opportunities to learn about the experiences of people from disadvantaged groups and how oppression is institutionalized. Often, firsthand encounters with real people and situations and information that they uncover themselves will be most powerful. People in resistance need the chance to delve more deeply into issues of injustice, find support for their growing consciousness, and develop ways to effectively channel their energy and feelings about social injustice. Those in redefinition benefit by being able to explore their cultural background and by learning about or talking with others who are social change activists with a positive sense of their own identities. By offering a range of information, experiences, and choices, we can most likely meet the needs of our different students.

Conclusion

For those unfamiliar with developmental theories, it can seem overwhelming to try to apply them all at once. I suggest that readers choose one they find most interesting and begin there. I have found over time that the more lenses I have to view a situation, the more ways I have to think about it and to develop strategies to address it. Various developmental frameworks help us to appreciate the behaviors of our students and to improve our educational effectiveness. These perspectives may also enhance our empathy and improve our attitudes toward students. Upon learning the Perry scheme, Robert Kloss (1994) notes, "I then both understood them and judged them less harshly as a result" (p. 152). This can move us away from blame or frustration and toward more constructive engagement. Learning about diversity and social justice presents tremendous emotional and cognitive challenges for our students. The process of growth and change in these areas is especially profound. For educators, managing not only individual but intragroup dynamics is a formidable task. Fortunately, developmental theories provide us with maps and guides for meeting and leading our students through this rocky terrain.

4

Understanding Resistance

In the previous chapter, I described the phase of contradiction, where the intention is to help people engage in critical thinking and the development of critical consciousness. People are encouraged to question assumptions, explore new ideas, and consider alternative perspectives. In diversity and social justice education, this process involves examining power relationships, structural inequalities, and ideology. It includes personal reflection and critical analysis that usually challenge how people view the world and see themselves. Although some individuals may embrace this exploration, others resist. Consider the following situations:

- Whenever stories are shared that illustrate how racism affects people of color, a White male asserts that he is really the one being discriminated against.
- A student sits in class with arms crossed, does not participate, and appears inattentive. She then turns in well-written papers that echo progressive perspectives on diversity issues.
- A lesbian teacher who discusses heterosexism, along with racism, sexism, and classism, is accused of always talking about gay issues and imposing "her" cause.
- While rejecting any information describing institutional barriers to overcoming poverty, a middle-class person insists that if people just worked harder they could succeed and that most people on welfare are just enjoying a life in which they don't have to work.

- Any discussion of patriarchy or male privilege is immediately labeled "male bashing" by the men in the group.

These examples illustrate some of the ways in which people express resistance to social justice issues. Many educators have written about their experiences with resistance (e.g., Chan & Treacy, 1996; Chavez & O'Donnell, 1998; Higginbotham, 1996; Sleeter, 1992; Williams, Dunlap, & McCandies, 1999). Often it is overt—discrediting people, discounting information, challenging every fact, changing the focus, avoiding assignments, or disrupting the class or meeting. Other times, it is subtle—conforming to assumed expectations or not participating. In any case, people resist learning and change.

Resistance grows out of social realities and reflects psychological issues. In this chapter, I will explore how societal and psychological factors underlie resistance. Because the social and psychological are so intertwined and their interplay is so powerful, the factors can be hard to isolate. Some of the distinctions seem blurred and, at times, somewhat arbitrary. Nonetheless, my intention is to try to identify the various forces that create resistance. Although many of these dynamics are accurate for people from disadvantaged groups, my focus is on people from advantaged groups. I will discuss reasons for resistance that are applicable to different forms of oppression and to social justice in general. In the next chapter, I will suggest ways to prevent and address it.

Just as there are differences among different types of oppression, there can be particular kinds of resistance to specific isms. For example, I have found that people become defensive during discussions of classism when there are challenges to the class system. People immediately interpret this as advocacy for socialism or communism (which are considered dirty words and of which they usually have distorted views). They also perceive it as a threat to their desire for upward mobility and "making it." In addition, there is frequently resistance to issues related to heterosexism because of religious beliefs. Resistance to exploring ableism often involves the fear of facing one's own vulnerability to becoming disabled. I will not address resistance to specific forms of oppression. Instead, readers can refer to the resources listed in the appendix. Even though some of these topics require particular insight and strategies, the perspectives and approaches I am presenting can be helpful in most circumstances.

What Is Resistance?

When people are resistant, they are unable to seriously engage with the material. They refuse to consider alternative perspectives that challenge the dominant ideology that maintains the status quo. They resist information or experiences that may cause them to question their worldview. They may dismiss the idea that oppression or systemic inequalities are real.

Resistance stems from fear and discomfort. Because we are asking people to question their fundamental belief systems, it makes sense that people feel threatened and act resistant. Defensiveness, specifically, is a way to mitigate anxiety, assuage guilt, or protect against other painful feelings. It is irrational, an automatic reaction rather than a considered choice (Clark, 1991, p. 231). When people's needs for safety and stability are not met, they turn off, shut down, and avoid new information—hardly conditions for education to occur.

In some educational literature, the term *resistance* is used in a different way (Apple, 1982; Giroux, 1983). *Resistance theory* refers to a student's unwillingness to learn as being a political act. Students from oppressed groups may refuse to participate in their education when they perceive the school and the curriculum to be culturally inappropriate or oppressive. This is not the type of resistance I am referring to. In this book, I specifically focus on resistance by people from dominant groups.

Let me further clarify what I mean by resistance. Resistance is not the same as prejudice. Prejudices are prejudgments—attitudes and beliefs about particular social groups. Resistance is not about people's specific views but about their openness to consider other perspectives. Prejudice reduction asks that people identify and reevaluate the messages they have received and the assumptions they make. The unwillingness to participate in that type of personal exploration is exactly what resistance is. Some people may not hold negative views about individuals from certain dominated groups, yet they deny the existence of social oppression. Needless to say, as we educate about social justice issues, we must help people examine their prejudices. But addressing resistance is the precursor to that endeavor.

I also do not consider questions and debate about the material done in the spirit of open inquiry to be resistance. Genuinely grappling with issues can reflect engagement. In fact, critical thinking can involve analyzing, questioning, and challenging ideas. My goal as an educator is not to have everyone think the same way or think as I do. Rather, I want them to engage with the material in a critical and self-reflective way and to develop a more informed and thoughtful understanding of themselves and their world.

There is the danger of mislabeling certain behaviors as resistance because of our own fears or cultural ignorance. Some educators are uncomfortable with strong emotions, conflict, or challenges. Their own discomfort leads them to see these behaviors as resistance and unproductive. The communication styles of some cultural groups (i.e., Jews, African Americans) tend to be more emotional and confrontational (Kochman, 1981; Tannen, 1990). Challenge and debate can actually be a sign of engagement and learning. Trying to suppress these types of exchanges may unintentionally undermine educational goals. On the other hand, other cultural groups (i.e., Asians) may be more quiet and deferential to the teacher. This might be construed as a type of passive resistance; the educator might assume that the student is not engaged and is simply trying to please the teacher. We need to be careful not to misinterpret these various kinds of behaviors and presume resistance when there is none. Gaining knowledge of different cultural styles is one way we can help ensure we don't mislabel behavior. We can also see whether people, despite their particular style, are willing to consider new perspectives, reexamine their assumptions, and reflect on what others have to say.

Resistance can be one of the most difficult aspects of educating about diversity and social justice. Often we feel angry at resistant behavior and frustrated with the individuals. They can make us feel incompetent. It becomes hard to like or connect with people who are being resistant. Most of us are painfully aware that we are least effective when we feel this way.

We can address those feelings and enhance our effectiveness by better understanding resistance. Rather than viewing resistant individuals as stubborn or obnoxious, we might see them as people who are afraid or in pain. This can increase our empathy and help us to develop strategies for intervention.

Sociopolitical Factors

We cannot understand resistance without understanding the social context in which it occurs. If we consider the realities in which we live, it is hardly surprising that people become defensive when social justice becomes a topic of discussion. Our social, political, and economic systems create and reinforce worldviews and ways of acting that undermine openness to true democracy and equity.

Most broadly, social relations in this country are structured on the basis of a *power-over* model (Kreisberg, 1992; Eisler, 1987). This top-down model is characterized by inequality, ranking, domination, and intimidation. It fosters a dualistic, win-lose mentality and the belief that people need to compete for scarce resources. Coming out "on top" or "ahead" is the primary measure of personal value. People assume that dominating others is natural, normal, inevitable, and desirable. Therefore, this view erodes the possibility of investment in fundamental change or true social justice. (I discuss this further in Chapter 10.)

Although this type of social system perpetuates oppression, certain aspects of it are especially relevant to understanding resistance to social justice issues. The structures and values of hierarchy, competition, meritocracy, individualism, and the material benefits to people from dominant groups are one aspect. A second aspect is the social climate and norms that dehumanize oppressed people and deny differences. I will discuss each of these more specifically.

Structures and Values

In general, the system is set up to the advantage of dominant groups. People from these groups gain *material benefits* from oppression. The very nature of being part of an advantaged group means that one has greater access to resources, opportunities, and unearned privileges because they are denied to others. Social change threatens these privileges that have been taken for granted and alters the rules of the game. As Wellman (1977) noted, White Americans want to attend to Blacks' demands while avoiding the institutional reorganization that might cause them to lose ground (p. 216).

Like oppression, which is grounded in dominant and subordinate relations, our social dynamics and institutional structures are based in *hierarchies*. Schools and workplaces are organized hierarchically; some people are considered either better than or superior to others (or both). Higher positions generally confer greater status and privilege. No matter where people are in the hierarchy, they usually strive to be above others and to stay one up. The only alternative seems to be the one-down position. Because people from disadvantaged groups are usually at the lower levels of the hierarchy, they serve to elevate people from dominant groups. Continuing to see people from subordinate groups as inferior justifies and maintains this stratification.

Competition is embedded in our hierarchical structures. To advance in the hierarchy, one needs to beat out others. This serves to create a zero-sum dynamic; one person's gain comes at another's expense. We often need to compete for status, power, and resources—be they material (e.g., jobs) or emotional (e.g., attention or respect). Because we are encouraged to see others as threats to our achievement or well-being, we have little incentive to enhance their situation.

A *belief in meritocracy* makes this competitive system seem fair. Increasingly, people from dominant groups assume that the playing field has been leveled and that people therefore get what they deserve. People from advantaged groups maintain that anyone can succeed if they have the ability and work hard. Lack of success is attributed to incompetence, laziness, or cultural deficits. The existence or impact of inequalities and discrimination is minimized or discounted. "People who believe in a just world are most likely to see victims as meriting their misfortune and/or asking for it" (Rubin & Peplau, 1975, p. 71). A victim-blaming culture undermines concern for those in disadvantaged positions and reduces the perception that the current system needs to change.

Moreover, our culture promotes *individualism*. Unlike other cultures that emphasize group membership and a collective sense of self, the United States glorifies the autonomous individual (Bellah, Madsen, Sullivan, Swidler, & Tipton, 1985; Sampson, 1988). "Look out for number one" and "Pull yourself up by your own bootstraps" are common expectations and advice. This individualistic orientation fosters a preoccupation with self-sufficiency and advancing oneself, regardless of the impact on others.

Individualism also impedes our ability to see ourselves as part of a privileged social group that unfairly benefits from inequality. Most people tend toward individualistic analyses of oppression. They attribute inequities to individual prejudices and discrimination. The focus, therefore, becomes on trying to change bigoted individuals, rather than on examining the cultural values and institutional structures that maintain oppression. There are those who claim that they are already treating everyone nicely and fairly and so do not need education about diversity. Some people may resist exploring social issues for fear of feeling guilty or personally accountable for social inequities. People from privileged groups are invested in retaining this individualistic perspective. If people acknowledge a system that advantages their group, they may come to question their own accomplishments. This lack of a larger social and historical perspective also allows some people from immigrant White ethnic groups whose families "made it" to assume that others today could do so as well if they just worked as hard.

Competition and individualism are mutually reinforcing. As people become focused on themselves, they increasingly view others as rivals. The more people are defined as rivals, the harder it is to build an overall sense of community or to establish genuine connection. This leads to a greater focus on self and the erosion of social responsibility. Similarly, the more people are self-oriented, feel responsible for their own survival, and become obsessed with their success, the more they see others as competitors. Dominant groups may have the most intensified self-absorption because they have the most opportunity for mobility and aggrandizement (Derber, 1979).

Competitive individualism is fostered by the dominant culture, rooted in institutional structures, and exacerbated by economic forces:

> People are cut adrift from any community providing economic security and thrown into a labor market that rewards individual performance, while making employment precarious and highly competitive; each individual must become self-oriented simply to subsist and succeed. (Derber, 1979, p. 91)

Lerner (1996) expands on this critique of our economic system. He maintains that the competitive market and its bottom-line mentality shapes the way we deal with each other. People are encouraged to see others in terms of what they can do for them and how others can satisfy their needs. This builds mutual distrust, erodes community, and impedes solidarity. As a result, it is easier to turn one's back on people who are oppressed. This creates a cycle in which people need to build emotional walls to protect themselves from the pain of others and, in so doing, become more isolated. As a result of this isolation, they receive less caring from others and increasingly need to look out for themselves.

Furthermore, Lerner maintains that the economic and political institutions of this society often frustrate our "meaning needs" (for love, recognition, and the opportunity to contribute to the higher good) by privileging selfishness, cynicism, materialism, and the isolated individual. At the same time, it makes us feel that a life based on our highest values is either impossible or self-destructive (because while we are going for own highest values, everyone else will be advancing his or her own narrow self-interest). You will be left out of the game or taken advantage of. If you can't swim with the sharks, you will be eaten by them.[1]

Social Climate and Norms

Public *scapegoating and the dehumanization of oppressed groups* further promotes resistance to social justice. Immigrants, people of color, gays and lesbians, and women (especially feminists) are frequently blamed for the ills and breakdown of society. Oppressed groups are often portrayed or discussed in less than fully human ways. For example, the *New York Times* reported that while debating a welfare bill, House Republicans compared welfare recipients to alligators and wolves (Pear, 1996).

Not only are people from oppressed groups scapegoated, they are blamed for their own social situation. To account for social problems or inequality, this "blaming the victim" ideology (Ryan, 1970) locates problems in the individual rather than in the social structures. The marginalization of groups of people is attributed to their own failings; they are somehow deviant. Consistent with a individualistic orientation, the focus is on changing the individual, not society.

A *conservative political climate* contributes to this thinking. Since the 1980s, social programs have been dismantled, and governmental efforts to address inequality have been eroded. Hate radio has boomed. Claims of political correctness have become popular, and progressive social causes are no longer in vogue. The religious Right has gained enormous popularity and political power (Pharr, 1996).

Despite this public noise about racism and other types of inequalities, there are *taboos against acknowledging differences and discussing oppression.* People are generally taught not to notice differences; to do so implies that one is prejudiced. The preferred stance is colorblindness (or other types of denials of differences), what Ruth Frankenberg (1993) refers to as "color-evasion" and "power-evasion." In a country where most people consider themselves middle-class, despite huge ranges in income and wealth, one is not supposed to acknowledge our class system. The publicly perpetuated norm encourages avoidance of honest, meaningful discussions about our social identities, about social inequities, and about our experiences because of them. People enter our classrooms and workshops with this internalized taboo and a lack of skill or comfort in having these types of conversations.

These various interlocking factors provide little institutional or cultural support to engage in an exploration of social justice. We are discouraged from recognizing and discussing systemic inequality and from developing a sense of community or social responsibility. Needless to say, this is not absolute; we receive contradictory messages as well—to help those less fortunate, to be kind to your neighbors, to treat others as you want to be treated. Nonetheless, the dominant values and social structures push us to act otherwise—to maintain the status quo and reserve our positions of power. Thus, this provides rich soil for the growth of resistance.

Psychological Factors

These social, cultural, political, and economic factors affect our psychology and worldview. There is an ongoing dialectic between the psychological and the societal, the personal and the political. Dominator models of social organization not only generate certain structural dynamics, they also produce what Koegel (1997) refers to as "dominator intelligence." As our consciousness is shaped by the dominant ideology and institutionalized practices, it influences how we act, how we view ourselves, and how we perceive others. We become conditioned to see the world in particular ways and to act accordingly.

Clearly, there is much in the dominant culture that lays a foundation for resistance to social justice. To some extent, we are products of our environment. However, these cultural values and institutional practices get internalized in personal and idiosyncratic ways. Because of our particular psyches, social identities, cultural backgrounds, and circumstances, we respond to these influences differently. Thus, although resistance has social roots, it is ultimately a psychological phenomenon. There are numerous psychological processes at work that help explain this need to resist new perspectives about social reality. Although there may be intrapsychic dynamics involved, I will primarily focus on what I see as social-psychological issues.

Focus on One's Own Pain and Plight

In the previous section, I discussed how our economic and social systems, which reflect an "ethos of selfishness, materialism and cynicism," fuel fears, pain, and insecurities. Many people feel underappreciated and underrecognized. Accepting the notion of a meritocracy, they blame themselves for not being more successful. People often become resistant to social justice issues or the plight of others when they are focused on their own distress or anxiety. A generally narcissistic culture also contributes to people's absorption with their own lives and personal struggles. Preoccupation with self and self-concern can reduce one's attention to or caring about others (Staub, 1978).

I regularly hear people from privileged groups express concerns about their own well-being, some clearly tied to societal situations, others to more personal issues. Few people from dominant groups feel powerful or greatly advantaged. Even though they are the so-called benefactors of oppression, they may feel victimized as well. Many have personal stories about how they were discriminated against, excluded, or stereotyped. They often feel angry and hurt by those experiences. White people have recalled how they were snubbed by people of color and assumed to be racist. Others recount aspects of their socialization that have had negative or painful consequences. People from wealthy families have discussed how they have felt isolated from other people and received material goods instead of love and family connection. Men talk about how they were taught to hide and ignore their feelings and pretend to be someone they weren't.

People from privileged groups may also perceive that it is they who are really at a disadvantage in many cases. They complain that low-income people or people of color get various kinds of financial, employment, or academic support for which middle-class and White people are ineligible. Some White men feel that they are unfairly losing jobs to White women and people of color because of affirmative action and that they are cast as the scapegoats in society. Heterosexuals may believe that gays and lesbians are getting special rights. Regardless of the accuracy of these beliefs, their emotions and experiences are real. Even when not directly blaming others, people still have worries about paying for their education, getting affordable housing, dealing with quality childcare, or keeping their job in the midst of downsizing. This focus on their own concerns affects their openness and ability to participate in a self-reflective and critical educational process.

People from privileged groups who are strongly identified with one of their subordinate-group identities may have little interest in exploring the oppression of other groups or the areas of their lives in which they are privileged. They may be narrowly focused on the pain or difficulty they face as a person from a disadvantaged group. Because the experience of victimization or oppression is usually more salient, they may have difficulty acknowledging privilege. In Chapter 2, I discussed how people in privileged groups often try to minimize their dominant identity and emphasize their targeted identity. Being the victim is usually more attractive than being the oppressor. This focus on one's subordinate identity to the exclusion of other aspects of one's identity may also be related to one's process of social identity development, which I discuss below.

In some cases, it is unacknowledged pain that becomes the source for resistance. Swiss psychoanalyst Alice Miller (1984, 1990) describes the "hidden cruelties of childhood" and "poisonous pedagogies"—the various ways children are abused, manipulated, objectified, and used to satisfy their parents' needs. She maintains that unless people have the opportunity to examine and work through these hurts, they are unable to acknowledge the suffering of others. They deny others' pain to resist facing their own pain. Unless people consciously deal with their mistreatment, they are more likely to lack empathy and to mistreat others.

Stage of Social Identity Development

In the previous chapter, I outlined some models of social (racial) identity development that can be useful in understanding people's self-concepts and worldviews (Hardiman & Jackson, 1992, 1997; Helms, 1992, 1995; Jones & Carter, 1996; Tatum, 1997). Resistance may be related to where people are in their development of social (racial) consciousness. Individuals are more likely to be resistant at certain stages, in particular, reintegration (Helms model, 1990, 1992,

1995) and acceptance (Hardiman & Jackson model, 1997). At these stages, individuals have internalized the dominant belief system about themselves and others. They may be invested in the status quo and most resistant to alternative ways of construing social relations.

During reintegration (in the Helms model), as people deal with their awareness of racism, their feelings of guilt or denial may be transformed into fear or anger directed toward people of color. They revert to blaming the victim and to beliefs of superiority. There is the effort to restore their sense of privilege by idealizing Whites and White culture and denigrating people of color and their cultures.

In the acceptance stage, people also support the dominant ideology. In passive acceptance, people unconsciously collude with the unjust system. They participate in maintaining inequality, often without ill intent, simply by going along with the status quo. Although there may be some resistance from people at this stage as their assumptions are challenged, they are less vehemently entrenched in a worldview that maintains oppression. People in active acceptance, however, consciously subscribe to a worldview that supports domination and subordination. They intentionally perpetuate attitudes and actions that oppress other people. They are invested in a belief system that preserves their dominance. We can expect the most resistance from people with this perspective.

When people make the transition from acceptance to resistance (meaning, in this case, the resistance to an oppressive ideology), they become more aware of systems of social injustice and more critical of them. In many cases, this state of disequilibrium creates an openness to new information. However, this period also can be marked by fear and uncertainty. People may worry about the implications of this questioning and self-examination. If the discomfort or fear is too great, they may feel overwhelmed and close down.

People in active resistance in a subordinate identity may also avoid dealing with their dominant identities or have minimal concern about people from other disadvantaged groups. At this point, many are steeped in their own feelings and process. They have little attention for things outside this scope. For example, a heterosexual Latino man in active resistance regarding racism may not be willing to recognize his heterosexual or male privilege or to connect to the experiences of heterosexism faced by gays, lesbians, or bisexuals.

Cognitive Dissonance

Another psychological factor that underlies resistance is cognitive dissonance. It is the discrepancy between what we currently believe to be true and other contradictory information. "One way to think about cognitive dissonance is as psychological discomfort" (Elliot & Devine, 1994, p. 67). We often resist things that challenge our views of self, other, and how the world operates. Thus, social justice education can be a very threatening process. If you've always believed that the United States was a just place or that certain groups were inferior, it is understandable to want to shut out contradictory information that forces you to question your whole view of the world and your place in it.

There are several ways people try to reduce cognitive dissonance (Simon, Greenberg, & Brehm, 1995). One way is to change the attitude, value, opinion, or behavior. Once individuals receive information that convinces them that their current view is inaccurate, they change their belief.

Another way individuals deal with dissonance is to seek out information to reduce the inconsistency. People may try to discount or explain away the discrepancy. Some will look for facts to support their opinion and discredit the other view. Others find ways to blame the victim (they're less intelligent or lazy) as a way to justify the oppressive conditions.

A third way to reduce cognitive dissonance is to trivialize the issue to reduce the importance of that which is creating discomfort. For example, people may argue that the oppression experienced is not that bad, that things have really changed, or that another group has it worse. Sometimes they complain that people from disadvantaged groups are being oversensitive, that they are making a big deal out of nothing.

Last, some people simply try to avoid or distance themselves from the issues. They may psychologically or physically withdraw. In educational settings, this may include cutting classes, not doing the assignments, or being inattentive or disruptive. All the above strategies serve to reduce the dissonance and restore psychological comfort.

The emotional ramifications of cognitive dissonance also can lead to resistance. Cognitive dissonance can be particularly threatening when it involves questioning beliefs or values learned from one's parents or other respected individuals. This can disrupt one's trust in these people and precipitate a potential rupture in relation-ships. This concern may be especially salient for college students who are just beginning to forge their own identity apart from their parents. It is also discomforting to acknowledge the limitations or prejudices of people who have been held in high esteem and with whom there is a desire to have a close relationship. In addition, al-lowing oneself to fully acknowledge the injustice and suffering in the world can be painful, saddening, and disempowering.

Protection of Self-Integrity and Self-Worth

Like cognitive dissonance, in which people's beliefs and values are challenged, individuals may avoid situations that they fear will challenge their self-concepts. Social justice issues are resisted to pro-tect self-integrity. Most people believe that they are good and caring. They consciously hold an egalitarian, nonprejudiced self-image (Gaertner & Dovidio, 1986). Therefore, many people resist experi-ences or information that might induce guilt or awareness of nega-tive aspects of themselves. They are often concerned that they will find out how prejudiced they are or feel bad when they realize their role in perpetuating the oppression of others. Moreover, many peo-ple, especially professionals, see themselves as competent, capable, and sophisticated. They are invested in maintaining this image to themselves and others. Consequently, in educational settings, they may be reluctant to appear ignorant, foolish, or naive. This prevents them from being open to new perspectives and activities that chal-lenge their sense of competence and control.

Another reason to become defensive is to preserve one's self-worth. If one's identity is precarious and built on feeling supe-rior to others, then questioning that system threatens one's sense of self. Even unconsciously, people may feel that their social group is more "normal" or better than others. Truly valuing and validating the traits and cultures of other groups diminishes this sense of supe-riority. Moreover, in a competitive and presumably meritocratic sys-tem, we need to constantly prove ourselves and fend off feelings of worthlessness (Kohn, 1990). Putting down others is often a way to bolster self-esteem and a sense of self-worth.

Fears About Change

Most people fear change. The unknown is scary. Especially if one accepts the dominant worldview, there is greater reason to fear social justice. People from dominant groups frequently imagine that the sharing of power and greater equity will mean that they will become oppressed. The assumption is that the same social dynamics will be in place but that they now will be in the disadvantaged role. If the only alternative is to be in a less desirable situation, it makes sense that individuals would resist the notion of social change. From this perspective, it also makes sense for people to want to ally with the oppressor rather than the oppressed.

Other Factors

Reactions to the Educator

Resistance can result from various types of reactions to the educator. Some people struggle with authority, regardless of the specific content or leader. They do not want to feel in a lesser position and thus seek to assert their power. Certainly, diversity issues are provocative and evoke resistance, yet the underlying dynamic is to challenge anyone who is in a role of authority and who is seen as telling them what to do or think. This can occur with students in a classroom or participants in a workshop within an organization. Their reaction is likely to intensify the more they assume that this will be a lesson in political correctness.

Others tend to blame the messenger for bringing them unsettling or painful information. The instructor becomes a target for their fear and anxiety. The leader is attacked for presenting issues that make them feel uncomfortable. It becomes the educator's fault that she or he "made" them become aware of certain personal characteristics or social realities.

There are also dynamics that arise between students and teachers because of their social identities. Allsup (1995) suggests that there is a "bond of unstated but understood affirmation between White male students and a White male instructor" (p. 89). When a White male teacher reveals and challenges the system of White male privilege, White male students may feel betrayed. They may become angry when the educator acts in ways that violate the implicit norms that maintain oppression and the assumption that "he is one of us." Similar reactions can occur with other isms when the educator from the dominant group does not espouse the expected perspective and breaks the assumed sense of solidarity.

When a teacher is a member of a subordinate group, students from the dominant group are more likely to challenge that teacher's authority and credibility. A sense of superiority and entitlement (particularly from White men) allows them to feel freer to do so. White women and people of color, especially women of color, are often viewed as less competent and less qualified. Students may not take them as seriously and question their expertise. When educators address a form of oppression in which they are in the disadvantaged group, they may be perceived as self-serving, complaining, oversensitive, bashing people from the privileged group or imposing their opinion. In these various ways, people use the educator as an excuse or vehicle to avoid dealing with the material.

Religious and Cultural Beliefs

Many people use their spiritual/religious beliefs as a foundation from which to do work for social justice. (I discuss this further in Chapter 7.) Individuals with strong religious or cultural convictions can be open to and respectful of other views, even if they ultimately do not accept them. Many people find ways to integrate new understandings and changing social dynamics into their religious or cultural belief systems. However, these beliefs can also promote intolerance and closed-mindedness, which may manifest as resistance. Some people who hold strong religious or cultural beliefs use these as reasons not to consider other points of view. They rigidly maintain the correctness of their positions and dogmatically reject the validity of other perspectives or experiences.

White Men and Resistance

Given the various societal and psychological factors discussed above, it is not surprising that many educators often find White males to be most resistant to social justice. Male psychology, socialization, and social position encompass and often epitomize the previously described reasons for resistance.

First, White men tend to have an individualistic and separate sense of self. Landrine (1992) describes two ways of identifying with "self": the *referential self*, which is egocentric and Western in origin, and the *indexical self*, which is sociocentric. The referential self focuses on the rugged individualist, a stereotype that is usually associated with White, male, middle-class Americans. Rarely do White men see themselves as part of a social group or understand how, as a group, they benefit from social inequality. Therefore, it is hard for them to understand oppression as a social system or their role in it by virtue to their social identity.

Second, they tend to imagine relationships as hierarchies with an emphasis on competition and maintaining or advancing oneself in this hierarchy (Gilligan, 1980/1993; Tannen, 1990). Their identity often has been based on a sense of superiority and on "making it" in society. Creating more equity changes roles and expectations, throwing into question their sense of identity.

In addition, most men have been socialized to suppress their feelings and fears. In an effort to deny and block feelings, they may resist emotion-generating experiences. It is threatening to acknowledge the pain of participating in an oppressive system and the ways in which they feel vulnerable or hurt others. They are generally less skilled in accessing their feelings and more constrained in expressing them. The denial of their own pain and emotions makes it more difficult to identify with the feelings of other people. This reduces their capacity for empathy, an important component of social justice work.

Several studies have reported that White men increasingly feel that they are unfairly blamed for social problems (Cose, 1995; Gallagher, 1997). White men often believe that other groups are getting advantages or special treatment that they are denied. I frequently hear White male students in my classes express anxiety about getting or keeping a good job. Narrowly focused on their own concerns about security, they have little interest in worrying about others.

Moreover, White men have received the greatest benefits from oppression and therefore have the most to lose. Because they have been the norm against which others have been measured, it can be frightening to become "decentered" and lose some of the privileges and superiority they have taken for granted. They often experience this shift toward equity as unfairness (because they're not getting as much as they used to). This generates a backlash against social justice efforts.

Conclusion

Clearly, the institutional structures and values of the dominant culture lay a strong foundation for resistance to social justice issues. Our society encourages people to be self-focused, to gain their sense of self-worth by feeling superior, to see others as threats, to protect their resources, and to blame people for their failures. These messages and worldview become internalized, to which people add their own personal issues. Psychologically, resistance is more likely when people are focused on their own struggles, are in particular stages of social identity development, try to avoid cognitive dissonance, and need to protect their sense of self. Despite this litany of reasons for resistance, all hope is not lost. By considering the range of societal and psychological reasons people may be resistant, I believe we can be more compassionate and more skillful in how we work with people. As we know, we are able to reach many (if not most) individuals. We *can* help them become more open to a process of change. In the next chapter, I'll discuss how.

Note

1. Thank you to Rob Koegel for suggesting this analogy.

5

Preventing and Reducing Resistance

The previous chapter discussed how many sociopolitical and psychological factors underlie the resistance we encounter when discussing social justice issues. Our dominant cultural values, structures, and social climate emphasize competitive individualism, hierarchy, meritocracy, blaming the victim, material benefits, and the denial of differences. These increase people's drive for self-preservation and advancement at the expense of others. Psychologically, fears, pain, cognitive dissonance, and protection of one's self-concept fuel defensiveness. In the long term, we need to work for systemic change to transform the societal beliefs and structures that maintain inequality and create the context for resistance to social justice. In the short term, we can look at how we can reduce the factors that promote defensiveness and resistance.

Resistance is an expression of fear, anxiety, and discomfort. It blocks people's openness to explore alternative viewpoints that question the status quo, analyze systems of oppression, and offer new possibilities of social relations. To address resistance, we need to create "psychological safety and readiness" (Friedman & Lipshitz, 1992). As discussed in Chapter 3, before people can deal with challenges to their current worldview, *contradiction*, they need an affirming, supportive environment, or *confirmation*. As educators, we need to provide people with a balance of challenge and support.

> If someone needs challenge and they get too much support, they
> don't learn anything. If someone needs support and they get too
> much challenge, they will flee the learning situation. People in de-
> fense are heavy on challenge and need support. (Bennett &
> Bennett, 1992, p. 4)

Therefore, in this chapter, I'll discuss how to provide support
and confirmation to prevent, reduce, and address resistance. Some
general approaches, as well as specific interpersonal and curricular
strategies, will be described. (Also see Bohmer & Briggs, 1991; Chan
& Treacy, 1996; Chavez & O'Donnell, 1998; Higginbotham, 1996.)

Shifting Our Perspective

As educators, the way we view resistance and people who act
resistant affects how much resistance we encounter and how effectively we deal with it. Moreover, when a student is being resistant,
we tend to locate the problem solely within the psyche of the student. This tends to lead to blame and judgment. We need, however,
to look at ourselves as educators and at the teacher-student relationship. It is helpful to consider what is happening between the instructor and the participant that is either facilitating or impeding the person's openness. I offer two metaphors from which to think about
resistance and our relationships with students.

I have done an exercise with educators in which I ask them to remember a time when they got defensive or acted resistant. In report-
ing their feelings in that situation, they mention, among other
things, feeling angry, frustrated, invalidated, and misunderstood.
As a result, they withdrew, attacked back, defended themselves, or
shut down. They felt that the other person made assumptions,
blamed them, and didn't listen. They wished the other person had
really listened to them, checked out their assumptions, and treated
them respectfully.

As their responses are listed, it becomes painfully clear that their
feelings and responses are very similar to how resistant students act
and feel. Imagine a resistant person as someone who has shut the
door and won't come out. Our first impulse may be to try to convince the person to come out. When that fails, we sometimes start
talking louder. As we do, the student locks the door. As we start yell-
ing and banging on the door, insisting that the student open it and

come out, the student starts adding bolts. As the situation escalates, the student begins pushing furniture in front of the door, barricading himself or herself in. In our zealousness for students to "get it," we can end up "banging" so loudly that students feel they need to protect themselves. When they feel attacked and blamed, they are likely to try to defend their position rather than question it. Because most of us who teach about diversity issues are personally invested and passionate about these concerns, we can easily end up trying to convince students of the importance of these issues. A more useful image is that of gently talking with the student and developing enough trust, safety, and validation that the student gradually opens the door, further and further, until he or she is ready to come out.

A second metaphor is that of a dance. The martial art aikido teaches that instead of trying to directly confront or block the force of the opponent, one should try to move with the energy. *Aikido* actually means "a way of blending energy." Thomas Crum (1987) has applied this concept to conflict resolution, and I think it apt in this context also. Often, we experience resistance as an attack, and our impulse is to fight back (not physically, I assume, but verbally or psychologically). This is reflected in the banging on the door in the above metaphor. Rather than opposing the energy, aikido offers us three main principles. First, honor and acknowledge the energy given. Second, accept the energy. By aligning with the direction of the attack, the power of the attack is dissipated, and the person can be led in another direction. Instead of trying to get rid of the energy, work with it. When we direct the flow instead of being pushed around by it, this creates a dance. Third, get out of the way and remove the object of attack. Expecting but not getting a rigid target, the attacker becomes off balance. When people express resistance, they are often testing the reaction of the educator and expect a strong response. When they don't get it, the intensity of their attack is usually diminished. If we push back, we set up a confrontation and usually block progress. If we acknowledge the feelings and work with them, we can create movement. Dance rather than struggle.

Both of these images, the door and the dance, provide ways for us to conceptualize how to respond to resistance. Instead of setting up an adversarial relationship in which we become more forceful, we can think about how to engage and dance with the student. I know how difficult it can be to do this. There are several times, despite my best knowledge, that I have gotten emotionally hooked and found myself doing exactly what I knew I shouldn't be. In my conversations with educators about resistance, I have found a pattern among those for whom resistance was not particularly a problem. They conveyed the deepest sense of respect and empathy for the student and a centeredness in their role as educator. I'll explore this further in Chapter 9 in "Issues for Educators." For now, let's consider how to apply the metaphors above and establish the kind of context that will most allow people to feel safe and take risks. I will first discuss ways to prevent and reduce resistance, then discuss how to address it when it occurs. (Table 5.1 at the end of the chapter provides a summary of these ideas.) I offer these as suggestions, not formulas or guaranteed solutions. Even though I've tried to describe them simply, the approaches are not meant to seem simplistic given the complexity of our situations, our students, and ourselves. The suggestions are geared for dealing with people from privileged groups, but most are relevant to all students. Similarly, many of the examples refer to classrooms, though the principles apply to other situations.

Preventing and Reducing Resistance

The key to preventing and reducing resistance, as I've said before, is creating a safe, respectful, and supportive environment. Most important is the stance of the teacher and the relationship between teacher and student. The more we are able to join with the students or participants, the less resistance we will encounter and the more able we will be to constructively offer challenges. In Chapter 3, I briefly mentioned ways to create a confirming climate. I will now discuss in more detail some specific ways to do so.

Talk With Participants Beforehand

When I anticipate that I will encounter a lot of resistance, I try to meet with people before the actual sessions. If I will be training in an organization in which I know there is hostility around the issue, I try to do some needs assessments or data gathering that provide me with an opportunity to talk with people that will be involved in the training. This usually helps to diffuse some of the resistance because those individuals get to be heard. It also allows them to get to know me, to see that I'm a reasonable person, and to understand what I intend to do. It also alerts me to what some of the particular issues might be. Knowing the root of the resistance provides opportunities to develop ways to address it. This approach can also be used before other types of meetings, classes, or workshops. When possible, talk before the session to people on the committee or in the group who are likely to block what you want to accomplish.

Design the Sessions With the Participants

Beyond just meeting with the participants beforehand, actually involve them in designing and planning the sessions. In addition to utilizing information gathered during the needs assessment, work with a small group of participants to create the training or class. If resistance is expected, try to include some key people who can influence how the training will be received. If they have a role in designing it, they will be more likely to set a more positive tone and encourage people to be appropriately engaged. We are also more likely to address issues that people will find relevant and useful.

This strategy was particularly effective when I was doing some training with a police department. They felt that more training, especially by a non–police officer, was being forced upon them. I worked with a couple of officers from the department who were well respected and in positions to potentially sabotage the whole thing. Not only did they have input into the entire design, but I specifically asked them to create a few case studies that they felt would be most meaningful given their situation. The training was now seen as something done in collaboration with their department, not simply as something that was imposed from the outside.

Get to Know Students or Participants

During a class or training, we can make an intentional effort to connect with individuals who are being resistant. Chat during breaks or before or after class, and encourage visits during office hours. Developing some rapport reduces the resistance. Even if students don't agree with some of the material, they feel less need to be defensive or disruptive if they can trust or like the educator. I have also found that the greater the rapport with a student, the easier it is for me to effectively deal with the person. When I am in touch with my caring for the student and I know that the student believes that I care and have the student's interests at heart, it provides a greater range of educational options. I feel freer to use (appropriate) humor and physical contact and to be more direct. I can more easily trust my responses and know that the student will take my actions as intended and, in turn, be more responsive.

Self-Disclose Appropriately

Self-disclosure on the part of the teacher can enhance teacher-student rapport and help increase safety. Appropriately sharing personal experiences with discrimination, our own process of coming to understand oppression, our mistakes made in dealing with diversity, and our struggles to overcome prejudices can make the teacher more human, less perfect, and easier to identify with. It also can make students feel more comfortable about disclosing or acknowledging their concerns, feelings, and vulnerabilities. Some educators will be very intentional about when and how they self-disclose. They will choose some things to share at the beginning of the class and choose others to reveal as the course progresses. Particular stories will be saved until predetermined points in the class to correspond with the issues that are being addressed. Teacher self-disclosure is a way to promote and sustain openness and trust. However, educators should always be thoughtful about what they share, ensuring that it is for the benefit of the students, not simply self-serving.

Build a Safe Educational Climate

Class or workshop ground rules are a central part of developing a confirming climate. Although these guidelines can be suggested by the teacher, I prefer to let the group develop them. Given the content and structure of the class, I ask students to identify the things that would make this a safe and productive educational environment for them. Invariably, students include items such as respect, confidentiality, no put-downs, really listening, and being nonjudgmental. Often, I will ask people to clarify what they mean by certain general terms, such as *respect* or *being nonjudgmental*. I will also make suggestions to the list as necessary and as agreed to by the students, often including the importance of speaking from one's own experience. Trust is built in the process of constructing the list because they get to discuss some of their needs and concerns and come to agreements. Furthermore, students subsequently feel greater ownership and investment in the rules they have created. Throughout the course, students and I will refer back to the list, especially if we are embarking on a difficult discussion or if some guidelines have been violated.

It is also helpful to acknowledge the feelings people have as they begin the class or training. Frequently people are concerned about saying the wrong thing, what others will think of them, finding out how prejudiced they are, conflicts in the group, or being forced to accept information they don't believe. Surfacing these concerns lets people know they're not alone and that it's all right to have some reservations. One activity I do that addresses this is called *hopes and fears*. Give each person an index card and ask each to anonymously write on one side a hope she or he has for the class or session, on the other side a fear or concern she or he has. Then collect and redistribute the cards, asking each person to read the card she or he has received. People just listen to what others have written. We can then discuss how to address the hopes and concerns people have (often, the guidelines are a good way to do this). In groups with higher trust, I'll ask people to share this information in pairs and then have them report out.

Other types of icebreaker activities also allow people to get to know each other and become more comfortable. There are many activities, usually fun and engaging, that loosen people up and begin to get them involved with the class or training. Exercises that give people the opportunity to work in pairs or small groups, to share (low-risk) things about themselves, and to begin to think about the content of the class are usually effective. A particularly adaptable format is *rotating pairs*. People are asked a series of short questions, each time pairing up with a new person and answering the question. (They can also do this in concentric circles, with those in the inner circle facing a partner in the outer circle. After each question, the outer circle rotates to the right, so everyone gets a new partner.) The questions can range from asking about a favorite activity, where people would rather be than here, one thing people like about their cultural background, a challenging situation in dealing with diversity, a time each person experienced discrimination or stereotyping, or when each person first became aware of racism. The questions can be geared toward both getting acquainted and generating content for the class.

Discuss Common Reactions and Social Identity Development

We can also discuss with students at the beginning of the class some common feelings and reactions people have as they learn about multicultural issues. We can go beyond just acknowledging their feelings at the moment to helping them anticipate what they might experience as the class progresses. Describe the tendency to want to avoid threatening material, the anger, guilt, or sadness that may arise, or the desire to discount information that challenges currently held views. Have them think about how they might deal with their feelings should they occur in the course of the class.

Sharing the stages of social identity development can help students make sense of their experiences as they explore social issues. (See Chapters 3 and 9 for a review of social identity development models.) They can better understand their own attitudes and responses as well as those of their classmates. As is the case with educators, when students have a way to understand their own and others' perspectives and experiences, it can make these attitudes and responses less threatening because they are seen as part of a normal process. This can preempt some of the resistance, normalize students' feelings, and provide language to discuss resistance as it occurs in class.

Provide Clear Structure and Expectations

Some people enter learning situations with a host of concerns about what will happen and what will be expected of them. They may assume that they will have to espouse what is considered politically correct, unwillingly reveal personal things about themselves, participate in embarrassing activities, or face arbitrary grading or evaluation based on whether or not they agree with the instructor. In any educational situation, it is helpful for people to know up front generally what will occur and what is expected. It allays people's anxiety and their related resistance to hear what the agenda is. It reassures them to know that they will not be forced to do anything they do not want to do (they have the option to pass on any activity) and that the point is to learn and consider new information, not to blame people or convert them. If the instructor conveys this with genuineness and respect, most people feel somewhat relieved and are more able to be open to the experience.

In classroom situations, where grading is an issue, we need to be especially clear about how students will be evaluated. They need to be assured that they will not be pressured to adopt particular beliefs or graded on how prejudiced they are. Instead, grading can be based on their ability to understand, articulate, and apply the material; to engage in critical analysis; to write effectively; and so on. It is important to have a syllabus that clearly describes assignments, grading procedures, and class expectations.

Affirm People's Self-Esteem

People with positive self-concepts can more easily sustain threats to their worldviews without becoming defensive (Steele, Spencer, & Lynch, 1993). Many people from privileged groups enter classes or workshops on multiculturalism feeling concerned about the prospect of being made to feel bad about themselves and therefore immediately become self-protective. If people's self-esteem is sufficiently intact, they can more easily engage in the sometimes difficult self-reflection required in social justice education. We can create ways to support a positive self-concept as people examine dynamics of oppression. People can explore their own ethnic or cultural background, becoming more aware of the specific traits and strengths of their culture and ways in which their social group has overcome obstacles. They can discuss ways they have effectively dealt with diversity, supported equity, or acted against injustice. They can read about or research people from their dominant social group who have worked for social justice (reinforcing that just because they're White or men does not make them bad people). We can move away from personal blame and guilt and instead focus on the systemic nature of oppression and individual responsibility for creating change. Throughout the course, people can have opportunities to participate in socially responsible activities such as letter writing, boycotts, petitions, fund-raising, volunteering, mentoring, or other kinds of activism. These kinds of activities not only build self-esteem but also counter powerlessness.

Acknowledge Feelings, Experiences, and Viewpoints

The opportunity for people to voice their feelings, experiences, and viewpoints and have them acknowledged is central to the process of confirmation. It validates their concerns and communicates that divergent perspectives are welcome in the class. Not only does this help people feel heard and respected, it provides educators with information about the needs and concerns of students. This can inform the class content and process. In addition, it allows students to hear themselves. This process can help them to sort out and work through some of their experiences and reactions and can provide a point from which to compare their views later in the course. (See Tatum, 1992 for a good illustration of using student self-interviews at the beginning and end of the course.)

There is another reason students need the opportunity to voice their feelings and concerns in a confirming environment: When people are focused on their own pain and needs, they are frequently unable to attend to or care about the misfortune of others. As noted in the previous chapter, people also may need to become more conscious of their past mistreatment and how this has affected their current attitudes and behavior. Therefore, we need to provide the opportunity for individuals to explore some of their feelings about their own experiences before they move on to consider those of others. Alice Miller (1990) suggests,

> It's not possible for someone really to clarify his situation and dissolve his fears until he can feel them rather than discuss them. Only then is the veil lifted and he realizes his true need: not a tutor, not an interpreter, not a confessor; he needs space for his own growth and the company of an enlightened witness on the long journey on which he has set out. (p. 184)

The importance of bearing witness is illustrated in the now-popular video "The Color of Fear."[1] Though this video can be read and interpreted in many ways and on multiple levels, it struck me as a powerful example of how people need to acknowledge their pain to reduce their resistance. The video documents a gathering of men from different racial backgrounds who come together for a weekend to discuss racism. Several of the men of color try to get one White man, David, to acknowledge the existence of racism. They repeatedly provide information, tell their stories, and share their experiences with various types of racial discrimination. They speak calmly, angrily, rationally, passionately; they do everything short of standing on their heads. David remains steadfastly unmoved. He continues to minimize and invalidate their experiences. He maintains that they are being oversensitive, assuming racism where there is none, and not making the effort to fit in or take advantage of opportunities that do exist. He continually blames the victim. Near the end of the weekend, there is some progress. David reveals that he was abused as a child by his authoritarian father. He emotionally recounts how he heard racist comments and jokes, learned to obey to survive, and protected himself from emotions. He realizes that as an adult he has tried to avoid dealing with the pain and strife of the real world; thus, he has minimized the feelings of the men in the group so that he would not have to deal with them. He admits how unaware he is of the dynamics of racism. It was not until David acknowledged his own mistreatment that he could begin to recognize the pain systematically inflicted on people of color.

Of course, people have various kinds of pain, degrees of mistreatment, and levels of need to address them. For some people, dealing with one's experience of discrimination and prejudice may be a prerequisite for engaging in the exploration of the mistreatment and oppression of other people. People from a privileged group who also have a subordinate identity often need to express their experience with that oppression and have it validated before they can allow other oppressed groups to be the focus of discussion. If not, they may feel that the others' oppression is seen as more important than their oppression. For example, White Jews can be reluctant to fully engage in a discussion of racism if they feel their experiences with anti-Semitism have not been recognized as another legitimate form of oppression. Similarly, men of color may resist discussing sexism and owning their own involvement in it until they feel racism has been adequately acknowledged.

In talking about experiences, people from privileged groups may need others to recognize how their lives have not been full of benefits and the ways in which they have been hurt by social inequity. As noted in the previous chapter, they usually have personal stories about how they were mistreated and how they feel that they are now the ones being discriminated against. The issue is not whether we agree with their interpretation of events or how we feel about their situations. The point is to help them deal with their feelings so they can become engaged with exploring social justice issues. We are trying to create an openness to self-reflection and alternative view points. Although it is important to acknowledge different experiences and perspectives, this, of course, does not mean they need to be accepted as the only reality. Students, as well as teachers, need to develop the skills to actively listen and to be empathic, without having to accept all views as equally valid. Listening empathically and understanding does not necessarily mean agreement. We can assist students in linking the personal with the political to consider how their individual experiences are related to social conditions.

As teachers, we need to make careful choices about the best way to allow students from dominant groups to voice their feelings of pain and mistreatment without alienating other students or derailing the class. We should not be therapists or attempt to make the class into a therapy session (though referrals for some people may be appropriate). There have been a variety of ways that I have tried to allow students to express their experiences and perspectives. These choices depend on the dynamics and makeup of the class, time available, personalities of the students, and my state of being, among other factors. Students should be reminded of the class ground rules as necessary.

Time can be created in the class for people to share their feelings and experiences as part of the regular, whole-class discussion. Another option is to have paired or small-group discussions. Students initially could talk with others who share their background, or students could participate in self-selected, heterogeneous groups of people with whom they have a personal relationship. In these contexts, students could have greater time and freedom to discuss their experiences with people likely to be supportive. Subsequently, there could be a more limited sharing with the whole class.

Students can also do freewriting during class in response to the readings, discussion topics, or focus question; these writings could then selectively be shared with the whole class. Journal writing is another effective way for students to express and reflect on their own experiences without the concern for other students' reactions and judgments. Responding to (not evaluating) their journal entries enables us to recognize the students' feelings and can allow a dialogue between student and teacher. We can invite students who require more attention than is available or warranted in the whole class or in these assignments to speak with us after class or during office hours.

It can be one of the more challenging tasks to listen to people from privileged groups talk about their concerns and mistreatment, especially when those may seem relatively insignificant or distorted. Nevertheless, I have seen important growth and openness occur as a result—for the students themselves, for their classmates, and for me. Even students from marginalized groups have reported that hearing experiences and feelings has helped them to humanize and better understand people from privileged groups. We can also help all students make links between their own feelings and experiences and those of other people, promoting empathy and a broader understanding of the dynamics of oppression.

Validate and Build on Current Knowledge

One way to both convey respect and minimize resistance is to acknowledge and build on what people already know. This avoids us coming in as the expert who is going to tell them the right way to think. It reduces people's issues with authority and their concerns about political correctness. Adults especially respond well to having their experiences and expertise validated. Case studies are particularly useful in letting them share what they already know about an issue, about what is effective or ineffective, and about solving problems. As they struggle with and debrief the case, it also allows them to notice where they need more information or ideas.

Often, people make generalizations on the basis of their own experiences (e.g., my immigrant family succeeded in school without bilingual education; therefore, other immigrants don't need it). Thus, their views may be limited and incomplete. We can acknowledge their pieces of the truth and expand on them, offering a broader and more complex picture. Other times, people may share information that is only partially correct. Again, we can affirm the correct aspects and provide a more accurate perspective.

Allow People to Discover Information Themselves

In general, and especially when there is resistance, people learn the most when they discover the knowledge for themselves. When information is presented that people disagree with, it can feel to them like it is being imposed. Instead, let them acquire the information independently. They can gather statistics (e.g., the race and gender breakdown of employment in various levels and positions in an organization or the ratio of students of color in tracked classes or special education classes); review the representation of people in the media (e.g., the number and types of roles of gay and lesbian characters); find out how much welfare recipients actually receive and the constraints on their lives; interview people from a particular group about their experiences (e.g., what it's like to be a person with a disability on campus); conduct research on a topic, using various sources; do a survey (e.g., of people's experience with sexual harassment); or observe in an organization (watch for gender or racial bias in classrooms).

In one class, after watching the video "Still Killing Us Softly," about the images of women in advertising, a number of male students discounted the validity of the video. They claimed that the ads portrayed were exaggerated and biased, that they didn't fairly represent current advertising. I asked the class to do their own research and bring in ads from the magazines they read to compare them with what they saw in the video. They were amazed at how sexist the ads were; the males acknowledged it was worse than they thought.

People's learning can also grow out of their own experiences, whether real life situations or simulations. Telling people information is never as convincing as actually experiencing it. The effects of inequality and the inaccuracy of blaming the victim are more powerfully conveyed by spending time in a homeless shelter, a battered women's shelter, or a poor inner-city school—and then discussing those experiences. Trying to convince teenage girls not to have babies is not as effective as having them spend several days taking care of a programmed doll that simulates the care a real baby needs![2] Attempting to explain the effects of exclusion has less impact than having people go through an exercise in which they are excluded or asking them to draw on their own experiences of exclusion. Star Power (Shirts, 1969), Bafa Bafa,[3] and the Blue Eyed/Brown Eyed exercise developed by Jane Elliott (Peters, 1971) are examples of effective simulations that allow people to experience the ideas we are trying to teach. Providing learning experiences in which people can come to their own insights and conclusions reduces resistance and creates more meaningful learning.

Provide Opportunities for Frequent Feedback

Resistance often occurs when people feel they do not have a voice. In addition to sharing ideas and experiences in class, it helps to provide people with opportunities for frequent feedback about the class process and content. We can do this through short, anonymous written evaluations at the end of each class (or every few classes) or with longer ones periodically; through journals; or through verbal check-ins at the beginning or end of classes. This provides several advantages: Less will be stifled that may erupt inappropriately in the classroom, it allows for a connection with quieter students, it allows engagement with students in a less public way (possibly providing more safety for them to express their views), and it reaffirms that we value students' feelings and opinions. It is then essential that students' feedback is acknowledged in some way and that the educator is seen as responsive to their views. This can be done by summarizing the feedback, by making changes in the class, by allowing for some flexibility, by responding in writing in the journals, or by inviting students to talk with the educator further about their concerns.

Frame Diversity Issue in Terms of Shared Principles and Goals

Resistance is likely if people see the class or training as interfering with, irrelevant to, or contrary to their goals and values. If we can frame the issue in a way that is consistent with their principles or mission, people usually are more receptive. There will be greater buy-in if people see it as useful and aligned with their philosophy.

In organizational contexts, I will try to relate the training to their mission statement, goals, or long-range planning. (The more relevance the mission statement has, the more effective this is. Unfortunately, there are often great things written on paper that have little connection to actual practice.) Agencies or businesses are usually concerned with productivity, effective teamwork, and good service to customers or clients (not to mention avoiding lawsuits and bad public relations)—all of which affect the bottom line. Sensitivity to diversity and equity therefore helps people to work more productively in teams and helps the company attract and retain diverse clients and customers (and talented employees) and foster a positive public image. Schools tend to highlight meeting the needs of diverse students, creating a safe and respectful school community, and fostering high achievement. In this context, attention to multiculturalism enhances one's ability to teach diverse students (improving their test scores and their attentiveness in class), decreases intergroup tensions, reduces fights, and creates a more inclusive environment. I find there is always a way to connect social justice issues to a wide range of goals. In Chapter 8, under "Self-Interest," I discuss ways to address particular needs and concerns of individuals and organizations.

More broadly, educators can appeal to people's commitment to democracy, fairness, and equality. Most people believe in these core national principles. The class can be framed as examining what these words mean and how well our country lives up to these goals (for example, see Andrzejewski, 1995). There is ample evidence that convincingly demonstrates that we have not yet reached these ideals despite the many justifications for various inequities. Allow people to do their own assessment of how well reality matches these stated values. In general, the educator should discuss social justice issues in the context of already-established goals and commitments rather than risk being seen as anti-American or as against national or organizational principles.

Explore Their Self-Interest in Social Justice and Alternatives to Systems of Domination

By helping students to reconceptualize social change, we can reduce the defensiveness that often occurs when we propose challenges to the status quo. Students are likely to resist perspectives or strategies that they deem detrimental to their current or future status or well-being. Although people from marginalized groups tend to be more able to see how changing the status quo can be positive for them, often people from dominant groups see efforts at progressive social change as a win-lose situation (in which they will lose). Given this vantage point, it is not surprising that we encounter defensiveness.

One approach is to help reframe the discussion from a win-lose model to a view that everyone could benefit from the elimination of oppression. As students from privileged groups see how they have been limited by oppression and why it is in their self-interest to foster social change, it can help reduce resistance and increase their investment in social justice.

In classes and workshops, people have shared a range of stories that reflect their understanding of some of the costs of oppression. White students have spoken about being ostracized from their families for dating a person of a different race and about their fear of engaging with people of different races or cultures. Heterosexuals have acknowledged how their homophobia has led to the loss of friendships and family relationships with gays and lesbians. Men have expressed feeling pressure to assume certain "masculine" roles and behaviors that limit who they can be. People from wealthy families have talked about the guilt they experience about their privilege and the inability to relate to those from other class backgrounds. Many people can see that violence and social decay are directly related to unfair social and economic systems. This is not to pretend that there are not real advantages to their privileged status. Nonetheless, we can help individuals from dominant groups understand what they have to gain, not just what they have to lose, by creating greater social equity. In the following chapter, I describe at length the costs of oppression to people from privileged groups.

People from privileged groups also need to have a sense of alternatives. If they can only imagine win-lose dynamics and systems of domination and subordination, there is little reason to give up what dominance they have. People need help developing and exploring alternatives to this model. They can read about the various alternatives others have proposed. It is even more inspiring to know about actual examples of organizations, businesses, communities, or societies that operate on more egalitarian, democratic, and cooperative principles (see list of organizations in the appendix). In Chapter 10, I discuss further alternatives to our current system and the benefits of justice to people from dominant groups.

Responding to Resistance

Even with our best efforts to prevent and reduce resistance, we still may be faced with it throughout the course or sessions. This is a good time to remember the images of the door and the dance. The more we can maintain our perspective and composure, the more effective we will be, and the more we will enjoy our work.

Be Aware of Getting Hooked

Because resistant behavior is likely to trigger our own feelings, we need to be particularly careful not to fall into certain traps. For each of us, there are probably particular types of resistant individuals and resistant behaviors that are more likely to hook us. Although we may try to avoid or ignore these individuals, we often end up focusing our attention on them at the expense of attending to the rest of the group. One trap is arguing with them and trying to convince them of our position or prove them wrong. Another trap is trying to engage someone who does not appear interested or attentive. We zealously may try to capture the person's attention and generate some responsiveness. Usually we are reacting to our own issues and needs and are not considering what is best for the whole group.

Assess Reason for Resistance

As previously noted, there are many reasons why people become defensive. They may be feeling blamed, overwhelmed, forced to accept things they're not ready or willing to accept, or trying to protect their self-concept. Their reactions may be related to their stage of intellectual or social identity development. The more we understand what is going on, the better able we are to decide how to respond. It can be helpful to revisit the ideas suggested in the section on preventing and reducing resistance. Often, we need to reestablish safety and connection, acknowledge people's feelings, affirm their sense of self, and slow the pace.

Invite Exploration of the Issue Raised

If someone makes a statement that you perceive as resistant, you can ask that person to further elaborate on why she or he thinks or feels this way. Many times, if people aren't immediately shut down and do have a chance to be heard, they can then listen to others. So when a student says angrily, "The problem isn't with discrimination. Someone just has to be willing to work hard," instead of immediately trying to prove them wrong, we could say calmly, with genuine interest, "It sounds like you have some strong views about this. What has led you to feel this way?"

In the course of the person's explanation, we can acknowledge his or her feelings and perspective and look for ways to lead the conversation into a broader exploration of what might account for differences in achievement or success. It is extremely important to invite other perspectives, especially if an individual's resistance is tending to dominate the group. We can ask, "What do other people think? Are there any other opinions?" If people are reluctant to speak, we can offer some other alternatives, such as, "Some people think that people have internalized a sense of inferiority and therefore feel hopeless, lack self-confidence, and don't bother trying; others believe that people face systemic discrimination in hiring and promotion, especially when they don't fit the cultural norms or expectations. They need to be twice as good to be seen as competent. What do you think of these possibilities?"

I handled it another way when Brian, a White male undergraduate student in my class on diversity once became agitated that there is so much sympathy for people on welfare. He said that if he could make it, other people could too. When asked why he had such strong feelings, he briefly recounted his own life history: growing up in a single-parent dysfunctional family, running away from home, becoming involved with drugs, and finally getting himself straight and struggling to work and pay for school. Both other classmates and I validated his experience and the strength it took for him to be at this place in his life. After that process, I asked the class to brainstorm reasons why other people might not be able to do what Brian was able to do. In the course of 10 minutes, the board was full of ideas, including discrimination based on race, gender, disability, or sexual orientation; having children; internalized oppression; limited English skills; poor communication or writing skills; addictions; lack of connections; mental illness; and homelessness. (There were many obstacles on this list that Brian did not confront.) We did not discount Brian's experience or try to convince anyone of anything. But brainstorming other reasons allowed people to think about this issue more broadly and from other perspectives.

If you perceive that something is said to intentionally be adversarial, as bait and challenge, there is little likelihood that this person really wants to engage in an open, productive discussion about it. Instead of debating someone's personal view, raise it to a larger issue and explore it as a commonly held viewpoint. Don't bite the bait. Instead, use it constructively. Rather than responding to their particular comment, such as, "Women can avoid being sexually harassed if they wanted to, and they really just like it," use this remark to explore aspects of sexual harassment. We could say, "That's an interesting point. Some people feel women are responsible for the sexual attention they receive and should just say no if they don't like it. Let's look at the dynamics involved in sexual harassment." Then discuss responsibility in sexual harassment, power relationships, blaming the victim, laws and policies, and so on. Don't engage with whether they are personally right or wrong, but use their comment to look at the issue and the feelings that many people hold. Use the comment as a point of departure, shifting the discussion from the personal to the general.

As an issue is being explored, and even as we acknowledge different opinions, we need to provide accurate information and have people adequately support their views. We cannot simply allow an opinion to be accepted as fact. Invite the expression of views and feelings and acknowledge them, but then help people to do more critical thinking. As mentioned before, people can be given information or be asked to do research themselves.

Contain the Behavior

When one or two individuals are disruptive and continue to assert their views or raise inappropriate questions, their behavior needs to be curtailed. Often, the squeaky wheel gets the most grease. It is easy to get pulled into allowing one or two individuals to derail the class and to become the focus of attention. After they have had ample opportunity to express their views (see above suggestions), acknowledge and summarize their perspective and indicate the need to move on: "I understand that you feel that affirmative action is reverse discrimination, and you don't believe anyone deserves preferences. Clearly, people hold different opinions about this issue. Let's leave this topic now, and move onto talking about other laws intended to prevent discrimination." The individuals can also be given a time limit to address the issue before moving onto other topics: "Take a couple of minutes to finish what you'd like to say about this, and then we need to discuss other issues." We can also invite them to discuss the issue further at another time (outside the session). In a group situation, other people and other issues need attention. People in the group will appreciate your efforts not to allow one person to control the class.

If Group Is Resistant, Go With the Flow

I have found that when the whole group or a large part of it is being resistant, there is little I can do in the moment to stop it. I have realized that you can't fight the tide. When this occurs, the aikido principles become particularly helpful. Be flexible and work with the energy. Allow the group to discuss their issue and see how you can connect it to the class topic. One time, when I was trying to do training on diversity with teachers in a school system, I encountered a lot of resistance. Every time I would try to engage people in exercises or discussion, they would complain about how they were forced to be there and how the administration was really the problem. After unsuccessfully trying to push them to be involved, I stepped back and allowed them to vent their feelings and concerns. This led to some strategizing, some connections made between their feelings and those of the students, and some thought about how this was related to diversity issues.

As most trainers can attest, there is a favorite game of some groups that is informally called "kill the trainer." Whatever anger, resentment, fear, or powerlessness the group is feeling toward management or their institution gets projected onto the trainer. The trainer becomes a convenient target upon which to vent their emotions. Trainers who attempt to confront this head-on and get into a struggle with the group will surely lose. Again, it will likely be more productive to try to dance with the energy and not be a rigid target, to try to join with the group and move with them to address relevant issues. In training situations, I have learned to try to do as much assessment as possible before I go in to determine if this is an appropriate time and manner to do training, so I can avoid being "set up." With adequate preassessment, some of this can be avoided.

Provide a Time-Out

If resistance becomes intense and either the group or we need some time to think about how to handle it, we can call a time-out. This can take the form of a break during which people get a few minutes to cool off, talk informally, and just break the flow of energy. We can create a more structured process by having people react for a couple of minutes in pairs, freewrite about what they're thinking and feeling right now, write their opinion of the issue with supporting evidence, or come up with how they would like to proceed with this issue (continue in a particular way or revisit it at another time). We can also lead with a few minutes of breathing and silence. Time-outs provide people with a chance to cool off and refocus. They allow both the educator and the participants to collect themselves and to decide how to move forward.

Arrange a Private Meeting

If there is strong or ongoing resistance, a one-on-one meeting with the individual or individuals might be warranted. It is important to do this in an inviting, not a punitive, manner. If people feel

Goal	Interventions
Preventing and reducing resistance	Talk with participants beforehand
	Get to know participants—develop rapport
	Self-disclose appropriately
	Build a safe classroom climate
	Discuss common reactions and social identity development
	Provide clear structure and expectations
	Affirm people's self-esteem
	Acknowledge feelings, experiences, and viewpoints
	Validate and build on current knowledge
	Allow people to discover information themselves
	Provide opportunities for frequent feedback
	Frame diversity issue in terms of shared principles and goals
	Explore their self-interest in social justice and alternatives to systems of domination
Responding to resistance	Avoid getting hooked
	Assess reason for resistance
	Invite exploration of the issue raised
	Contain the behavior (e.g., set a time limit, summarize and move on)
	If group is resistant, go with the flow
	Provide a time-out (e.g., journaling, free writing, reactions in pairs, a break)
	Arrange a private meeting

Figure 5.1 Addressing Resistance to Social Justice Issues From People From Privileged Groups

they are going to be scolded or attacked, they will become more defensive. Expressing interest and concern sets a different tone. Saying something like, "I notice you're having a hard time with the [class or training]; I'd like to talk more about it with you and hear some of your concerns. Could we find a time to talk?" During the meeting, try to express genuine interest and respect, and listen empathically. We can affirm the person's view while also helping him or her understand our perspective and the impact that she or he is having on the rest of the group. Try to problem-solve about how to address the situation.

Conclusion

Although there may be no magic answers, clearly there are a range of things we can do to prevent, reduce, and address resistance. Most people, if given the right opportunity, would rather be engaged than anxious and defensive. Those who are unable to participate appropriately and enjoy a disruptive role can be dealt with in ways that do not prevent others' learning. Although we cannot make people grow in the ways we might like, in my experience there are few cases where someone has begun and ended in the same resistant manner. When sufficient trust and rapport have been built and interesting material and activities presented, people often become productively involved, sometimes despite themselves. Making and sustaining these connections can sometimes take a tremendous amount of energy and patience. Yet unless we can approach people with respect and compassion, we will likely face more difficulties. It is to our students' and our advantage to create a space in which people are engaged.

Notes

1. This video is available from Small Fry Seminars and Consulting, 470 Third St., Oakland, CA 94607, (510) 419-1097.

2. The Baby Think Over program provides dolls for this purpose and is available from Health Ed. Co., P.O. Box 21207, Waco, TX 76707-1207.

3. Bafa Bafa may be purchased from Simile II, P.O. Box 910, Del Mar, CA 92014, (619) 755-0272.

6

The Costs of Oppression to People From Privileged Groups

The previous chapter discussed how resistance could be reduced if people from dominant groups reconceptualize how they think about social justice. Although change for most people tends to be difficult, it is even more so for those who feel they are on the losing end. People from privileged groups often see social change as a win-lose situation in which they lose. Even though greater equality would undoubtedly involve giving up and sharing power and resources, social justice could also enrich their lives.

Living in a society where there are systematic, institutionalized inequities affects everyone, whether they are in advantaged or disadvantaged roles. It has profound ramifications that influence and limit how we think about ourselves and others, how and with whom we interact, and the opportunities and choices we have about how to lead our lives. Although in some instances there are positive effects, there are costs and harmful consequences for all of us, though in different ways.

Most efforts to understand the social and psychological effects of oppression have focused on the experiences of those in disadvantaged groups. Yet systems of oppression also affect people in advantaged groups. When the experiences of people in privileged positions are considered, they tend to be compared with the experiences of those who are oppressed. The focus is usually on how people from dominant groups oppress others or benefit from the inequalities. Most theorists have paid less attention to how oppression has negative consequences for people in the advantaged group. However, our understanding cannot be complete unless this is fully explored as well. As members of an interdependent society, what affects some people inevitably affects us all. Martin Luther King, Jr. (1991) reminds us, "All men [sic] are caught in an inescapable network of mutuality, tied in a single garment of destiny. Whatever affects one directly, affects all indirectly" (p. 7).

One way to address resistance and to foster meaningful, long-term involvement in social change is to help people in privileged groups understand how they are harmed by oppression. In this chapter, I will first present specific ways in which people from dominant groups are adversely affected by oppression and ways in which they could benefit from its elimination. Then, I will consider how oppression more generally undermines their sense of humanity and human potential. As I have said before, most people are part of both advantaged and disadvantaged groups. The focus here is on their experience as someone from a privileged group, even though their other social identities always affect this experience.

Specific Costs of Oppression
to People From Dominant Groups

We need to name the damaging effects of social injustice on people from advantaged groups without ignoring the larger dynamics of social power in which they occur. Recognizing the ways in which privileged groups may be negatively affected by oppression in no way equates that reality with the experiences of people in oppressed groups. Whatever the costs are to those in dominant groups, it is not the same as the loss of power, dignity, opportunities, and resources faced by people in disadvantaged groups. In this sense, I am not suggesting that people who are in privileged groups also are oppressed; they still have disproportionate social power. While keeping this in mind, I still believe it useful to discuss the price paid for privilege and dominance to more fully understand the dynamics of oppression and to develop strategies and visions for change.

In general, there has been little written about the particular costs of oppression to dominant groups. The profeminist men's move-

ment has probably most clearly articulated the harmful consequences of sexism for men (Kaufman, 1993; Kimmel & Messner,
1989/1995; Kivel, 1992/1998) and offered new models of masculin-
ity. Others have described some of the negative ramifications for
privileged people in relation to classism (Bingham, 1986; Mogil &
Slepian, 1992; Wachtel, 1989), racism (Bowser & Hunt, 1981/1996;
Feagin & Vera, 1995; Kivel, 1996), and heterosexism (Blumenfeld,
1992; Thompson, 1992). Even though each form of oppression has its
own particular effects on those in the advantaged group, there are
numerous similarities that illustrate some common dynamics of systems of domination.

Drawing on the works cited above and my own teaching experiences, I will discuss the psychological, social, moral/spiritual, intellectual, and material/physical costs of oppression to people from
privileged groups. Although these different consequences will be
discussed separately, their overlap with and impact on each other is
extensive. In addition, even though people may experience these
costs on an individual basis, they are the result of larger social patterns, structures, and ideology. They grow out of our particular systems of domination and inequality. Other oppressive societies with
different forms of social organization may have both similar and different negative effects on those from privileged groups.

The themes cited highlight consequences or issues that pertain
to dominant groups across different forms of oppression. The quotes
are taken from participants in classes and workshops I have conducted in the past several years. Some of the effects are very personal and center around the individual and her or his interpersonal
relationships. Others involve societal ramifications that affect the individual as a member of society.

Psychological Costs: Loss of
Mental Health and Authentic Sense of Self

Systems of oppression constrain the ability of people from privileged groups to develop their full humanity. Pressures to fit pro-
scribed roles and to limit one's emotional capacity hinder one's
self-development. Diminished self-knowledge and fears further
thwart healthy psychological growth. I will describe several aspects
of how overall mental health is compromised.

Socialization Into Roles and Patterns of Behavior

People in dominant groups are socialized to conform to certain rigid standards of behavior. This impedes the exploration of aspects of themselves that do not fit with these expectations. For example, heterosexuals may constrain their feelings and relationships with people of the same sex, whereas men may block their emotional expressiveness or pursuit of interests considered feminine. People from upper-class families are prevented or discouraged from considering nonprofessional occupations or career interests outside the family's established sphere. Individuals' efforts to conform to expected roles can undermine their ability to know who they are, what they can do, and what they really need.

Denial of Emotions and Empathy

Personal growth is further limited when people attempt to deal with the contradiction between what they are often taught (equality, love, and kindness) and what they are expected to do (treat people inequitably). This may occur when they divert their eyes from a homeless person or treat a person in a service role as a lesser human being. As a result, people may disregard or not perceive the feelings of other people. Although clearly damaging to people in disadvantaged groups, it also requires people in advantaged groups to deny their own emotional capabilities, sensitivity, and mutuality. This stifles emotional honesty and hinders the development and use of empathy.

Limited Self-Knowledge and Distorted View of Self

People from privileged groups are routinely denied information and opportunities to understand their role in an unjust social system as well as honest feedback from people in oppressed groups. As a result, they are denied self-knowledge. This skewed self-awareness has numerous ramifications.

People from privileged groups often obtain a positive sense of self (consciously or unconsciously) based on the diminishment of others. They feel good about themselves because they can point to someone else who they believe is inferior. However, this positive self-esteem is shallow, artificial, and false. After marrying a Latino from Central America, one White woman reports,

Because of my own "privileged" background, I felt somehow better than him and his people. When I began to accept responsibility for myself, I had to "eat" my own response to this racism. It wasn't easy, but it was necessary.

People from advantaged groups often develop a sense of superiority or a distorted sense of self to rationalize the inequality. Promotions, opportunities, and access to resources are inequitably distributed in an unjust, hierarchical system. Often, these are not truly gained by merit but by connections or by belonging to a certain race, sex, or class. To justify these greater advantages, people from privileged groups often convince themselves that they are better than other people and therefore more deserving, even if they are somehow aware that this is not so. To reconcile themselves to this situation, they may maintain the belief in their own superiority. They can easily draw on the dominant culture to create and reinforce this view.

Despite these efforts, they may find it hard to trust their gains and to believe in their abilities. They may wonder whether their achievement was based on privilege or merit. McIntosh (1985) labels this "feeling like a fraud." Although these feelings can arise for a variety of reasons, success in a rigged system can rob people of faith in their capabilities and diminish their sense of accomplishment.

Discrepancy Between External Perceptions and Internal Realities

There is often the discrepancy between external appearances and internal realities. Individuals do not feel like the powerful, privileged people they are presumed to be. On the surface, it may appear that privileged people "have it all," especially those with wealth. Yet internally, people often feel isolated, lonely, and cut off from one's self, others, and "the real world." Even though there may be material success, there can be emotional and spiritual emptiness.

Fears and Pain

There are numerous fears, many of which have social ramifications (and are addressed in the following section). Even when people recognize the irrationality or unfoundedness of some of their fears (of certain types of people, of new or different situations), they still find that these fears inhibit their lives and cause psychological distress. Some people are afraid of losing entitlement and privileges.

They worry that people in oppressed groups may retaliate and mistreat them as they have been mistreated. If marginalized groups are given greater social power, they fear this will be used against them (i.e., women will deny men employment opportunities, people of color will subjugate Whites to second-class treatment).

For those with close relationships with individuals from dominated groups, there can be fear for the others' well-being. People from dominant groups find it painful to witness and share in their suffering and mistreatment. Whether this involves common encounters with discrimination or a more dramatic occurrence, it can be distressing to see and feel the effects on one's friend or relative. This is particularly evident when a daughter or wife gets raped, a friend of color is harassed by police, a low-income friend is unable to find work or housing, a gay friend gets beaten, or a Jewish friend's synagogue is defaced. Parents from dominant groups who have children from disadvantaged groups (of color, gay or lesbian, or with a disability) are often concerned about those children's treatment and safety.

People from privileged groups who support justice often describe the pain they feel when they hear offensive remarks made about disadvantaged groups. Others from their social group often assume that they will share the prejudiced view. It is both psychologically and emotionally upsetting to listen to such disparagement about other people. When there are other, more serious acts of hatred, it is even more painful to realize that fellow human beings are capable of such cruelty.

Diminished Mental Health

Thomas Pettigrew (1981) identified six criteria for positive mental health. Among them, he cites self-awareness and self-acceptance, degree of actualization of one's potential, relative independence from social pressures, adequate perception of reality, and the integration of psychic functions. As reflected in the above costs, being socialized into an unjust system negatively affects our ability to obtain these components of psychological health. In particular, people from dominant groups tend to develop unhealthy psychological mechanisms (such as denial, false justification, projection, disassociation, and transference of blame) to deal with their fears of minorities or people from oppressed groups (Fernandez, 1996). One woman describes this process: "As a White woman, I cannot easily own the negative parts of myself. I disavow them and project them onto others (people of color). As a result, I am cut off from important parts of myself." Middle-aged people, in an effort to deny their own mortality, may marginalize and discard elderly people; or heterosexuals who cannot accept their feelings for members of their own sex may act out in homophobic ways.

Social Costs: Loss and Diminishment of Relationships

The lack of trust between groups, a social climate that rarely supports relationships across differences (except for between men and women of the same backgrounds), and our socialization, which has fed us misinformation about ourselves and others, undermines relationships. Internalized oppression and social taboos often interfere with positive interpersonal relations among diverse people. Fears, avoidance of different people, and limited experiences and knowledge of others result in less human connection and more isolation. The social costs are immense.

Isolation From People Who Are Different

The separation people experience from those who are different may be due to an individual's psychological or emotional issues and to the social structures and norms in society. In the former case, fear and discomfort prevent people from reducing the distance. "I often felt so isolated from most people and yearned to be able to connect but my fear of the 'unknown' was so prevalent. It overpowered me. How very sad and how I regret this!" Opportunities for deep, important, gratifying relationships with diverse people are lost.

An able-bodied man recounts,

> I literally often avoid contact with the disabled because I'm unsure how to act—to walk the line between acknowledging a difference in ability and being rude; between helpfulness and patronization. My social distance grows as I don't make efforts to interact fully with the disabled.

In the latter case, various forms of oppression restrict where we work and play and the ease with which we can have meaningful relationships across differences. Often, we have no contact with certain groups of people or have contact only in limited ways:

As an able-bodied person, I did not come into contact with handicapped people until I was old enough to participate in volunteer work in junior high. Though I have done extensive work with them, I still don't feel natural being around them. They are not part of my life. I feel like I am missing out on the opportunity to be friends with a certain number of the population.

Barriers to Deeper, More Authentic Relationships

Even when there is contact, it is difficult to have meaningful relationships. It is often hard to develop deep, genuine relationships with people from diverse backgrounds. Numerous barriers interfere with this process.

First, people from privileged groups often carry a host of fears because of their social position and socialization in an unequal society. Very common fears are of people who are different and of participating in other cultural experiences. Because privileged-group members have had limited contact with and have received negative messages about people who are different, they are fearful of going places or having relationships across social-group boundaries. When and if they do deal with people from dominated groups, people from privileged groups worry about saying or doing the wrong thing and being offensive:

> I hear negative messages about racial groups that my grandparents used to say and I fear that someday I will use them out of my subconscious. On a conscious level, I do not want to believe or use the terms they used, but I fear some aspects of racism were ingrained at an early age.

Often, people talk of "walking on eggshells." With the constantly shifting social norms, even many well-intentioned people are confused or frightened about what is acceptable and what is not. At times it can seem easier to do nothing at all than to risk pain or embarrassment.

Second, stereotypes or prejudgments may prevent contact in the first place or impede real relationships once there is contact. People from disadvantaged groups can hold prejudices toward people from advantaged groups and vice versa. People from the dominant group often complain that they are stereotyped and not seen for who they are. They may be judged and avoided on the basis of their social group identity, which may feel frustrating and unfair. Quite at odds with these individuals' own experiences and self-images, a man may be seen as a potential rapist and not trusted by women, a wealthy person viewed as an elitist snob, or a White person as an unconcerned racist. Two White women describe this experience:

> When attempting to assist with problems of others that are not White, it is looked upon as charity or I'm told that I don't care because I'm White, or that this trouble doesn't concern me. This was said without regard to my feelings about the situation or my beliefs as an individual. There was a simple presumption that I would only offer to help because I believed I was superior to them, solely based on the color of my skin.

This was echoed by another person:

> Not being taken for who I am but assuming I am part of the stereotypical dominant race who are stereotyped as uncaring, rich, selfish, biased, unaccepting of other cultures, rude, snobby, better than others, etc. by the minority race who holds negative opinions of the White race.

As a result of feeling like they will be judged, people from privileged groups choose to hide aspects of themselves. Hiding aspects of who one is undermines an open and honest relationship. People most often discuss this in terms of class:

> As a product of a middle/upper class environment, I often feel that I am pre-judged. People think I'm spoiled or have been given everything on a silver platter. They think I'm pretentious or a snob or that Daddy is going to do everything for me. Consequently, it is an aspect of my life that I don't usually reveal.

People from dominant groups also recognize that their own stereotypes of others (especially in a context that encourages segregation) inhibit their ability to get to know people from oppressed groups or to develop those relationships. One White woman spoke of her loss of a potentially important relationship due to her own racism and the segregated social environment:

> I had a male friend in college who was African American, and my friends told me he really liked me. I never made any advances (and

neither did he) because the idea of going out with a Black man made me nervous. I think I missed out on an opportunity to become involved with a sensitive and caring man because of how separated/segregated my experience was when I was growing up. If I were confronted with why I didn't go out with him, I would have denied racism vehemently. But in hindsight, I know that this is the truth.

Third, people from privileged groups recognize a lack of trust. They realize it will be harder and slower for people from oppressed groups to be open and honest with them. In relation to heterosexism, one person writes, "I lost out in the ability for people to share their [gay men and lesbians] lives fully."

In addition, the lack of trust makes it less likely that they will broach difficult subjects or try to work out troublesome interpersonal dynamics. A White woman spoke of how racism affects her ability to have real and honest interpersonal relationships with people of color:

> I am hurt or limited by the fact that I cannot honestly state some of my feelings and concerns about the subject for fear it may be considered racist. I feel that if there is not honest dialogue about people's true concerns, we will never be able to reach real solutions. We will just walk politely around the issues and put band-aids [sic] on problems as they jump up and hit us in the face. This is no different than communication between a couple or close friends. If you're not really honest about how you see things, you will either just learn to live with things as they are or pull away even farther from the situation. You will not really make a positive long-term change.

Disconnection, Distance, and Ostracism Within Own Group

As people from privileged groups speak about barriers to relationships, they often refer to the distance that is created in their own communities and families. As before, this distance may be because of their own or others' attitudes. One type of disconnection is due to differences in other social identities.

Among people with a shared subordinate identity, some individuals may also have a dominant identity that creates a rift within the social group. Middle- and upper-class people of color frequently mention feeling disconnected from poor and working-class people from their own racial/ethnic group. Sometimes, it is they who feel excluded: "As a Black woman, it is a constant issue that I am upper-middle class. I am often made to feel that I must hide this fact because of the attitudes and judgments from Blacks." Other times, people feel they have little in common with people from lower socioeconomic classes. The distance is due to their own discomfort, estrangement, privilege, or any combination of these factors: "As a upper-class Black person in a wealthy White community, I often ended up oppressing people who looked just like me but didn't have money."

These dynamics, which lead to disconnection, also occur within families. A woman recounts how this occurred in her family because of class differences:

> As a result of classism, I don't know my father's side of the family. My mother's family is middle class and educated. Dad's are farmers and fishermen. They are seen by Mom's side as "not worth knowing," so I don't even know cousins I have.

In addition, because of heterosexism, heterosexual siblings or parents may reject a gay child, forfeiting that primary relationship.

Other times, people are ostracized for the choices they make that violate the accepted norms of behavior within their own group. This strains or breaks bonds with family members, friends, peers, and coworkers. Men can be teased and become social outcasts for not being "one of the guys":

> In my peer groups at work, I often get "knocked" because of my feelings and values, and my openness and willingness to express them. I definitely feel my male peers expect certain "male" behavior and attitudes from me.

If individuals date or marry outside their own racial or class group, they can be disowned by or estranged from their family. One White woman from the United States tells how after she married a Guatemalan man she "experienced the pain of rejection, abandonment, discrediting, and almost complete discounting" from her family. Another woman relates the "numerous issues with my father due to his belief that I should not date out of my race. His anger at my dating of a Black man has also led to physical violence toward me by him."

Moral and Spiritual Costs: Loss of Integrity and Spiritual Center

Most people like to see themselves as decent, caring, and having principles of fairness and justice. However, they live in a society where there are pervasive inequities, reflected in homelessness, poverty, violence, and job discrimination, to name a few. Many people grapple with the discrepancy between the reality in which they live and their moral/spiritual beliefs.

Guilt and Shame

Some people feel uncomfortable with the fact that some people have so much while others have so little. They may feel embarrassed or guilty for having more than others. People frequently feel guilt when they know that others do not share their privileges or standard of living. In response to these increasingly apparent inequities, people often "blame the victim." Yet for many people, the guilt and shame still haunt them. They may ask questions such as,

> Do I deserve to have so much when some people have so little?
> What is my responsibility to "them" and to myself and my family?
> How can I see myself as a good caring person, yet do nothing to really change the system or the conditions of the oppressed?

As people become more aware of injustices, these feelings and questions become harder to ignore, and these moral naggings intensify. People from advantaged groups may feel bad or defensive about who they are ("I may be White but some of my best friends are Black"). It is shameful to think about how one benefits from the pain or exploitation of others. Often, people feel guilty for not doing more to change inhumane or unjust conditions, for not responding to offensive comments and jokes, or for not taking a stand against an injustice.

Moral Ambivalence

Often, people feel torn between acting in accordance with their personal integrity and risking family or societal disapproval, such as giving up significant money to social-change efforts or marrying "one of them." They may be faced with decisions between doing the "right" thing and going along with social pressure—selling their home to gays, Jews, or people of color in an otherwise (apparently) homogeneous neighborhood or hiring a person with a disability, knowing that clients or staff would be uncomfortable and resistant to accommodations. They may also question their negative feelings about a person from an oppressed group, wondering whether their personal dislike or perception of incompetence was due to prejudice or to a fair and reasonable judgment.

Spiritual Emptiness or Pain

Many people's religious or spiritual beliefs maintain that we are all "Children of God," part of the same Oneness, or interconnected and interdependent beings. Perpetuating oppression violates this sense of connection. It also belies the notion of God or Spirit in each person, and undermines the inherent integrity of each individual. As one person stated, "I believe when one group suffers, we all suffer for it is an indication of our own lack of 'soul.' "

Intellectual Costs: Loss of Developing Full Range of Knowledge

Neither their formal education nor their own experiences tend to provide people from dominant groups with sufficient and truthful information about their own or other social groups. The lack of relationships and the lack of (accurate) knowledge about people from dominated groups furthers ignorance. People's ability to expand their minds is thwarted.

Distorted and Limited View of Other People's Culture and History

People from privileged groups are uninformed or misinformed about much of the human race and the contributions of many other kinds of people. These include aspects of culture such as music, food, arts, values, philosophies, and social systems. When people in privileged groups are only exposed to the ways and accomplishments of people like themselves, they develop a distorted worldview. When history is recounted from the perspective of the dominant group, they receive only a partial picture of our past. This ignorance leads to limited and skewed views of different lifestyles, viewpoints, perspectives, and people. They become out of touch with reality and lose the ability to consider other, more productive and effective ways to live their lives and to understand the lives of others.

A White woman recounts her experience in an African American community:

> I was so enriched when I worked with African American families and came to see a different worldview of collectivism—families taking care of family members, communities, themselves. What a loss had I not experienced this other possible worldview. It has changed my life and my priorities.

However, more often, ignorance allows people to retain the misinformation and stereotypes about people of other social groups. This, coupled with fears, fosters the avoidance of people and experiences that might challenge their view of the world. This distorted perspective also has social consequences.

> As a member of the upper middle class, classism and "blaming the victim" prevented me from knowing and reaching out to those who are less privileged than I am. I was prevented from seeing others as "human" until I learned more about my own privilege.

Ignorance of Own Culture and History

People from privileged groups lose not only a clear understanding of others but of themselves. History books, in addition to omitting and distorting the experiences of people from oppressed groups, misconstrue the experiences of people from dominant groups. In the section on psychological costs, I discussed the loss of individual self-knowledge. However, people also miss a more accurate understanding of their own cultural group. For example, racism has caused many Whites to let go of their particular ethnic backgrounds to assimilate into mainstream White society, with its resulting privileges. In addition, when we ignore the wisdom and stories of our elders, we lose important perspectives and information, particularly about one's own history: "Ageism has cost me a rich resource of knowledge from the past. From the mouths of elders in my own family, I have lost their life experiences which I cannot pass on to my own children."

Material and Physical Costs:
Loss of Safety, Resources, and Quality of Life

Oppression creates social conditions that affect people from privileged groups not only personally and directly but indirectly as well. Because of social injustice, we lose and waste both material and human resources.[1] Many factors related to one's safety and quality of life are negatively affected.

Social Violence and Unrest

Oppression and inequality tend to breed social unrest. As people feel increasingly mistreated, hopeless, and disconnected from the larger society and its benefits, violence and antisocial behavior increase. Although people from privileged groups often have more opportunities to try to hide from this reality, its effects are inescapable. They may try to avoid people and experiences that make them uncomfortable, creating a smaller and smaller world in which to live. People may put up walls and live in gated communities, becoming prisoners in their own homes. Their access to places is restricted as they increasingly feel that it just isn't safe to go there. People become more fearful about moving about in the world and spend more time, money, and energy trying to protect themselves and their belongings.

Higher Costs

As it becomes more difficult to find homes and schools that are safe and of good quality, the ones that do exist become more expensive. It becomes more challenging to maintain a good standard of living. Basic economics teaches that when there is high demand and short supply, prices go up. This also occurs in the labor market. When groups of people are systematically excluded from the labor pool (because of stereotypes, discrimination, or lack of preparation), there are fewer people to choose from, which creates higher wage costs. Employers therefore need to spend more to attract qualified people.

Waste of Resources

Keeping an unjust system in place is also extremely expensive. A significant amount of our taxes and economic resources goes to supporting law enforcement and the judicial and penal systems, to providing social support services, and so on. Economic and human resources are directed at addressing the effects of social inequalities as opposed to ensuring opportunities for all. Frequently cited examples are the special programs or college loans available to people of color. White students are left to struggle to fund their education, instead of having education available to all who desire it. As one person stated, "I've faced the inability to access services as a middle class child/adolescent/college student, due to the 'status' of 'being able to pay for everything' when in fact that wasn't the case."

Loss of Valuable Employees, Clients, and Customers

When groups of people are impeded from having decent jobs and earning living wages, they are less able to purchase goods and services. This in turn negatively affects the economy. When restaurants, universities, businesses, and other organizations are seen as inaccessible, discriminatory, or unfriendly to different oppressed groups, they lose clients, customers, and students. This tends to translate into financial loss for the owners and less job security for employees. Similarly, it is more difficult to attract and retain talented employees from marginalized groups who would enhance organizational success. When they are hired, if they are unable to bring their whole selves to work (including aspects of their identity or culture) or have to constantly deal with prejudices, they are less creative and productive.

Loss of Knowledge to Foster Societal Growth and Well-being

When groups of people are disenfranchised, given limited opportunities, or have their cultures ignored or obliterated, the society as a whole loses their contributions. We know that different cultures and life experiences can bring fresh perspectives to current problems and issues. When these are discounted or individuals are not given the chance to develop their abilities, we have lost the potential for new ways to think about old and new concerns. We also miss the contributions to the arts and sciences that enrich and advance our country and the world. As one person noted, "I believe that we simply 'miss out.' As a culture we lose some of the inventive, creative contributions that could be made by many people who are denied a chance to flourish."

Diminished Collective Action for Common Concerns

When attention and energy are directed at addressing the effects of oppression and at individual (or group) survival, they are diverted from other issues that would enhance societal well-being. This keeps us separated and impedes our ability to work together to address larger common concerns (education, health, or the environment). Even collective action in a narrower sense, such as in unions, is hindered by the intentional or unintentional exclusion or marginalization of oppressed groups.

Negative Health Implications

People in privileged groups experience high degrees of stress and stress-related illnesses as they feel increasingly fearful and disconnected from other human beings. Pressures to achieve and maintain status in a hierarchical and competitive social and economic system further undermine health. A recent study also found that there are higher mortality rates for both wealthy and poor people in metropolitan areas with high income inequality (Lynch et al., 1998). Metropolitan areas with the largest income differences between the top and bottom 10% of the population have the highest overall death rates. The larger this discrepancy within a geographic area, the higher the area's death rate is likely to be for people in both rich and poor communities.

Interconnections and Variations

Though described separately, many of these costs in fact are overlapping and mutually reinforcing. They build and feed on each other, often creating a vicious cycle. When people do not have contact with others who are different and do not have accurate information about themselves or others, they develop fears and stereotypes that make it harder to establish contact. This leads to more discomfort, avoidance, ignorance, and fear. They therefore are more likely to support social policies that are oppressive or ineffective at addressing the issues, which in turn helps to perpetuate the inequality.

Even the same general cost may affect various areas of one's life. The disconnection from others may have psychological, social, moral/spiritual, intellectual, and material costs. For example, one is likely to develop fears or be limited in one's self knowledge, to lose

Table 6.1 Costs of Oppression to People From Privileged Groups

Cost category	Effects
Psychological Costs: **Loss of mental health and authentic sense of self**	Socialized into limited roles and patterns of behavior Denial of emotions and empathy Limited self-knowledge and distorted view of self Discrepancy between external perceptions and internal reality Pain and fears (of doing and saying wrong thing, of retaliation from oppressed groups, of revealing self for fear of judgment, of different people and experiences) Diminished mental health (distorted view of self and reality, denial, projection)
Social Costs: **Loss and diminishment of relationships**	Isolation from people who are different Barriers to deeper, more authentic relationships Disconnection, distance and ostracism within own group if one acts differently
Intellectual Costs: **Loss of developing full range of knowledge**	Distorted and limited view of other people's culture and history Ignorance of own culture and history
Moral and Spiritual Costs: **Loss of moral and spiritual integrity**	Guilt and shame Moral ambivalence (doing right thing vs. social pressures and realities) Spiritual emptiness or pain (disconnection from fellow human beings, violation of one's spiritual values)
Material and Physical Costs: **Loss of safety, resources, and quality of life**	Violence and unrest (restricted ability to move about freely; increased fear for self and others; limited desirable places to live, work, go to school, recreate) Higher costs (e.g., for good and safe schools and homes, for qualified employees) Waste of resources (to address effects of inequality: prisons, law enforcement, social services, welfare) Loss of valuable employees, clients, and customers (because of inhospitable environments, discrimination) Loss of knowledge to foster societal growth and well-being (the underdevelopment, exclusion, and marginalization of the talents of people from oppressed groups) Diminished collective action for common concerns (e.g., education, health, the environment) Negative health implications (e.g., stress and stress-related illnesses)

out on meaningful interpersonal relationships, to feel cut off from other human beings who are subject to injustice, to not know about others' lives and perspectives, and to miss out on valuable talent or knowledge. As one woman aptly summed it up, "This separation causes a kind of blindness to others' suffering and experiences, and a narrowness of viewpoint which can affect one's political, social, intellectual and spiritual development."

How people from privileged groups perceive and experience the costs varies among individuals. Sometimes people may not even recognize something as a cost until it is named by someone else (e.g., the expense involved in maintaining oppression). They may take for granted certain ways of being or social arrangements, assuming these are normal (e.g., sex roles or conflicts among different groups). One's other social identities clearly play a role in what is seen or felt to be a cost. I wonder about gender differences. In general, males may be less likely to identify costs because they are more advantaged by our current social system. Yet because males are socialized overall into roles of dominance and are more constrained by rigid sex roles, those who are socially conscious may be more sensitive to the pressures to act in ways that deny their own and others' humanity. Women, who are allowed (and encouraged) to be more emotionally expressive and often experience more flexibility in their ways of behaving (and thus experience less of a cost), may be more attuned to the loss of connection with others (because of being White, heterosexual, middle/upper class, etc.). We cannot expect all individuals to experience the costs in the same way. It is useful, however, to be able to illustrate the various effects and to help people to identify the relevant ways in which they as individuals and as members of society are negatively affected by oppression.

General Costs to People From Privileged Groups

When we collectively consider the range of costs of oppression to people from privileged groups, it becomes clear that they cannot escape the consequences of systems of injustice. To maintain inequality, people from advantaged groups must be psychologically conditioned to assume their roles in the social order. The current ideology and social structures reinforce the kind of thinking and behavior that perpetuate injustice that ultimately diminishes all human beings (see Chapter 4). As we participate in the dehumanization of others, which we inevitably do by participating in institutions, practices, and social relations that support societal inequality, our own freedom, authenticity, and humanity are limited. Several prominent social activists have acknowledged the intertwined fate of the oppressor and the oppressed.

According to Paulo Freire (1970), humanization is the vocation of human beings: "As oppressors dehumanize others and violate their [the oppressed's] rights, they themselves also become dehumanized" (p. 42). Freire further states, "Dehumanization, which marks not only those whose humanity has been stolen, but also (though in a different way) those who have stolen it, is a *distortion* of becoming more fully human" (p. 28).

Nelson Mandela (1994), in his book, *Long Walk to Freedom*, adds,

> I knew as well as I knew anything that the oppressor must be liberated just as surely as the oppressed. A man who takes away another man's freedom is a prisoner of hatred, locked behind the bars of prejudice and narrow-mindedness. I am not truly free if I am taking away someone else's freedom, just as surely as I am not free when my freedom is taken from me. The oppressed and the oppressor alike are robbed of their humanity. (p. 544)

Martin Luther King, Jr. (1991), also noted this connection.

> I can never be what I ought to be until you are what you ought to be, and you can never be what you might be until I am what I ought to be. (p. 7)

In his writing about racism, Robert Terry (1981) addresses the loss of authenticity. He maintains that authenticity "describes the press in all of our lives to make sense out of our world and act purposefully in it" (p. 121). This involves being true to ourselves and true to our world. Like other forms of oppression, racism distorts authenticity because it distorts our relationships to ourselves, to others, and to our society.

One of the fundamental human desires is to know and be known. We seek relationships with others that allow us to see them fully and have those others see us fully. We want to be recognized for who we truly are. Oppression prevents this process of mutual recognition. It thwarts our ability to become our authentic selves and to fully know ourselves. It also impedes others from knowing who we are. It is often with much pain that people from privileged groups recount stories of how they feel mis-seen and misjudged, especially by people from oppressed groups. The full complexity of their history, backgrounds, and experiences is not acknowledged. Instead, they are perceived more one-dimensionally. Certainly we know that this occurs to people from subordinate groups. Even though they are not experienced in the same way by people who are in advantaged and disadvantaged positions, dehumanization, inauthenticity, and misrecognition are inherent aspects of all forms of oppression.

Conclusion

As discussed in Chapter 2, McIntosh (1988) makes the distinction between conferred dominance and unearned advantage. The first is the way in which society gives people in dominant groups the power to control and disadvantage others. These so-called privileges "distort the humanity of the holders as well as the ignored groups" (p. 78). They are the products of unjust hierarchies. Unearned advantages are the conditions that currently are available to people in privileged groups (access to decent food, housing, education, and respectful treatment) that should be had by everyone. These privileges we need to make available to all. The goal is not for people in privileged groups to be punished or diminished as human beings but to eliminate the conditions that hurt them and others and to increase the conditions that benefit all our lives.

As people from privileged groups gain an awareness of these costs, it can lead to their understanding of how systems of oppression are not necessarily or fully in their best interest. From there, one can more readily think about the benefits of greater equity. As the costs imply, with greater social justice, people could have a fuller, more authentic sense of self; more authentic relationships and human connection; greater moral consistency and integrity; access to cultural knowledge and wisdom; and improved work and living conditions. There would also be the potential for real democracy in our government and institutions. (I will discuss these further in Chapter 10.)

Yet simply helping people from privileged groups to understand the personal and societal limitations of oppression does not mean they will readily work to change the current system. There are many incentives to maintain the status quo. However, it does create an opportunity for critical thinking and for challenging the win-lose paradigm. The following chapters discuss ways to build on this perspective and engage people in social justice efforts.

Note

1. See Glyn, A., & Miliband D., (Eds.). (1994). *Paying for inequality: The economic cost of social injustice.* London: IPPR/Rivers Oram Press. There, they provide a more thorough discussion of how social inequality negatively affects various sectors of public life and decreases efficiency.

7

Why People From Privileged Groups Support Social Justice

There are obvious reasons why people from dominant groups resist challenges to the status quo. There are also plenty of reasons why they remain apathetic and uninvolved. Yet we know from history and our current experiences that people from privileged groups also support and often lead struggles for social justice. Instead of just focusing on why people from privileged groups don't support equity, I have been exploring what motivates people to do so. Why do some people from dominant groups act as allies, supporting the rights of an oppressed group of which they are not part? Why do some men support feminist initiatives, some heterosexuals work for gay and lesbian rights, or some Whites challenge racist practices? I have been asking people in classes and workshops that question. How would you answer it?

People's responses tend to fall into three distinct, though interrelated, categories. Some speak about a personal relationship they have with an individual from an oppressed group, of how they can relate their own experiences to the experiences of others, or how they feel a sense of connection or "we-ness." I call this type of response *empathy.*

Others speak of their need to act morally and their discomfort with the discrepancy between what they believe and what they observe around them. Some talk of unfairness, of how certain groups don't deserve their plight, and of their desire to fulfill the American ideal of equality. A spiritual belief in the inherent worth and dignity of all people motivates others. I call this type of response *moral principles and spiritual values.*

Still others focus on how oppression affects them as members of the dominant group and on the potential benefits of greater equity. They speak of wanting to live in a society with more harmonious intergroup relations, of wanting a world safe for their children, and of seeing the survival of the planet predicated on creating greater justice. Others personally desire more diverse friendships, broadened knowledge, and more varied cultural experiences. Some acknowledge the benefits to their organization through increased enrollments, retention, or profits. This group of responses I name *self-interest.*

I will first describe and discuss each of these factors individually.[1] I will then explore the interconnections among them. In the following chapter, I discuss how to actually foster and appeal to empathy, moral or spiritual principles, and self-interest to gain support for social justice concerns. I am not suggesting that these are the only qualities needed to be an ally or to work for equity but that these are key factors that encourage people to do so.[2]

Empathy

Empathy involves being able to identify with the situation and feelings of another person. It incorporates affective and cognitive components, requiring both the capacity to share in the emotional life of another as well as the ability to imagine the way the world looks from another's vantage point. Chinua Achebe refers to this as "imaginative identification" (as cited in Lazarre, 1993, p. 4). It is "our capacity to understand and feel the suffering of others even though we have never experienced that particular suffering ourselves" (in Lazarre, 1993, p. 4). Being empathic, or taking the perspective of another person and imagining how that person is affected by his or her plight, can be useful for promoting more positive attitudes and inspiring action. Research suggests that empathy and the desire to help are natural human inclinations (Kohn, 1990).

Empathy is not the same as pity. With pity, we hold ourselves apart from the other person and his/her suffering, thinking of their plight as something that makes the person fundamentally inferior or different from ourselves. Pity is seeing a homeless person on the street and, while feeling sorry for that person, thinking, "that never could be me." Empathy, however, is more like compassion. It recognizes our shared vulnerability while also acknowledging the differences between one's self and the other. Compassion is seeing the homeless person and thinking, "that could be me." We acknowledge our susceptibility to situations or conditions of misfortune as fellow human beings.

Empathy and Social Justice

Many theorists have discussed the significance of empathy in social relations (see Kohn, 1990, for a review of the literature). The presence of empathy can foster positive social action whereas its absence can perpetuate injustice. Suppressing empathy for people in oppressed groups is a powerful tool in maintaining oppression. When we fail to see our common humanity with people we perceive as different from ourselves, we can more easily ignore their plight. It also allows us to dehumanize others, seeing them as less than human or as unworthy of care and respect. This sets the stage for the acceptance or perpetuation of violence (a common strategy during wars; Grossman, 1995). The more one dehumanizes people, the more likely one will do violence. This in turn increases the need to dehumanize them. "By making the objects of our violence less than human, we do not experience the guilt associated with killing or harming fellow human beings" (Sampson, 1991, p. 322).

There are many ways in which people from oppressed groups are depersonalized and dehumanized in our society. Depersonalization and dehumanization occur through stereotypes (defining gay men as child molesters), images (depicting African Americans as animals) and language (using derogatory names—*gook, bitch, wetback*). In sum, perpetuating the sense that the Other is sufficiently different and less human than ourselves erodes the capacity for empathy and, thus, the propensity for care and action.

On the other hand, empathy can be a powerful tool in promoting social responsibility. Empathy helps us connect with and subsequently care about others who seem different. "Coming to see others as more simply human than one of Them, represents so drastic a conceptual shift, so affecting an emotional conversion, that there may be no greater threat to those with an interest in preserving inter-

group hostility" (Kohn, 1990, p. 145). Empathy makes it more difficult to use derogation as a means of maintaining a belief in a just
world—vilifying or blaming victims for their circumstances to continue to believe that society is fair. Instead, empathy tends to encourage prosocial action to remove the injustice (Batson et al., 1997). It
also helps to counter the egoistic desire to avoid personal costs and
maintain relative advantage.

There is an important difference between using empathy to motivate altruistic or helping behavior and using empathy to encourage social activism and support for social justice. Most research on
empathy and altruistic or prosocial behavior is confined to studies
of people responding to someone's immediate distress (often in lab-
oratory conditions). A single act will often suffice to alleviate that
distress. It is usually focused on helping an individual in a particular
situation, regardless of his or her social group membership or connection to social oppression. Prosocial activism, on the other hand, is
"sustained action in the service of improving another person's or
group's life condition by working with them or by trying to change
society on their behalf" (Hoffman, 1989, p. 65). People are more
likely to be engaged in prosocial activitism when they respond
empathically to a victim's or group's long-term plight, rather than
just to an immediate situation. This involves understanding that the
other person or persons are part of a social group and recognizing
the chronic nature of the victim's or victims' distress.

Although I will draw upon the research on empathy and
prosocial behavior to discuss why people act in caring and socially
responsible ways, the research on prosocial activism is most relevant to social justice efforts. As I will discuss, it is important that we
encourage people to see beyond just aiding an individual in a particular situation. We need to foster their support for societal changes
that will improve the lives of those who suffer systemic victimization.

Types of Empathic Responses

An empathic connection with someone who is suffering tends to
elicit two kinds of affective responses (Hoffman, 1989). One is
personal or *empathic distress*. This is when the empathy generates uncomfortable feelings for the people who are empathizing. This negative arousal may make people feel anxious, upset, disturbed, guilty,
or shameful. With empathic distress, individuals have a personal re-

action of distress to the situation of another. For example, when I see the unsafe, overcrowded, and inadequate conditions of the schools for children in the inner city near where I live, I often feel guilty and upset.

A second kind of affective response is *sympathetic distress*. This is what we tend to think of when we think of empathy or compassion. It involves caring about and feeling for the person in distress. In response to the above school conditions, I may also feel sorry for the children and families that must live with these circumstances (sympathetic distress). Hoffman (1989) has suggested that sympathetic distress may also elicit other related feelings. These can include feelings of empathic anger—anger on behalf of the victim toward the party responsible for the suffering—and empathic injustice—feeling that the victim's treatment is unfair and undeserved. For example, I may also be angry at the politicians who don't attempt to remedy this school situation (empathic anger). Or I may feel outrage because these children don't deserve to be forced into these oppressive conditions (empathic injustice).

Motivations to Care and Act

Once we have empathized and feel some kind of empathic or sympathetic distress, we have to decide what to do about it. Different types of empathic responses tend to produce different motivations to respond to the person (group) in need. Although these motivations are independent and distinct internal responses, they are not mutually exclusive and often occur in conjunction with each other.

Two main motives for acting on our empathy are egoistic motivations because they are primarily concerned with addressing our own needs (Batson, 1989). The first motivation is based on acting in *compliance with internalized standards.* Through socialization, we internalize standards or expectations for appropriate actions or behaviors. These may be based on social expectations (societal or group norms) or self-expectations (personal norms). Our motivation to act is driven by our desire to live up to these standards. By complying with these expectations, we can anticipate receiving rewards or avoiding punishment. These rewards or punishments may be explicit and obvious, such as obtaining an award, peer approval, monetary remuneration, gratitude from those helped, or public censure. Often they are more subtle and in compliance with internalized needs, such as avoiding guilt, seeing oneself as a good person, receiving esteem in exchange for helping, or gaining a sense of adventure. Continuing with the above example, I may decide to participate in a campaign for school finance reform because I think of myself as a caring person, my friends are involved in social justice causes, and I want to live up to the expectations of myself and my peers.

The second type of motivation is *aversive arousal reduction.* The motive is to reduce our own distress that was generated by empathizing. There is the desire to do something to reduce feelings of guilt, anger, or discomfort. From this perspective, I may work for school finance reform because I want to relieve my guilt that my children attend a high-quality school whereas other children do not, to dissipate my anger at their unjust treatment, or to relieve my discomfort at having to walk by there every day.

A third motivation is *altruism,* which is focused on addressing others' needs. The motivation to act is focused not on addressing our own distress, arousal, or needs, but on responding to the needs of other person (group). Our concern is simply to improve the welfare of the other, regardless of whether we will benefit. We may still experience some kind of positive effect, but that is not the motivating factor. My social action might be based on my care for the children and my desire that these children get the kind of education that all children deserve.

People's motivation to act on empathic responses can be based on any one or all of these factors, and often, the line is blurry. Though isolating the specific factors is not crucial, it can be helpful for educators to understand people's motivation to better foster and channel their emotional energy.

Moral Principles and Spiritual Values

Morality deals with questions of right and wrong. Research suggests that people are intrinsically motivated to behave fairly and to seem moral and good (Kelman & Hamilton, 1989; Tyler, Boeckmann, Smith, & Huo, 1997). Value systems affect people's judgment of a situation and their determination of whether it violates their moral or spiritual code. When someone considers something morally or spiritually wrong, that provides an impetus for the person to act to remedy that situation. Even though people from privileged groups may be inclined to justify their advantage as fair, studies demonstrate that concerns about justice affect both the feelings and actual behaviors of the people in privileged positions (Tyler et al., 1997). Despite the assumption that self-interest most influences people's decisions in the political arena, research suggests otherwise (Orren, 1988; Sears & Funk, 1990):

> What is far more likely to predict someone's position on an issue of public policy is a deeply held principle. Attitudes about issues ranging from desegregation to unemployment tend to reflect value commitments more than they do one's personal stake in a given policy. (Orren, 1988, p. 24)

In fact, many actions toward social justice are done to uphold ethical or spiritual values (Colby & Damon, 1992; Daloz, Keen, Keen, & Parks, 1996; Hoehn, 1983; Oliner & Oliner, 1988).

Types of Moral Reasoning

There are two commonly recognized modes of moral judgment. One is a person-oriented ethic of care; the other is a principle-oriented ethic of justice (Gilligan, 1980/1993; Lyons, 1988; Reimer, Paolitto, & Hersh, 1983). The dominant ideology in the United States, which espouses values of fairness, equality, and equal opportunity, reflects a justice orientation. Each of these moral orientations and their developmental sequences has implications for motivating support for social justice. I discuss each of these below.

A morality of justice, long believed to be the only system of moral reasoning, is focused on rights and fairness. This form of morality is concerned with upholding principles or standards. It is rooted in a formal sense of equality and reciprocity (treating others as you would want to be treated). When using this type of moral reasoning, people make moral decisions by applying logical, abstract, and impartial rules or principles. People contend that something is unjust when it violates these accepted standards, which often involve equal rights, equal opportunity, or role-related obligations.

A morality of care is focused on relationships and responsiveness. This form of morality is concerned with promoting the welfare of others, preventing harm, and relieving physical or psychological suffering. Using this type of reasoning, people arrive at moral decisions inductively, motivated by the desire to maintain connections and avoid hurt. From this perspective, individuals contend that something violates their moral code when people are being harmed or not cared for.

People may therefore agree that something is morally wrong but arrive at that determination in different ways. Take, for example, a situation of housing discrimination based on race. A justice perspective might focus on its unfairness because it violates laws that assert equal opportunity. A care perspective might focus on the harm to the family looking for a home and the suffering it causes them.

Most people tend toward one type of moral orientation, though they often use both. Because a morality of justice is the norm, even people who prefer an ethic of care are fluent in and can use a ethic of justice perspective. Studies have suggested that women tend to use an ethic of care more frequently than men (Gilligan, 1980/1993; Lyons, 1988).

Developmental Sequences

Even within the same moral orientation, there is a developmental sequence of moral reasoning that reflects distinctions in how people make moral judgments within that framework. Again, although people may engage in similar actions, their reasons for doing so may differ. I'll use an example of a college administrator charged with recruiting and hiring more faculty and students of color to illustrate the different perspectives.

Within an ethic of justice, there are three levels, each with two stages, that reflect the development of moral reasoning. Reasoning at the first level, *preconventional*, is concerned with the concrete interests of the individuals involved, not with what society defines as the right way to behave in a given situation. People here consider what the specific consequences would be for acting in a particular way. An administrator reasoning from this self-oriented level might not even feel that there is a moral problem (racial discrimination or exclusion) to be addressed. However, he may comply because he fears losing his job if he doesn't or because he thinks that he will be more marketable if he does increase diversity. He might also believe that this will give him more leverage with the student organizations or faculty groups that support diversity when he has to deal with other issues, such as an alcohol policy.

Moving away from a self-centered focus, the second level, *conventional*, involves an identification with the expectations of others and the rules and norms of society. This level is most common among adults. The administrator might pursue this effort because it is what his peers are doing at other colleges, people he respects expect him to do so, and it is commonly recognized in academic circles that there needs to be more inclusion of underrepresented groups at colleges. He also might be concerned with conforming to affirmative-action laws, campus policies, or other statutes that mandate equal opportunity and outreach.

At the third level, *postconventional* or *principled*, the focus shifts to abstract ideals of justice. These may include abiding by the social contract (laws, rules, and values), which considers the welfare of all and protects all people's rights. Individuals may also be guided by universal ethical principles that involve the equality of human rights and the respect for the dignity of human beings as individuals. People will abide by laws and social agreements to the extent that those correspond with their universal principles. The administrator reasoning from this level might support efforts to create a more diverse and inclusive college to benefit all—providing a better-educated workforce that can value diversity and use the talents of more of its citizens. He may believe that all people should have the freedom to pursue knowledge and be able to fulfill their potential.

The ethic of care also has a developmental sequence of moral reasoning. This three-position sequence begins with *survival,* a position in which the concern is for caring for oneself to ensure survival. The second perspective is *goodness,* a position that involves caring for others and being good according to conventional definitions. The last perspective is *truth,* in which care for oneself as well as others is considered and the interconnection between self and others is recognized. Care becomes a self-chosen moral principle with the injunction to prevent or condemn harm and violence.

Similarly, different considerations might motivate the administrator using a care perspective. From the view of survival, he may comply with this strategy to keep his job so he can pay his bills and support his family. From the view of goodness, he may feel that being a good administrator means caring about all potential students and faculty and being liked and respected by his colleagues and the campus community. From the third perspective of truth, he may realize that exclusion hurts people of color by denying them opportunities and harms Whites by denying them a fuller educational experience. He may feel that, ultimately, our collective well-being is better served by a more diverse campus.

Spiritual Values

Spiritual beliefs may fall within these moral frameworks or have their own ethical codes. Spirituality or religion always has an ethical orientation because it seeks to respond to the moral question of how we ought to live our lives (Daloz et al., 1996). Some talk of upholding the Golden Rule, of treating everyone as a child of God, of the importance of relieving suffering, or of recognizing that "there is that of God in every person." In their study of people committed to working for the common good, Daloz et al. found that for many individuals, religion and spirituality played an explicit or implicit role in their development of commitment and in their larger meaning-making system. People frequently alluded to a principle of interdependence. This sense of the interdependent nature of life informed their public commitment. These individuals also found a way to continually reframe and expand their religious understanding and practice to include and respect others and the complex diversity of the world. Some spoke of a sense of spiritual imperative, of feeling called and compelled to respond to the needs of the world. Despite their many differences, most religious or spiritual belief systems share a common mandate to care for those less fortunate and to treat people humanely.

We can be more effective at appealing to moral and spiritual values if we understand how people determine what is ethical or just. As these frameworks and sequences suggest, different moral orientations and reasoning can motivate people to support social justice. The early stages in both moral frameworks are self-oriented, more focused on one's own needs than those of others. However, as we'll see in the next section, self-interest is not necessarily selfish concern. Self-interest can also be a healthy aspect of being an ally.

Self-Interest

I previously discussed some of the many costs of oppression to people from dominant groups. These various psychological, moral/spiritual, intellectual, social, and material/physical costs provide a basis for why people from privileged groups might support greater equity. They may seek greater authenticity and integrity, better interpersonal relationships, safer communities, or more effective organizations. These reasons highlight how justice can be in the self-interest of dominant-group individuals.

However, the term *self-interest* tends to have a negative connotation. In fact, the primary dictionary definitions explain it as selfish concern and personal advantage. These common definitions of self-interest imply that one gains at the expense or exclusion of others, that it is a zero-sum game. This is consistent with economic exchange theory and with the dominant worldview that envisions people as separate individuals competing for positions of advantage or superiority. Although this may reflect one aspect of self-interest, it ignores the possibility that what may be in my interest might also benefit others.

People also tend to assume that there is something inherently wrong or less pure about considering one's own interests or needs, especially in doing work as an ally. As Carol Gilligan (1980/1993) has suggested, in interdependent relationships, we need to put ourselves in the "web of care" and consider our own needs as well as the needs of others. A healthy self-concern is not the same as selfishness. We do not need to ignore or act against our own needs in the process of working for justice. But to do so, we need a broader understanding of self-interest (see Kohn, 1990, and Lappe & Du Bois, 1991, for a discussion of alternative conceptions of self-interest). The term *enlightened self-interest* has been used in a general way to describe the understanding that the interests of the individual and the common good can converge. I will propose a more complex conception of self-interest and suggest that it is a useful, if not necessary, component of motivating people from privileged groups to support social justice.

Continuum of Self-Interest

Instead of defining self-interest simply as selfish concern, we can define it more broadly to include benefits to oneself that do not necessarily exclude benefits to others as well. Self-interest can incorporate the interests of others as well as one's own. It can range from a very narrow, selfish perspective to a more inclusive, interdependent perspective. There are two key factors that distinguish different types of self-interest: one's conception of self (separate and autonomous or connected and relational) and a short- or long-term perspective (whether one focuses on immediate or long-run interests). Moreover, as evidenced in the costs of oppression described earlier, the benefits for people from privileged groups may take various forms, from the psychological to the material. I will describe a continuum of self-interest (see Figure 7.1) and provide some illustrations of the various perspectives.

On one end of the continuum is *individualistic*, or "me-oriented," self-interest. This coincides with the common equation of self-interest with selfish concern. People operating from this type of self-interest may support social justice efforts solely for their own perceived personal gain. The concern is for the self; the fact that it benefits someone else is incidental or secondary. The prime motivation to support social justice is seen in terms of "what it will do for me." Appealing to this type of self-interest may be getting someone to do the right thing for what may seem to be the wrong reason. It is a short-sighted and short-term perspective, concerned with immediate, and usually material, benefits.

For example, a politician may support rights for people with disabilities because it will provide votes among a needed constituency. Similarly, an individual or organization may give money to a shelter for battered women or antipoverty program because it will be good public relations and help their reputation. A male student may help organize campus events against violence against women as a vehicle to meet women or fulfill an extra-credit assignment.

Farther along the continuum, self-interest involves a consideration of what benefits others as well as oneself. A *mutual* perspective sees benefits for both—"you *and* me." Moving away from a narrow, self-oriented perspective, this reflects a more relational view of self-interest. The action is based on real concern for others. The personal benefits may be of many types. People may volunteer in a food kitchen because it makes them feel good about themselves and allows them to feel they are doing something helpful (psychological) or to learn more about homelessness (intellectual). At the same time, they may also genuinely want to do something to address the disadvantaged situation of others. People may join the Peace Corp or other service organizations both for the sense of adventure and to meet new people (social), as well as to aid in the development of poor communities. Individuals might work on campaigns for wel-

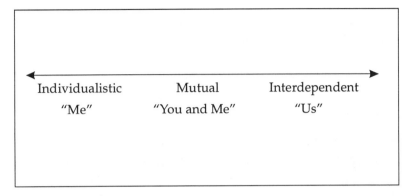

Figure 7.1. Continuum of Self-Interest

fare reform and living wages to relieve their guilt about their privileged economic background (moral), in addition to assisting people in need. A heterosexual father of a gay son may be involved in passing gay nondiscrimination laws. It reduces his own anxiety over his son's experience of homophobia and benefits his son and other gays and lesbians. There may be material benefit when the decision to sponsor a Diversity Week is based partly on the desire to respond to the concerns of marginalized groups and also based partly on seeing it as a strategy to quell greater demands and accusations that the organization doesn't care about diversity.

My assumption is that for the majority of people who support social justice efforts, there is some sense of mutual benefit. Even though they might like to believe or have others believe that the support is solely on behalf of the oppressed group (in which case it would be pure altruism with no self-interest), I suspect that most of us get some other personal satisfaction from engaging in such actions. This in turn motivates further involvement.

The *interdependent* perspective has a greater relational view that blurs the boundaries between you and me and sees "us." As Sampson (1988) explains, "When the self is defined in relation, inclusive of others in its very definition, there is no fully separate self whose interests do not of necessity include others" (p. 20). Various feminist theories have been developing relational theories of self (Gilligan, 1980/1993; Jordan et al., 1991). Work on behalf of others is simultaneously work on behalf of ourselves. From this interdependent perspective, because our lives and fates are intertwined, social justice efforts are being done for our collective benefit. A heterosexual person who fights against homophobia might feel that all of us need to be free from rigid sex roles, limits on sexual expression, and lifestyle constraints. Likewise, a person without a disability might champion the humane treatment of people with disabilities, believing it reflects on how society views and values all human beings.

Interdependent self-interest may require that people work against what appears to be their immediate self-interest. However, a relational sense of self and a more long-term perspective allows them to see the benefit to themselves and others in the long run. Wealthy people may support higher tax rates or caps on executives' salaries (which affect their earnings) to create a more equitable distribution of wealth. They may believe that because a more peaceful society depends on people having quality educational and work opportunities and decent living conditions, there needs to be a fairer allocation of resources. White men (or women) may support affirmative action, even though in the short run it reduces the likelihood that they will be hired. They support a practice that they feel will lead to the kind of world they want to live in—one with great equity and the inclusion of important voices that have been silenced. People who have an interdependent sense of self-interest are likely to recognize their privilege and to seek ways to give it up, to not take advantage of it, or to use it to promote social justice.

The Connections Among
Empathy, Morality and Self-Interest

By themselves, empathy, moral and spiritual values, and self-interest can provide an impetus to support social justice. However, they often operate in conjunction and can be addressed in combination to strengthen the appeal to action. I will provide some examples of how they can be used to bolster each other.

Empathy Joined With Moral Principles and Self-Interest

The use of moral values along with empathy can help transform feelings into action. Instead of just making people feel bad, moral or spiritual principles can create a sense of responsibility to act to alleviate the suffering or injustice. The experience of empathy may lead to the invocation of moral principles. In addition, because empathy generally requires that people see the situation or suffering as unjust, moral principles can allow people to come to that understanding or interpretation.

Self-interest is implicit in much empathically motivated behavior. People often act in socially responsible ways to address their empathic distress. They are motivated by a desire to reduce their negative arousal or to be consistent with their internalized standards. After an empathy-generating experience, self-interest can be useful in helping them deal with their reactions. It can motivate and sustain action once their empathy has been aroused.

Moral Principles Joined With Empathy and Self-Interest

Empathy can help move one's moral concern out of the abstract and impersonal. Some people are rule-, not person- or other-, oriented. Kohn (1990) suggests that if people are overly concerned with rules, ideology or abstract principles, this actually may interfere with their sensitivity to the suffering of real people. In these cases, empathy can help put a human face and a personal connection on the moral injustice and thus enhance these individuals' commitment to address the situation. Feeling a human connection can also help expand one's sense of who is included in one's moral community. The more others are seen as similar or sharing a close relationship, the less able one is to maintain the cognitive distortion to justify the status quo. Also, empathy may be evoked once some human contact has been made, after the initial action was taken out of moral principle.

Moral values promote action in part to maintain self-integrity. It is in people's self-interest to protect their self-esteem and self-image. Self-interest can also be tied to one's level of moral reasoning and motivation to act morally.[3] For some, as earlier examples illustrated, self-interest is central in their process of making moral judgments. For those with more principled reasoning, a more mutual and collective sense of self-interest strengthens their ability to follow through on their moral convictions. Because people generally weigh the personal costs before acting on their moral values, increasing the sense of personal benefit helps shift the balance toward acting.

Self-Interest Joined With Empathy and Moral Principles

Empathy can shift people out of narrow, individualistic self-interest by fostering a concern for others. It can strengthen their feelings of connection and promote interdependence. This can help move them toward a more mutual and collective sense of self-interest.

Moral principles can encourage people to act not just out of selfish motives or short-term advantages but also out of ethical considerations. It provides people with other guidelines to make decisions about their behavior. Because we want people to be engaged in social justice work with commitment and integrity, enhancing their emotional and intellectual investment leads in this direction.

Research on activists (though the activists are not necessarily working on issues in which they are part of the dominant group) suggests that they are highly developed in their senses of empathy, morality, and collective self-interest (Berman, 1997). Indeed, these factors are intertwined. Activists have a sense of self that is defined by moral values and a sense of connectedness with others, especially with those suffering injustice and with the world as a whole. This relational sense of self fosters a sensitivity to the feeling of others and an understanding of the connection between others' well-being and one's own and leads to a commitment to relieve suffering and oppression. This connected sense of self underlies and promotes empathy, a morality of care, and an interdependent sense of self-interest.

For most activists in the research, seeing themselves as moral beings was also a central part of their sense of self. This unity of self and morality fostered activism and erased feelings of self-sacrifice. "No one saw their moral choices as an exercise in self-sacrifice. To the contrary, they see their moral goals as a means of attaining their personal ones and vice versa" (Colby & Damon, 1992, pp. 300-301).

In addition, studies suggest that "roots of activism also lie in the desire for a sense of meaning that takes one beyond oneself. To be bigger than oneself, to feel that one is contributing to the welfare of others and society, not only motivates action but sustains it over the long term" (Berman, 1997, p. 68). Commitment to honesty and openness to new information and change were also cited as common characteristics of activists.

Conclusion

As reflected in this chapter, the reasons people from privileged groups may support social justice are varied and multilayered No one factor—empathy, moral and spiritual values, or self-interest—will motivate all people, nor will the same factor appeal to people in the same way. My impression is that educators often emphasize one of these aspects—usually empathy or morality—to the exclusion of others. Some people address these sources of motivation generally, without considering some of the complexities within each. Becoming more conscious about which we use, how we use them, and in what combinations we use them enhances our effectiveness with the various individuals and issues that we deal with. It provides some direction for our educational and social change efforts. When we build on empathy, moral and spiritual values, and self-interest in conjunction with each other, we also promote more long-term activism. In the following chapter, I will discuss how to develop these qualities in our students and how to encourage social action.

Notes

1. Kimmel (1993) found that one reason why men have supported the women's liberation movement was that it simply made logical sense. Although this may be true for some individuals, in my own research, I have found that this reason has rarely arisen, and therefore I do not include it in my discussion.

2. I wish to acknowledge the work of Steve Wineman (1984), which suggested a framework for these responses.

3. For an interesting discussion of the connections among moral reasoning, racism, and self-interest, see Terry, R. (1978). White belief, moral reasoning, self-interest and racism. In W. W. Schroeder & F. Winter (Eds.), *Belief and ethics* (pp. 349-374). Chicago: Center for the Scientific Study of Religion.

8

Developing and Enlisting
Support for Social Justice

In the previous chapter, I discussed how empathy, moral and spiritual values, and self-interest can motivate people from privileged groups to support social justice. This chapter will focus on how this framework can be applied to our educational and change efforts. I will further describe how to foster and appeal to empathy, moral and spiritual values, and self-interest to enlist support for social change efforts. I will also consider ways to encourage people to be allies and activists.

Empathy

Fostering Empathy

To increase empathy, both the intellect and the emotions need to be engaged. In general, to foster empathy, people need to maximize personal knowledge and heighten emotional attunement. By imagining another's point of view and feelings, we can better understand his or her situation. It is also helpful to minimize distance and anonymity by actually getting to know real people and experiencing their life circumstances. There are many things we can do to increase the empathy of people from privileged groups toward people from oppressed groups.

Expose People to Other Life Experiences

We can be exposed to others' realities through books, movies, panels, and personal testimony. Hearing the information in person tends to be the most powerful (though this has a higher risk because there is less control over what people say and do). Invite an individual or a panel of speakers to discuss their lives. One of the more effective programs in my work with faculty on addressing issues of diversity and equity in the classroom has been to have students from marginalized groups (students of color, gay and lesbian students, poor students) talk about their experiences in classes. After hearing the panel, faculty are usually more receptive to discussing how to be more inclusive and sensitive in their teaching.

It's important to include a variety of experiences from within a particular group or to discuss how this individual reflects the experiences of many others. There is the possibility of seeing an individual as an exception or atypical for his or her social group. In addition, because perspective taking fosters empathy, provide frequent opportunities for people to develop their ability to take the perspective of others and consider other points of view. This can be done through simulations, role plays, and case studies.

Have People Share Their Own Experiences

We can ask people to reflect on and share their own experiences with discrimination and oppression. Nearly all people are members of at least one oppressed group. And everyone has some experience of being stereotyped and treated unfairly. People can better understand the feelings of others through considering how they felt in similar circumstances. Individuals who have experienced the effects of oppression in one aspect of their identity can often use this to relate to the experiences of someone from a different oppressed group in which they are part of the dominant group. A heterosexual African American woman acknowledged that she was homophobic and expressed some discomfort at the prospect of listening to a panel of gay, lesbian, and bisexual people share their stories. After the session, she remarked, "They deal with a lot of the same stuff I do as a Black person!" She could relate to their feelings of internalized oppression, marginalization, and fear of violence. By using her experiences as a person of color as a reference point as a heterosexual, she now had new insight into (and tolerance for) gays.

This can be a helpful starting place to make some connections and develop compassion, but further discussion is needed so that it goes beyond emotional catharsis. We don't want people to overlook differences or equate isolated incidents with systematic, socially sanctioned mistreatment. Just because the woman above could use her experiences as an African American to connect with the experiences of gays and lesbians, this does not mean that she knows what it's like to be gay (or vice versa). Moreover, a man's exclusion from a women-only support group is not the same as women's exclusion from men's organizations or from positions that serve as vehicles for the sharing of social power and promotion.

Furthermore, if we want people to be engaged in social action, they need to understand that a person's plight is not just an individual issue. His or her lack of opportunities or disadvantage is due to larger societal conditions that require addressing social inequalities. People need to understand that the distress of this individual is symptomatic of some form of oppression that also affects many others like them.

Give People the Opportunity to Have Firsthand Experiences

Provide people with the chance to get to know actual people and experience others' situations directly. In a diverse class, cooperative learning and group projects can help achieve this end. Internships, extended visits to different neighborhoods, volunteer work, and service learning can reduce both emotional and physical distance. Even helping that is initially done nonempathically can lead to empathy (Kohn, 1990). People who help tend to develop a more positive view of those they have assisted, become more concerned with their well-being, and feel a greater responsibility to continue to help them (Staub, 1989). In conjunction with these activities, it is important that students are engaged in a process of self-reflection and in discussions of privilege and social inequality so that they can make sense of their experiences and avoid paternalistic attitudes.[1]

Hoffman (1989) found that activists' direct and repeated contact with disadvantaged groups intensified their initial empathic and sympathetic distress. It also diminished their intellectual remoteness and challenged their stereotypes. Their empathic and sympathetic distress was transformed, in part, into empathic feelings of injustice, empathic anger at society, and guilt over their own relatively privileged position. This led them to question their own ideology that assumed that society was basically caring and just.

A recent newspaper article (Bole, 1997) suggests the power of empathy. In Tennessee, after failed efforts to get Whites to support additional funds for poor Black schools, a group of African Americans invited a group of Whites (though an interfaith organization) to visit their schools. After this firsthand experience, Whites were willing to support the additional funds and also joined forces in fighting for school-based management. The politicians were unable to split the Black and White communities on these issues.

Potential Pitfalls of Empathy

Although empathy is a powerful force in acting for justice, we need to be careful in our efforts to help people from dominant groups empathize with the experiences of people from marginalized groups. Elizabeth Spelman (1995) spells out some of the paradoxes of these efforts and dangers to watch out for.

In Spelman's *paradox of appropriation,* there is the tendency, in the process of seeing oneself in the experiences of others, to erase the specifics of the others' experience and to equate the two experiences. Although we want people to connect to the experiences of another and to a sense of shared humanity, we do not want them to expropriate that experience. It is the danger of falling into the trap of thinking, "I know just how you feel!"

In the *paradox of identification,* the danger is overemphasizing the similarity of experiences by ignoring the differences and the larger social and historical context in which these experiences take place. This overlooks the implications of differential social positions and access to power and privilege. Because oppression breeds on highlighting difference and building barriers based on those differences, by identifying with others, we can break down those divisions. However, this poses the danger of coming to think, "We're all alike."

Consider the situation when a White person tries to empathize with the experience of an African American person in an all-White environment. The White person may recount how she also felt uncomfortable and marginalized as the only White person in an all-Black gathering. On the one hand, it may be helpful to focus on the similarities for her to relate to the experience of the Black person. However, she may ignore the particularities of the Black woman's experience and the differences between their experiences, given the larger context of racism. For example, the White woman can gener-

ally choose whether or not to be in the situation of being a racial minority, and it is an exception to her usual interactions where her
Whiteness is the norm.

While encouraging empathy, we need to be careful not to obscure differences as we emphasize similarities. We must acknowledge and discuss differences in power and social position. In addition, some people feel that by empathizing they are "doing
something." Empathy itself is not action; it is a starting place, not the
end product.

Impediments to Empathy and Empathic Responsiveness

The potential of empathy as a positive social force can be diminished in many ways. There are many factors that reduce people's
ability to be empathic, as well as to act on their empathic responses. I
will identify several of these and offer some brief suggestions for
how to address them.

Lack of Cognitive Ability

First, people need a certain level of cognitive ability to engage in
perspective taking. Although there are different kinds of empathy
displayed by children, the type of empathy discussed here requires
the ability to have a differentiated sense of self and the cognitive
flexibility to imagine the perspective of someone else. Most teenag-
ers and adults have that cognitive ability, though many still have a
difficult time with the cognitive flexibility that is required. People
who are dualistic thinkers (see Chapter 3) tend to see things as either-or and have difficulty considering experiences or perspectives
that differ from what they consider the truth. For these individuals,
it may be helpful to stress that being empathic does not mean condoning someone else's behavior. Because abstract connections may
be more difficult for these individuals, we can provide opportunities for them to concretely put themselves in the position of another
that require them to take on a different way of seeing the world (i.e.,
through a role play).

Lack of Emotional Flexibility

In addition to cognitive flexibility, people need emotional flexibility.

One who cannot tolerate his own feelings, or who is essentially a stranger to himself, is unlikely to forge an affective connection to someone else. A degree of self-knowledge and comfort with one's own affective life facilitates both knowing and being known to others. (Kohn, 1990, p. 152)

Generally, people who have difficulty acknowledging and experiencing their own feelings have difficulty perceiving and understanding the feelings of others. Although there is not conclusive research on gender differences and empathy (varying with how empathy is measured), it tends to be more challenging for males to make empathic connections. Male socialization usually does not foster the development of emotional self-knowledge, expressiveness, or sensitivity to others. As a result, men often have underdeveloped empathic abilities and overdeveloped emotional armor to protect themselves against feelings that might make them vulnerable and uncomfortable. In educational contexts, we can consistently model empathic behavior toward them and others and can provide opportunities for them to develop and practice empathic skills.

Lack of Psychological or Emotional Freedom

Third, people are less likely to feel empathy if their own needs feel more pressing than those of others. It can be hard to be empathic when feeling stressed or in pain. If people are self-absorbed, are anxious, or lack the psychological or emotional freedom to attend to another's needs, their empathic abilities will be decreased. As previously discussed, this can be the case when someone is focused on his or her victimization as a member of a subordinate group. We can provide the safety and opportunity for these people to share their feelings, concerns, or experiences so that they feel heard and validated. Once they feel recognized and no longer need to defend their own pain or disadvantage, they may have more psychological space to connect with another. (Also, review the suggestions in Chapter 4 for reducing resistance.)

Blaming the Victim

People often have little or no empathy for victims they see as accountable and deserving of their fate. Blaming the victim may in fact lead to feelings of indifference or hostility. Through a variety of educational strategies—providing information, role plays, personal stories, researching facts, or critical analysis—people can develop a more informed perspective that may shift their understanding or interpretation of the situation. This in turn can alter the way they see the victim and allow for some empathic connection. People who believe in a "just world," which assumes a close relationship between one's fate and one's merit, are more likely to react with compassion if they are asked to imagine themselves in the same situation as the victim (Rubin & Peplau, 1975).

Empathic Bias

People also tend to have difficulty empathizing with people that seem too different from themselves. There tends to be an *empathic bias*; individuals feel less empathy for those they perceive as different and more empathy for those they perceive as more like themselves. Empathic bias is reinforced by the stereotypes and prejudices people learn. It can be reduced by providing people with opportunities to increase familiarity with individuals or groups they see as different and encouraging a focus on the similarities between themselves and the others—shared characteristics, feelings, and experiences. Ultimately, despite all other differences, we share a common humanity.

Psychological Threat

Finally, although similarity of experience can promote empathy, it can also impede it when the situation is experienced as too psychologically threatening. It may touch on one's own unresolved issues, unconscious conflicts, or disappointments. A heterosexual woman may resist empathizing with an angry lesbian woman because of her inability to acknowledge her own anger about the sexism she herself faces. A man may have difficulty empathizing with a battered woman if he has not dealt with his own feelings about seeing his mother in an abusive relationship. We may be able to help him empathize with women in other situations that do not stir up such feelings but also involve sexism or the domination of women by men. And even though we are not therapists, we can appropriately allow people to express their feelings and help them understand why they are unable to empathize in this situation. We can also recommend referrals for counseling or other assistance.

Limitations of Using Empathy
to Promote Prosocial Activism

Not all empathy leads to prosocial action or activism. Even when people do feel empathy, there are several factors that reduce their motivation to act on this empathic connection. One is *empathic overarousal*. People can be overwhelmed by their own feelings of distress that are generated from being empathic. The level of guilt or anxiety can be immobilizing. Allowing people to process their feelings—through writing, talking, emoting, movement, or art—helps reduce the intensity of the feelings so that they can consider acting more constructively.

A second reason is *feelings of powerlessness*. When people are unable to relieve the suffering, they may rationalize their failure to act by derogating the victim. After an empathic connection with a homeless man, a person who feels powerless to help this man or to deal with homelessness might find ways to blame him for being in his situation (i.e., not trying to find a job, not going into rehabilitation). We can assist people in dealing with their sense of disempowerment by helping them to learn about and develop strategies for positive intervention and action.

Third, we live in an *unsupportive social context*, in a culture where people are encouraged to see victims as deserving their plight. Empathic abilities and the motivations to act are not commonly taught, encouraged, or valued in this society.

> What motivates people to help others is determined more by the social system in which they live than their basic nature. Absence of genuine altruism in the US should not be attributed to a fundamentally egoistic human nature, but to the highly individualistic, competitive and success-oriented nature of our social system. (Sampson, 1991, p. 275)

Even though we cannot simply change the dominant culture, we can continue to help people to develop their empathic abilities, to highlight the benefits of caring for others, and to provide examples of people who do act on their sense of empathy to improve the lives of others.

To use empathy as a motivation for progressive social action, we need to help people emotionally and intellectually relate to other's experiences and to understand that people may be motivated by their own personal needs as well as altruism, and we need to be able to address the various individual and societal impediments to people developing and then acting on their empathic responses. Because the effective use of empathy generally requires that people see the victim's situation as somehow wrong or unfair, moral principles become an important ingredient. It is to these that I next turn.

Moral and Spiritual Values

By invoking moral principles and spiritual values, people can be motivated to live up to and according to one's values and to right what they perceive as a wrong. For people to act on moral or spiritual principles, they need to be aware that there has been, in fact, a violation of their values. Everyone may not agree on how to remedy the moral infraction, but at least if people see that there is an injustice, they can become concerned and invested in addressing it.

First, it can be helpful to encourage people to identify and articulate their moral/spiritual values. This provides a standard from which to judge situations. It can also provide educators with useful information about how to speak to their concerns. Although not everyone has the same interpretation of justice or fairness, most people in the United States tend to support the notions of equal opportunity, meritocracy, and equal rights.

Next, we can educate people about the inequity. People often have little accurate knowledge about social inequities. In addition to providing facts, statistics, personal stories, and theories, individuals can be asked to conduct research themselves and to gain awareness from firsthand experiences. Often, students are more persuaded by information they uncover themselves. If people think that a life on welfare is one of luxury and an easy free ride, we can ask them to research the amount of the allowance, to live on that amount for a couple of weeks, or to try to apply for welfare to see how they are treated.

Once people are aware of an inequity, we can help them see that it is unfair, that it violates their moral/spiritual principles. Unless they perceive the discrepancy as an injustice, they will not feel that a moral wrong has been committed. Because there is pressure to cognitively distort situations in ways that justify the status quo, educators need to be able to challenge those distortions. We need to help people question the dominant ideology that makes inequities seem fair and to offer alternative explanations. People can be encouraged to reexamine their assumptions and beliefs that tend to blame the victim, deny discrimination, and presume a level playing field. We can help elucidate how institutional structures and practices violate stated principles of fairness and equity. Often, when myths are exposed and greater understanding of systemic inequality is revealed, people are more likely to feel that their values have been breached, that something isn't right. In the United States, many people accept the fairness of the free market system and the ideology that people get what they deserve on the basis of ability or hard work. Yet a study by Smith and Tyler (1996) with people who were economically advantaged found that the more respondents viewed market procedures and outcomes for the disadvantaged to be unfair, the more they supported redistributive policies. As in the above example of welfare, if people realize how inadequate most public assistance is in supporting families and in providing the necessary job training, transportation, day care, and employment opportunities for people to get decent-paying jobs with medical benefits, they are more likely to feel that people are being denied the opportunity to live a reasonable life off welfare and that this is detrimental to those individuals and society at large.

Because an ethic of justice tends toward an intellectual or cognitive orientation, providing information and facts is a useful strategy. An ethic of care tends to be more feeling or affectively oriented. In this case, an effective approach is to illustrate the harm of social injustice, thereby promoting empathy. This appeals to values of caring for others and alleviating suffering. The strategies discussed earlier to foster empathy—such as personal stories, relationships, and perspective taking—are useful with people who have a care-based morality.

After people recognize moral injustice, the next step is motivating them to take some action to remedy the situation. For some, the clarity of a moral wrong might be enough to elicit their support. For others, more particular appeals may be needed. We can be more effective at appealing to moral values if we understand the process through which people determine what is just and why they would act morally. Otherwise, we can offer a range of reasons that will appeal to people with different moral orientations and motivations. The developmental sequences within each moral framework can provide a guide for speaking to particular moral frameworks. Also, although individuals tend to be predominantly in one stage, they may use reasoning from other stages, depending on the circumstances.

I have often been asked to do diversity and sexual harassment training in schools with teachers, administrators, and other staff. Frequently, this is initiated by a teacher who sees a problem and wants to garner the support from the administration and fellow teachers. There are usually several ways to appeal to people's moral values. I will tend to include a variety of reasons, both to appeal to the range of concerns and to provide examples of more principled and caring considerations.

Those using moral reasoning from preconventional or survival perspectives may be most concerned with protecting themselves from accusations and legal liability. For them, addressing sexual harassment can reduce their personal or institutional liability as well as negative public exposure that could jeopardize their careers. For those concerned with being able to teach without as many discipline problems and conflicts, the training can reduce negative behavior and tensions among students.

Those at the goodness or conventional level tend to be interested in having policies and laws to ensure that people are treated fairly or are not subject to behavior that interferes with their right to an education. They want to follow and enforce established rules that help maintain order in the school and allow people to be treated respectfully. For those concerned with being good and caring teachers, the training can help them better meet the needs of their students, ensure their safety, and prepare them to deal with differences.

To speak to the concerns of people at the truth or postconventional level, I try to appeal to shared or stated values. These may include wanting every child to be able to reach his or her full potential or wanting to create a caring community in which people are not subjected to hurtful or demeaning behavior. These individuals are seeking ways to create an environment in which everyone can learn and work effectively.

Limitations of Appealing to
Moral Principles and Spiritual Values

Equity theory suggests that recognizing an injustice produces an uncomfortable and distressing emotional state (Tyler et al., 1997). People attempt to restore a sense of justice (a) behaviorally, by changing their behavior or the situation, and (b) psychologically, by changing their interpretation of events (such as assuming that people are lazy, incompetent, or undeserving). The psychological solution allows people to justify their advantage. People who view themselves and others as personally responsible for their success or failure are more likely to assume that societal inequities are legitimate. They accept the just-world hypothesis that people get what they deserve in life and consequently deserve what they get. Therefore, there is no motivation to remedy the situation.

Even when people do recognize an injustice, they will decide whether to act on the basis of two main factors. The first is practical concerns (e.g., the likelihood of success or of retaliation or the amount of self-sacrifice). People may want to see justice occur but may not be willing to incur the consequences of the imagined change. The second is the ambiguity of the situation—how clear it is that an injustice has occurred and what specifically needs to be done to address it. If people are not convinced that there is an unfair inequity or do not believe that what is proposed will remedy it, they are less likely to act.

In addition, there may be some groups of people who are seen as nonentities, undeserving, or expendable, and thus are morally excluded from one's scope of justice (e.g., migrant workers, the Japanese during WWII, gays; Opotow, 1990). This allows people to see the harm to these groups as acceptable, appropriate, or just. Moreover, the less one's sense of self is rooted in a moral identity, the less persuasive moral arguments will be.

Deciding whether to address a moral injustice is more than a simple instrumental decision, a rational assessment of the costs and benefits of a certain course of action. Emotional reactions may be the most important influence on whether or not people take actions. The type of action is more a function of cognitive judgements (Wright, Taylor, & Moghaddam, 1990). Therefore, eliciting emotions such as anger or moral outrage enhances an individual's likelihood of acting. Since people are more likely to act to restore justice when there is a clear injustice and when there is a particular set of actions that could correct the injustice, it is important that they have specific ideas of how to act that they feel will make a difference. Otherwise, they may feel hopeless and powerless and resort to psychological distortion.

Self-Interest

Most change agents know that you need to be able to answer the question, "What's in it for me?" People are concerned with how things will affect them. The previous chapter outlined how people may construe that question differently; yet in some form, people want to have their needs met.

A basic principle of conflict resolution is to identify underlying concerns and interests and to try to develop a solution that meets the needs of both (all) parties. This requires letting go of preconceived solutions and being willing to think creatively to come up with alternatives that would be satisfying to both. Often, conflicts persist because people cannot imagine alternatives to the present situation or do not believe that their needs would be met by the currently proposed solutions. Similarly, with issues of oppression, people often don't support efforts to eliminate oppression because they feel that it doesn't affect them or that nothing can really change, or they cannot imagine how it could be different and not threaten their well-being. Ultimately, we need to help people from dominant groups expand their sense of possibilities to see how their long-term interests and needs really can be met by social justice. (I discuss this in Chapter 10.) In the meantime, we may need to identify their present and short-term interests and find ways to address those while engaging them in actions for equity.

Some appeals to self-interest can be targeted toward a specific issue or action. In this context, self-interest is used as a strategy toward a particular end (at least for the moment). We are interested in getting support for a given program or project. It can also be used in a more educational or theoretical way to help change people's ways of thinking about social justice and to help them understand how oppression is harmful to all. In this case, the goal is twofold: consciousness-raising and changing attitudes and behavior. Strategic and consciousness-raising approaches can be used separately or in conjunction with each other.

Strategic Approaches

First, find out what people are concerned about. Then, *integrate people's concerns into the social justice agenda.* Try to show how those interests can be addressed by supporting your efforts. For some people, these concerns may be very self-focused; for others, they may be more inclusive of other people. The examples along the continuum of self-interest illustrate what might appeal to people with different conceptions of self-interest. The most important thing is to understand their viewpoints and to speak to their needs. From there, we can make the link to issues of equity and show how their needs can be compatible with social justice.

Even while appealing to more individualistic types of self-interest, offer a more interdependent perspective. This is a chance to raise consciousness, provide alternative ways of viewing the situation, and challenge the win-lose mentality. Because we do not want to reinforce individualistic thinking, the goal is to start where people are and help expand their perspective toward consideration of the common good. While providing additional examples of how to use self-interest to garner support for a current issue or project, I will also illustrate how we can expand on narrow self-interest, help people see their personal concerns in a larger context, and link their short-term and long-term interests.

As a university affirmative action officer, I needed to enforce affirmative action guidelines that many people felt were unfair and interfered with their right to hire who they wanted. To get their cooperation, I often pointed out ways in which hiring a person from an underrepresented group benefited them—not only were they more likely to get permission to actually fill the position, but that person might also help attract and retain students in their department, especially students from underrepresented groups (which was important for maintaining or increasing the viability and resources for their department). I also included ideas about how this new person's experience or perspective might enhance their own scholarship and thinking about their discipline and about how diversity makes the campus a more vibrant and attractive place to students and faculty. Finally, I challenged them to think about what it meant to be "most qualified" (especially when diversity is a goal) and provided information about how to more fairly evaluate qualifications. Regardless of the real reason for their compliance, I felt I needed to expose them to broader ways of thinking about and justifying the hiring of a candidate from an underrepresented group.

Another approach is to *link personal concerns to larger issues of equity and justice.* This shifts the dynamic from blaming the victim to blaming the system. Many college students, particularly at public universities, are concerned about paying for college and experience the stress of working and worrying about expenses. I have heard White students complain about the "special treatment" some students of color receive and about some of the scholarships that are set aside just for students of color (though this is quickly changing). This tends to lead some White students to blame students of color for White students' lack of financial support for college. The economic concerns of White students are valid. However, the real problem is not students of color (who also generally receive very little financial backing). Some White students realize this, and instead of working against scholarships for minority students, they have organized to challenge the larger system that does not make college accessible to all who want to attend. They have enlisted the support of other White students by addressing their concerns about college costs, but they have focused on the bigger issue of educational funding and opportunity. Through collective action and lobbying with students of color (and other allies), they have been more successful in addressing access to a college education (e.g., through lower tuitions and more state and other aid). So although their concerns may be about their own college tuitions, their solution has been to address the larger issue of economic and social equity. They feel that their self-interest is better served by more systemic change.

Last, we can *link people's short-term and long-term interests with the social justice agenda*. We can help people see that they will be better off both in the short term and in the long term by supporting efforts toward equity. Most people are concerned with juvenile crime and drug dealing. Some people believe that building more prisons is the answer. Alternatively, in many communities, people are trying to create comprehensive programs for youth that include education, training, and constructive involvement in recreational and community activities. One strategy to enlist support for these efforts is to help people see how these types of programs reduce violence, are far more cost effective, and improve their quality of life. In the short run, young people are less likely to be involved in illegal activity and create problems on the street. In the long term, they are more likely to become productive, contributing citizens as opposed to adult criminals, prison inmates, or welfare recipients who require further government money. It also maintains the integrity of the community and property values. Instead of some quick fixes, people's short-term as well as long-term concerns can be addressed.

Theoretical and Consciousness-Raising Approaches

The strategic use of self-interest clearly provides the opportunity for consciousness-raising. Educational contexts often offer us greater latitude in how we can educate people from privileged groups about their self-interest in social change. We can help them to explore the costs of oppression, the benefits of justice, and ways to move toward the kind of world they would like to live in.

There are many ways that people can be given the chance to *consider the costs of oppression to themselves and others from dominant groups.* I have engaged students in thinking from this perspective by asking them to identify the ways in which they feel negatively affected by some form of oppression in which they are part of the dominant group. This makes most sense once they have already done some exploration of oppression and multicultural issues. After considering this question individually, they then listen to the responses of peers, provoking further reflection and discussion. This may be one of the few times when the pain of people in privileged groups has been acknowledged and validated. For people who have never named or discussed these costs, it can be a powerful experience and provide great relief to let go of the secrets or of the feeling that they were the only ones. When I have conducted this exercise with groups, simply viewing the list of costs generated by the group has had a significant impact. It vividly illustrates the pervasive detrimental ramifications of oppression for members of privileged groups.

For some groups, responding to a general list of costs will be much easier and more effective than trying to develop their own because it requires less original thought. You can ask them which items they can relate to on the list and have them add their own examples. Even for people who have a difficult time identifying costs, it encourages them to think in a different way, it allows them to hear the stories of others, and it begins to broaden the way they think about oppression and their role in it.

People from oppressed groups may have difficulty seeing themselves as members of a privileged group. As discussed previously (Chapters 3 and 4), people tend to most identify with their subordinate identities because that is where they usually experience the most pain. I particularly have found that people of color initially tend to find this type of exercise challenging. They tend to be most aware of their experience as victims of racism and much less able to see themselves as members of a privileged group in another ism. Some of this may be due to their stage of identity development. It may also be related to the fact that the existence and impact of racism is so often minimized that people of color feel they need to consistently remind people (especially White people) of its significance. I have found it helpful to acknowledge the pervasiveness of racism and its widespread effects as well as how it mitigates other areas of privilege. However, because the focus of this exercise is not on privilege but on the costs of oppression to all, I encourage them to think about how they might also be harmed by an oppression for which they are not the direct target. In addition, before I begin the discussion of costs to the dominant groups, I usually review how oppression affects those in disadvantaged groups and review some of the privileges for those in advantaged groups. I then add the parts about negative effects on people from dominant groups, suggesting this as a way to provide a more complete and complex understanding of oppression. Naming oppression and recognizing privilege at the outset allows some people from oppressed groups to then feel more comfortable considering costs to the privileged group.

People may suggest situations in which they see themselves as the victims of reverse racism or of another form of oppression. Affirmative action is often a favorite example of how White people are negatively affected by racism. First, it is helpful to dispel the myths that there is currently a level playing field and that affirmative action has taken away so many jobs from White men. Then it's important to help them reframe this situation and understand it not as a victim of racism but as a result of racism in our society. A system of racial discrimination and bias has motivated the establishment of these kinds of programs and supports. If there were no racism, there would be no need for affirmative action or special consideration given because of race.

Encourage students to imagine what it would be like if there were no racism, sexism, or other forms of oppression and how that would be beneficial to them. Ask them to consider questions such as the following: How would their lives be enhanced if they did not have to deal with the results of systemic injustice? What would it be like if the list of costs were obliterated? What would it feel like to be rid of the limitations, pressures, conflicts, guilt, moral ambivalence, and ignorance? Visualizations, drawing, writing, discussion, and list making can make these imaginings more concrete.

A related approach is to *have people compare their vision of an ideal world with our current reality.* Ask people to imagine and describe the kind of world they want to live in—How would society be organized? What would work, housing, education, the environment, neighborhoods, or recreation look like? Then have them compare that ideal to this reality. They can consider the following questions: How is the vision different from our reality? What gets in the way of attaining that vision? How do oppression and inequality undermine this ideal? How might greater social justice help to reach those ideals? Because most people want to live in a world with peace, positive social relations, and material well-being, this can lead to discussions of various forms of oppression, as well as the larger dominant-subordinate power structure upon which injustice is based. This exercise can also be focused on a particular aspect of society, for example, one's community, school, or workplace. Similar questions and discussion could ensue. These types of discussions can help people think about their investment in social justice and lead them to consider ways to move toward that vision.

Help people to identify and experience more equal and satisfying relations in everyday life. Imagining a total transformation of society can seem too unrealistic or abstract to be useful. Yet, in most of our daily lives, we have the kinds of experiences that would be more available in a just and caring society. Encourage people to notice how they feel when they do have emotionally honest and mutually satisfying relationships with others; when they are behaving in accordance with their values; when they feel that they are acting out of their deeper sense of humanity and love; when they have positive, enriching relationships with people who are different from themselves; and when they feel a sense of personal integrity and moral consistency. Help them verbalize these situations and positively reinforce these kinds of connections and ways of being. We can provide opportunities in the class for these types of relationships and experiences through how we structure the class and the activities we do. These activities can be used to discuss how to create more of these kinds of experiences in our lives, how to change the systems and structures that undermine these ways of being, and how to replace them with ones that foster a more just and caring world.

Pros and Cons of Appealing to Self-Interest

Intentionally appealing to self-interest can be a controversial strategy. It has advantages as well as dangers. Although it can be a useful and necessary approach, we need to be thoughtful and careful in its use. I will first discuss some of its possible pitfalls and then consider some of its positive uses and benefits.

One of the major dangers of using narrow self-interest to motivate support is the distrust it breeds from people (both allies and people from oppressed groups) who are genuinely committed to the action. People appropriately may not trust the motives or the depth and longevity of the support of people who they suspect are acting on individualistic self-interest. If the motivation stays only at the level of narrow, individualistic self-interest, their support may be withdrawn when self-interest is reassessed as circumstances change. By appealing to individualistic self-interest, without trying to broaden the perspective or commitment, we may be reinforcing a way of thinking that is counter to our ultimate goals.

In addition, someone may engage in superficial involvement or low-risk commitment while undermining a more serious examination of the issues or more meaningful change. This often results in mere lip service, or it can trivialize or co-opt the issue. Many people are familiar with the token committee and unread report or with diversity training that never goes beyond understanding cultural differences to address inequities in organizational policies and practices. Sometimes strings are attached; support will be given as long as the work is not too radical or avoids certain topics.

Using self-interest to develop support also has advantages. Appealing to narrow, individualistic self-interest is probably most problematic; however, it starts where people are and addresses them in a way that makes sense to them. "Speaking their language" initially may be more effective than appealing to issues that hold little interest for them. Although we might prefer that people engage in actions from more lofty ideals and commitments, this is not always immediately possible. Obtaining support, even if it is with selfish motives, may allow a positive project to move forward instead of being blocked or impeded.

Joining narrowly self-interested people where they are can also provide an opening for more genuine change, a first step in real engagement. Involvement with an issue may expose people to individuals, situations, or information that they otherwise might not have encountered and that may, in turn, change attitudes and subsequent behavior. A White manager may initiate a program to address the hiring and promotion of people of color primarily because she sees this as a way to get more financial resources for her department. Yet in the process of participating in the task force, she may develop actual relationships with people of color, learn some important information about racism, and encounter people who challenge her stereotypes. This can result in a more genuine commitment to racial equity.

If the ally behavior is inconsistent with currently held beliefs or behavior, it may create cognitive dissonance and the need to rationalize the new behavior. Attitude change may occur to justify the behavior to oneself and others. For example, a heterosexual leader of a fraternity decides to be a representative on a committee to examine the treatment of gays on campus and to play a role in educating about homophobia. Although initially participating to deflect criticism of fraternities, through this experience he might gain some new awareness and justify his involvement by explaining to his friends that this really is something to take seriously.

Furthermore, recognizing one's self-interest, particularly from a mutual or interdependent perspective, can foster a more long-term commitment to social justice. Shifting the focus from only doing it for "them" to also doing it for oneself enhances the investment. It can be hard to maintain a commitment to social change, particularly when some issues are framed as against your immediate best interests. Acting for oneself, not just for others, can help deepen and sustain support for social justice efforts. A recognition of the collective benefit may reduce potential condescension and thus make one more trusted by the oppressed group.

Drawing on Empathy, Moral and Spiritual Values, and Self-Interest

In the previous chapter, I described how empathy, moral and spiritual values, and self-interest could be used in conjunction to strengthen the motivation to act for social justice. Similarly, when we try to implement strategies to foster support for equity, we can intentionally try to integrate these three dimensions. We can consider how we can appeal to these various aspects and have them build on each other.

After a workshop in which I presented this framework, a participant, Tim, developed an action plan that illustrated this integration. Tim was interested in creating interracial dialogues on campus, particularly between White fraternity members and other students of color on campus. There had been some incidents of racial prejudice from some fraternities. He decided to initially appeal to the fraternities' self-interest. He knew that the fraternities were concerned about their image on campus. (Another participant said that on his campus, the self-interest would be to increase membership in their fraternity.) He would initially propose a daylong retreat with representatives from the fraternities to discuss how they could improve their reputation of being racially insensitive. During this retreat, he would also do some consciousness-raising about racism, attempting to help these students become more sensitive to and empathic toward the experiences of students of color. Just as the fraternity members hate to be stereotyped, so do the students of color. By the end of the day, Tim expected to have some fraternity members willing to participate in racial dialogues, both as a mechanism to improve their racist image and as a way to actually better understand the issues for students of color. Through these dialogues, he hoped to foster their sense of empathy and their moral commitment to eliminate behavior that is racially offensive. In general, we strengthen our appeal and effectiveness when we can draw on the various sources that motivate people to support diversity and justice.

From Motivation to Action: Allies and Activism

Although not everyone we work with will become an activist, empathy, moral and spiritual values, and self-interest can help generate concern and the motivation to help. We need to assist people in translating this interest into action. As educators, we can support people in their desire to create more justice in the world.

Throughout the discussion of how to motivate people to support social justice, I have included various reasons why people might do so—from primarily self-serving reasons to altruistic ones.

When I speak of allies, I refer to people who make intentional choices to support or work for the rights of those from disadvantaged groups of which they are not part. They are committed to eliminating some form of oppression from which they benefit. Even though we may need the support of those who do not share these larger goals, allies are people with integrity and genuine concern. They attempt to have their behavior be consistent with their beliefs. Allies act out of their own values, not for the approval of people from the oppressed group. However, to ensure that their efforts are appropriate, allies should have some relationship with and accountability to the people they are seeking to assist.

By focusing on empathy, moral and spiritual values, and self-interest as the factors that tend to motivate people to support social justice or become allies, I do not mean to imply that that is all that is needed for people to be good allies. Despite good intentions and real commitment other qualities are also important. I consider some of these to be the following: (a) self-awareness—of one's personal characteristics and social identity, (b) an understanding of the structural and interpersonal dynamics of oppression, and (c) the ability to choose appropriate strategies given the situation. As part of our overall educational efforts in developing allies, certainly these and other issues need to be addressed.

There are a range of ways in which people can be allies—from more passive support to active leadership. We need to help allies find ways to be involved, support their increasing commitment, and deal with some of the blocks that undermine their best intentions. (See Adams, Bell, & Griffin, 1997; Ayvazian, 1995; Kivel, 1996; and Tatum, 1994, for examples of how people can be allies.)

Blocks to Taking Action

There are several things that tend to act as impediments to people following through with their support. One is that people feel inadequate, overwhelmed, powerless, or hopeless. As they become aware of the depth or pervasiveness of oppression, people may feel that it is useless to try to change things or that there is little they can do. Some people believe that they are not smart enough, educated enough, "together" enough, or somehow just not good enough to take action. Often people have a very limited perspective on the kinds of things they could do to make a difference. They would like to help but don't know what to do, and, therefore, do nothing. For others, guilt becomes immobilizing. They feel too embarrassed or ashamed of their background or privilege to get involved. Additionally, people frequently feel overburdened and busy with their lives as they currently are and resist adding more to their plates.

Many people also feel isolated or alone when these concerns or interests are not shared by their families, peers, or colleagues. This diminishes their courage to act and may impede their willingness to speak out, for fear of being viewed as crazy, silly, or a troublemaker. People face a variety of fears and risks in being an ally. These can include the disruption of relationships, reprisals at work, threats to one's current standard of living, and even violence.

Encouraging Action

One of our important roles is to help people acknowledge and address these concerns. In doing so, we need to respect where people are and what they feel ready to do. Like other endeavors, acting as an ally is a process. It can be useful to make people aware that there are numerous ways people can be allies. Although they may not be ready to take on high-profile leadership roles, they can still be involved with actions requiring less visibility or risk. Allow people to choose the kind of involvement that fits their level of comfort, commitment and risk taking, and their time and interests. In some cases, where and how to act will be clear (e.g., when one's support is being solicited in a particular situation). In other cases, people will need to spend more time thinking about next steps.

Help people deal with their guilt and reframe how they see their privilege. Instead of hiding the fact that they have privilege, people from advantaged groups can acknowledge it and use it responsibly—in the service of social justice. They can use their skills, knowledge, resources, and access to power to foster equity by working for change in arenas where they have influence. They can also share their expertise with people from oppressed groups and support the empowerment and leadership of people who have been marginalized. When people from privileged groups are aware of the dynamics of oppression, they can use their privilege in the spirit of collaboration as opposed to paternalistic helping. (See Crowfoot & Chesler, 1996, for a discussion of the role of White men in multicultural coalitions and the struggle to be appropriate allies.)

Because nothing succeeds like success, it can be helpful for people initially to be involved in efforts in which they can obtain a sense of efficacy and empowerment. In these cases, starting with a small and doable goal may be the best course. Furthermore, because people get overwhelmed thinking about trying to change the world, we can ask them to think about the areas in their lives where they do have an impact, their "spheres of influence" (Adams, Bell, & Griffin, 1997). These may include themselves, their immediate family, and their friends, neighbors and colleagues and move out toward their community and organizational affiliations, political leaders, and national or international groups. They can consider ways they can use their influence in any one of these areas to effect change.

People can also be encouraged to think about actions that target oppression on both the individual-interpersonal and institutional-cultural levels. At the individual-interpersonal level, they may choose to commit to educating themselves more thoroughly about oppression, interrupting offensive comments or jokes, pointing out inequitable group or classroom dynamics, or speaking up at meetings about diversity issues. At the institutional level, they may be involved with changing educational policy, workplace practices, tax laws, or welfare programs; working on media reform, the redistribution of wealth, or company boycotts; or instituting educational programs in their workplace, community, or religious organization. Because most people tend to reduce social change to addressing individual actions and attitudes without a systemic perspective, we need to continually encourage people to hold a larger vision of change. Remind them to consider how their individual actions can be joined with collective action to contribute to more comprehensive social transformation.

A critical element in taking and sustaining action for social justice is support. We all need people we can rely on to help us work effectively, deal with the risks, and keep us going in the face of adversity. Support from others reduces our sense of isolation and feelings of powerlessness. Collective action can also be some of the most effective action. Help connect individuals with shared interests with each other and with groups or organizations in their area. This helps reduce their isolation, provides ideas of how to be involved, and gives people the feeling of being part of a bigger effort. Communities and college campuses often have a variety of groups dealing with issues of social justice.

An historical perspective also provides many benefits. It helps people feel that they are part of a larger process and movement and provides role models and sources of inspiration. We can learn from past experiences, successful (and unsuccessful) strategies, and individuals who had wisdom, courage, and hope. In addition, a historical perspective reminds people that although change is possible, it takes time. It involves forward movement as well as setbacks. If people expect a quick victory, they will generally be disappointed.

Last, people tend to do some kind of cost-benefit analysis to see if it is worth getting involved or supporting a change. As discussed previously, we need to highlight and increase the sense of benefit and self-interest and find ways to decrease the sense of costs. Because people already want to be allies, we can highlight the possibility of increased self-esteem, moral integrity, personal connections, and knowledge, as well as the long-term benefits and their contribution to the greater good. If they are given what feel like viable options, most people would rather feel good about themselves than guilty and ashamed.

Conclusion

In conclusion, there is no one right way to engage people in social change efforts. We need to know our audience and our context. I've suggested a variety of approaches that can help develop people's sense of concern and encourage their support and involvement. Often, multiple tacks are most effective. We can build on the interconnections among empathy, moral and spiritual values, and self-interest to broaden people's perspective and strengthen their commitment. Overall, we can continually reinforce how supporting equity and diversity offers benefits to themselves and others and serves our collective well-being.

Note

1. Even though service learning can be beneficial for both students and communities, there is also the potential for it to undermine the goals it seeks, such as by reinforcing stereotypic beliefs and a colonialist mentality or superiority and by exploiting the community for the benefit of the student. (See Cruz, 1990; Kendall, 1990; Reardon, 1994.)

9

Issues for Educators

Throughout the book, I have reiterated the importance of creating a safe and confirming environment, of offering appropriate challenge, and of embodying respect and acceptance. As I have said numerous times, our own perspectives, attitudes, and behaviors are central to our educational effectiveness. Yet thus far, the primary focus has been on gaining insight into the students or people we work with. Characteristics of privileged groups, various developmental theories, reasons for resistance, motivations for supporting social justice, and how these affect educational strategies or pedagogy have been discussed. I've emphasized how more knowledge and insight about our students allows us to be better educators. However, our students are not the only ones we need to understand. So I now turn the spotlight on us as educators.

In Chapter 3, I referred to the qualities identified by Rogers (1980) as being necessary for growth-promoting relationships—genuineness, unconditional positive regard, and empathy. People need to be able to trust us to take intellectual and emotional risks. Stephen Brookfield (1990) refers to the trust between teachers and students as the "affective glue" (p. 163) that binds educational relationships together. We need to be perceived as authentic—as human beings, in our regard for the students, and in our commitment to equity. Students need to feel that we really do care about them and are their allies in the learning process. They also need to believe that we are genuine in our interest in the issues and in our desire to promote

social justice. In addition, trust is gained when people see us as credible and congruent: when we have sufficient knowledge and experience and when our actions match our words. If we talk about valuing individuals and cultural differences, we had better reflect that in
our practice.

Furthermore, through our own reactions and interactions with
students, we have the opportunity to model the principles of equity,
democracy, and respect that we espouse. Our classrooms are micro-
cosms of the larger systems of social relations and can be laborato-
ries for alternative ways of relating. On the one hand, we can engage
in classroom dynamics that mirror the societal dynamics of domination, competition, and win-lose conflict. We do this when we treat students disrespectfully, overpower their voices, or show off our expertise
at their expense. On the other hand, we can demonstrate how power
can be used in ways that enhances others and how conflict can be a
productive process. Our own behavior is a powerful educational tool.

In a similar vein, Shelley Kessler (1991) describes the "teaching
presence," the qualities in the classroom that allow students to be
vulnerable and discover new things, to be authentic and fully alive.
She identifies three components for generating this teaching presence: being fully present, having an open heart, and maintaining
discipline. When a teacher is fully present, she or he is "alert to the
circumstances of what is happening *right now,* attentive to what is
happening inside him-herself and what is going on in the room"
(p. 13). A teacher with an open heart is willing and able to care and
willing and able to be vulnerable—to feel deeply and to be moved.
Discipline refers to creating the safety needed to allow students to
take risks and be authentic with one another. The teacher ensures that
students follow the class guidelines and are not allowed to hurt each
other. These qualities transcend any particular methods or activities.
Although Kessler writes about her work with young people in a program to foster spiritual development, these ways of being correspond
to the nonjudgmentalness and compassion that I've stressed are needed
when educating people from dominant groups about social justice.

Without a doubt, cultivating this teaching presence is easier said
then done. When educating about diversity and social justice, who
among us has not at some point gotten our buttons pushed or gotten
hooked? How many of us have never disliked a person and found it
hard to work with him or her, become aware of our biases, or felt
very judgmental toward a student? Who has not at some point lost

their ability to think clearly, respond flexibly, really listen, and be understanding?

As we become aware of our own issues and reactions, we can better manage and transform our responses. Self-awareness is essential for any good teacher. There are many things we should know about ourselves to be competent and compassionate educators. Because of the intellectual and emotional complexity of educating about diversity, it is even more critical for social justice educators to be self-reflective. Insight into our own inter- and intrapersonal dynamics allows us to better monitor our behavior and address areas of limitation (see Bell, Washington, Weinstein, & Love, 1997). We then can more successfully create educational experiences that meet our goals.

In this chapter, I'll first examine some common attitudes and behaviors that may diminish our effectiveness in educating people from privileged groups. After considering some of these challenges, I will then suggest some ways to deal with them. Throughout this discussion, my focus will be on how to develop and sustain the patience, flexibility, and openheartedness needed for social justice education. I will explore how to cultivate the qualities that can enable educators to develop trusting relationships and offer constructive challenge.

Social Identity Development

Theories of social identity development are one way to develop insight into our attitudes and behaviors in educational contexts. Our stage of social identity development affects our views of self and our own social group, of others and their social group, and of social oppression. In Chapter 3, I described the process of social identity development for people from privileged groups. These models were presented in the context of understanding the thinking and behavior of students at different stages. Those same theories, applied to us, can help us to understand our own actions and reactions.

I will briefly review each stage of the Hardiman and Jackson model (1997), this time with emphasis on the social identity development of people from targeted groups. I will then explore how our levels of awareness, in both our dominant and subordinate identities, may affect our work with people from privileged groups. Even though I will focus on work with people from advantaged groups, it is essential to consider how our social identities and levels of awareness affect our work with people from oppressed groups, especially when we are part of privileged groups. I hope readers will use this discussion as an impetus to further explore these issues.

We simultaneously go through the process of identity development in each of our dominant and subordinate identities. We also tend to be at different stages of development in our different identities. Moreover, no one is solely in one stage or moves neatly from one stage to the next. We tend to have a predominant stage or worldview, although we will incorporate perspectives from other stages depending on the issue and situation.

I doubt any social justice educator would be in the first stage, *native*, in which people are unaware of structural inequities and of the social significance of our identities. This stage is most typical of young children, and older individuals at this stage would have little interest in engaging in social justice work. In *acceptance*, people (actively/consciously or passively/unconsciously) accept the current social arrangements and dominant ideology, along with its stereotypes and notions of subordinate-group inferiority and dominant-group superiority. People from oppressed groups in acceptance will attempt to ignore, deny, or rationalize the inequities they face. They will also internalize the negative messages about themselves and their social group.

Educators who are primarily in acceptance are not ready to be teaching about social justice. They have not yet developed a critical consciousness about power relationships and institutional oppression or the ability to offer more equitable alternatives. People in active acceptance are firmly committed to our present social relations. People in passive acceptance are less aware of how they perpetuate systems of oppression and maintain the supremacy of the privileged group. "Good liberals" are generally in passive acceptance and might teach about diversity with good intentions. Nevertheless, they will tend to point to individual reasons for inequities and imply that people from the oppressed group should be more like those in the dominant group. Even if this is not the educators' predominant perspective, they may still hold beliefs indicative of this stage. They need to continue to deepen their awareness of this form of oppression and make conscious efforts to check their assumptions about the privileged and oppressed groups. Students in acceptance may feel very comfortable with an instructor who is also at this stage. However, the educator is unable to offer sufficient challenge or contradiction to facilitate the participants' growth and may instead reinforce the status quo. She or he may lose credibility with and frustrate the people who are in resistance or redefinition.

In *resistance,* people become highly attuned to the dynamics of oppression. They are invested in unlearning the misinformation they believed in acceptance and in challenging unjust behaviors and social structures. People in active resistance tend to do this more publicly and vehemently than people in passive resistance. People from dominated groups attempt to purge themselves of the negative images they have internalized about themselves and their group. They generally want to associate with others from their social group and have little interest in or tolerance for people from the privileged group. As people become aware of their oppression and attempt to change it, they often experience strong feelings of pain, anger, and hostility.

At this stage, people often want to help others "see the truth" and to rally support for social change. Thus, they are motivated to be educators. Resistance is probably the most common stage of social identity development of social justice educators and is the most challenging one from which to do this work. Someone from a dominant group who is in resistance may glorify people from the oppressed group and excuse their inappropriate behavior, yet have little compassion for people from their own group. They may feel particularly punitive toward those who are in acceptance and lack an understanding of the oppression or a commitment to address it. They may project their own negative feelings about themselves as a privileged-group member onto others from their group. Because most would prefer to be with people from the oppressed group, they may not want to deal with people from their dominant group, especially if those people are not at a similar stage of consciousness.

These feelings are likely to be even greater for educators from a subordinate group. They tend to be highly invested in having people "get it" and may become overly emotionally involved in class discussions or in student outcomes. Such educators will often be perceived as having their own agenda or a chip on their shoulder. They may find it hard not to stereotype or dehumanize people from the privileged group (i.e., "those White men") or to value any aspects of the dominant group's culture. It is particularly difficult for educators in active resistance to have patience with the educational process and to maintain respect and empathy for people from the privileged group.

People in resistance also may have difficulty educating about other forms of oppression. In this moment in time, their ism feels the most important and compelling. Because they are most focused on this issue and their own experiences, they may not have the depth of understanding of other isms or the same level of commitment to address them. (Even though understanding one form of oppression can help in understanding others, most people in this stage are not yet ready to be making those strong connections. It also depends on their level of awareness in their other social identities.) In general, educators in resistance need to assess whether they are ready to be in an educational role.

This occurred with a colleague of mine in graduate school. Michael was from an upper-middle-class family and recently had become very interested in class issues. He was reading a lot about class exploitation and working people's movements. He was an activist on campus, particularly in efforts to ensure greater accessibility for poor and working class students. He was into "downward mobility" and looked the part. Michael was anxious to teach the weekend workshop on classism. After doing so a couple of times, it become clear to Michael as well as the other trainers that this was not a good match. He had a constant edge of anger in his voice, students found him overbearing, and cotrainers found him too inflexible. At this point in time, Michael needed to be able to immerse himself in the literature about and struggles against class inequality. Being a trainer was not most productive for him or the participants. Being an organizer was more appropriate.

People who are moving out of resistance and into *redefinition* are grappling with redefining their social group identity, independent of the oppressive system. People from privileged groups are trying to develop a positive identity that is not based on superiority. Instead of rejecting and reacting to the dominant culture, people from oppressed groups are seeking and reclaiming aspects of their own culture. The intensity of feelings has usually subsided.

Because educators from privileged groups are developing an affirmative sense of their social identity, they may have fewer negative feelings about others from their group. Educators from oppressed groups are still most interested in being with others from their group with a similar consciousness in order to forge a new social identity. However, they are in a proactive, as opposed to a reactive, mode. As they develop strength in their own social identity and efficacy at dealing with oppression, they tend to be better at managing their own feelings in order to educate others.

In *internalization*, people have internalized this new sense of their social identity. Although they may still feel passionately about social justice, they now have more emotional and psychological space to deal with others. They are less immersed in their own issues and are more able to take a broader perspective. People are able to see themselves as individuals with multiple social identities and make links among different manifestations of oppression. This makes it easier for them to relate to people who are from dominant as well as subordinate groups. They tend to have more tolerance for and understanding of people in privileged groups who are ignorant, resistant, or both.

Ideally, it would be nice if we all could reach internalization in all our social identities before being educators. Needless to say, this is not the case, nor would it be practical. We cannot afford to wait until we have it "all together" to educate others about issues of social justice. However, we can do some honest self-assessment and then make responsible choices about what we do. We can create ways to manage our feelings and behavior. Later in this chapter, I'll suggest some ways to do this.

Other Factors That Affect
Our Educational Effectiveness

Social identity theory is just one way to understand our thinking and reactions. Just as many forces affect students' openness to learning and growth, many things affect our educational responses and abilities. I will now highlight a few other factors that, in addition to or conjunction with our stage of social identity development, affect how we work with people from privileged groups.

Triggers

Most of us can think of words or behaviors that push our buttons—that make our stomachs tighten, our fists clench, our hairs stand up. There may be things that make us freeze and feel paralyzed. Thus, I'm calling these *triggers*. In addition to rolling the eyes and other body language, some common triggers are these: "You're being too sensitive." "Those people . . ." "They all look alike to me." "Why do they have to be so obvious?" "She asked for it." Triggers

can cause us to lose our composure, our clarity, and our ability to respond appropriately. People from privileged groups can trigger educators from both advantaged and disadvantaged groups. (People
from subordinate groups can also push our buttons, though I'll con-
fine my discussion to dominant-group members.)

I remember walking into a room to do a training on oppression
issues after a week of dealing with several incidents of rape and sexual harassment of women on campus. I said to my male cotrainer,
Jim, "If any of these guys say that men are as oppressed as women, I
may strangle him. You have to deal with it." Of course it came up,
and fortunately, Jim could address it. By knowing how I was feeling,
I could avoid acting inappropriately. Even if I had not been fortunate
enough to have a skillful cotrainer, I would have been somewhat
better prepared to respond realizing that I would have to carefully
watch my response.

Usually, the trigger hits upon our own issues. Often there is
something in our own experience that makes these words or actions
so potent. Sometimes it touches on our unresolved issues. This occurred when I was coleading a weekend workshop on classism at a
university. One woman in the group consistently said classist, insensitive things. People in the workshop tried to engage her, but she re-
mained narrow in her perspective. As people became more frustrated with her, she became more entrenched. At a break, a professor
who was observing suggested that one of us (the trainers) talk to her
because she seemed to be boxing herself into a corner. I said I didn't
want to be the one to do that—I didn't like her, and I wasn't feeling
at all empathic. She was an upper-middle-class Jewish woman who
pushed my buttons about materialistic, spoiled Jews, of whom there
were many in the town where I went to high school. I still had my
own issues about my experiences there and about my own identity
as an upper-middle-class Jew. Fortunately, my cotrainer had more
presence and was able to speak with the student, who was in fact
feeling judged and attacked. The student was able to return to the
workshop with more openness and more ability to participate productively. (I used the break to try to deal with my feelings.)

Other times, our reactions may be related to transference. This occurs when we project our feelings about an individual who is close
to us onto another person (in this case, someone from a privileged
group). A certain appearance, tone, comment, or interpersonal style
may set us off because it restimulates our emotional reaction to

someone else. It seems that people frequently have difficulty with individuals that remind them of their parents. Very often, transference occurs unconsciously. We may end up in a strange dynamic with a person, not quite understanding what is going on or why we are feeling so intensely. (Students also engage in transference, which sometimes explains their reactions to us.) A female colleague had an especially hard time with men who were condescending. Although few women appreciate this kind of conduct, it really set her off; that dynamic always seemed to hook her. When we discussed it, she began to realize how this was reminiscent of her relationship with her father and her struggle to be seen as an adult in his eyes.

Another kind of triggering situation occurs when educators from disadvantaged groups are working with groups of people from advantaged groups. In the course of educating about diversity issues, many educators ask people to identify stereotypes or prejudices they have about different social groups. How this is done warrants serious thought because the intent is not to inflict pain but to increase awareness. People from oppressed groups, including trainers, may find it particularly painful to hear negative things said about their social group by dominant group members because this replicates oppressive societal dynamics.

In one situation, I was coleading a daylong workshop on racism and anti-Semitism with a relatively inexperienced trainer, an African American woman whom I'll call Denise. The group was made up of highly motivated and concerned White psychologists from various religious backgrounds. As the day progressed, several participants shared some of their racist prejudices and misconceptions—this was done appropriately, honestly, and with an investment in overcoming these beliefs and attitudes. I (and others) began to notice Denise becoming more and more quiet and withdrawn. When I asked her what was going on, she explained how overwhelmed she felt hearing voiced the negative things such nice, caring professional people felt about people of color.

Another time, I was cotraining with a lesbian, whom I'll call Patty, who was not out to all members of the group. The 2-day workshop was on diversity issues and was with a group of people who were committed to social justice and who were (mostly) heterosexual (from what we knew). On the second day, we were planning to do several role plays to help participants develop skills to interrupt oppressive comments and behaviors. Together, we developed a role play about homophobic name-calling. I would be the one doing the name-calling, a participant would try to intervene, and Patty would process (discuss and debrief) the role play. We enacted the role play, and when it came time for Patty to facilitate the discussion, she sat there silently. I looked at her, waiting for a response, indicating that we were ready to end the role play. When it became clear to me that she was not responding, I began to debrief what we had just done. When we spoke about it afterward, she said she just had frozen when she heard the homophobic remarks.

I do not think that anyone really becomes impervious to hearing negative things about one's group, especially when they are from a dominant group toward a target group. Perhaps we become more used to it, develop ways to cope with it, and find ways not to absorb it. It can be easier to deal with when it is clearly done in the context of raising consciousness—bringing things to light for examination, instead of keeping them hidden and allowing them to grow and fester. Many people say that people from disadvantaged groups have heard all these words before and know that people have these thoughts. However, there is something very powerful about hearing them all at once, especially from the mouths of nice, caring people. The educator is even more vulnerable when she or he is one of the few people (if not the only person) from that targeted group present. Becoming immobilized may be related to inexperience or one's stage of social identity as well as to what else is going on in one's life at that time. Although we can't always anticipate our reactions, we can try to think through the impact of our activities on both our participants and ourselves.

Becoming the Advocate or Missionary

Another common pitfall in educating for social justice is falling into the role of missionary. This is when we try to convert people to our point of view or argue with them in an attempt to get them to "see the light." When we feel strongly about an issue, it can be quite easy to slip into this role. When we start trying to convince people, we take on the role of advocate and lose our ability to be an educator who assists people in their own learning processes.

I think this reflects one of the central challenges for social justice educators. Generally, people do this work because they care deeply and have a personal stake in the issues. This energy can be crucial to creating exciting educational experiences and to persevering through all the difficulties and risks. Yet there is a difference between passion and overzealousness, commitment and dogmatism, and integrity and self-righteousness. I couldn't teach without passion, but it needs to be tempered with respect and openness. Otherwise, when we act in ways that overpower or negate the views and feelings of others, we jeopardize our credibility as educators and our relationships with individuals. If people feel that something is being forced upon them, they are likely to resist or withdraw. This is counterproductive to our intentions.

Stereotypes and Biases

Just like everyone else, we educators have our own prejudices and assumptions about individuals from different social groups, including privileged groups. Appropriately, many educators are sensitive to and concerned about stereotypes about people from marginalized groups. However, they are often less aware of or take less seriously stereotypes about people from privileged groups. Like biases about people from oppressed groups, prejudices about people from dominant groups can grow out of messages from our environment (e.g., family, peers, or media) and our own experiences. The same principles regarding stereotypes about oppressed groups hold true for stereotypes about privileged groups—even when there may be a kernel of truth, it is exaggerated and applied to all members of that group, regardless of their individual qualities. Moreover, one or more experiences with individuals from a particular group does not give us license to then assume that those qualities fit all members of that group. Our stage of social identity development (especially resistance) may heighten our tendency to hold negative views about individuals from privileged groups. Even though knowledge about particular cultural groups and social positions (see Chapter 2 on privileged groups) can be useful, we lose our ability to really see an individual if we make blanket generalizations. Furthermore, when we objectify or dehumanize people from an advantaged group, we are doing just what we are asking them not to do with people from a disadvantaged group: We are distorting and diminishing their sense of humanity. We are perpetuating the very notion of "us and them" that we are attempting to overcome by social justice work. When our hearts and minds are clouded by biases, our ability to be open and fair is impeded. Our capacity to be empathic and accepting is diminished.

Increasing Our Educational Effectiveness

Educating about diversity brings together our own issues with our students' issues. This interplay is embedded in the context of the larger social dynamics. This highly charged mix creates opportunities for great stimulation and learning as well as frustration and challenge. To navigate and grow from this work, we need to engage in praxis—action and reflection (Freire, 1970). As we engage in teaching and reflect on our practice, we will encounter difficulties and disappointments. Instead of seeing these situations as negatives, we can try to view them as gifts. They provide an opportunity for growth. We can ask, "What can I learn from this? How can this make me a better educator? How can this experience help me develop as a person?" And even when it's hard to view the situation in such a way, we can always consider it an AFGO (Another F__ing Growth Opportunity).[1]

Ongoing Personal Work—Content and Consciousness

Being an effective social justice educator and having the qualities required for "the teaching presence" requires ongoing personal work. Educators need a commitment to personal and professional growth. We need to continually raise our consciousness, work through our issues, and stay current on the topics. There are numerous things we can do to improve our ability to be present, open, and informed.

We become more comfortable and flexible as we increase our knowledge of the content we teach and enhance our skills in managing the process. The better informed we are about our subject or subjects, the more easily we can respond to stereotypes, provide accurate information, and challenge misconceptions. The more skilled we are at dealing with conflict, working with emotions, and handling group dynamics, the more we can enjoy the process rather than dread it. These skills allow us to foster the conditions for safety and the development of trust. We also become better able to structure sessions to enhance the potential for learning and decrease the likelihood of resistance. When we feel competent and well-informed, we can be less self-conscious, anxious, or defensive. Information and skills can provide us with a confidence that allows us to be more relaxed and more present. We are less likely to be in situations where we think, "I didn't know what to do!"

As important as it is to be knowledgeable about the content and able to manage the process, it is just as important to be aware of and able to manage ourselves. Some honest self-evaluation is a key starting point. We need to determine whether we are ready to educate about certain issues, and if so, how, with whom, and in what context. As suggested above, models of social identity development provide one tool for this type of self-reflection. We need to understand the impact our identities and stages of development have on our self-awareness and our work with others. If we haven't done our own work around an ism, we won't be ready to educate others. If we are going to be working with people on an emotional as well as a cognitive level, we need to have had the opportunity to do this ourselves. As I've stated throughout, consciousness-raising is not just an intellectual endeavor. In addition to having the content knowledge and the process skills, we need to have explored our own baggage. Part of this exploration of readiness includes assessing our strengths and limitations. As much as possible, we need to try to anticipate our reactions and the situations that might be challenging for us.

Once we have determined what we're ready to do and how we might behave, we can create structures to support us. If we are unsure of our emotional or intellectual readiness to educate about a topic, we can try to work with a cotrainer or coteacher for the whole session or for parts of it. We can bring in guest presenters who can more skillfully address and facilitate discussion on an issue. It is very helpful to have people with whom we can debrief and share support and advice. Many people find it useful to keep a journal to record and process their thoughts and reactions.

Another aspect of our personal work is being conscious of and able to deal with our biases. We need to monitor the thoughts in our heads, check the assumptions that we make, and reflect on our behavior to ensure that we are being nonjudgmental, caring, and fair. When we notice our prejudices infiltrating, we need to take responsibility to address them. This might mean gathering more information to enhance our understanding, seeking more contact with people from this group, speaking with the student to get to know her or him as an individual, exploring why we hold such views, or just being extra vigilant in our interactions. Certainly, the more we can rid ourselves of our stereotypes and biases, the less energy we need to spend worrying about them, and the freer we can be. We can remain self-aware without being self-conscious.

We also need to examine our areas of resistance or defensiveness. One way to become aware of these is to notice which feedback we automatically reject or rebut. If a male student claims that we were being unfair to men, do we automatically dismiss it as male privilege speaking, or do we take time to see whether there is some truth in what he is saying? If a student claims that we are portraying people of color as victims, do we justify our curriculum by claiming we're just trying to illustrate the depth of racism, or do we take a second look at our syllabus to see if it is imbalanced? If a heterosexual person accuses us of promoting homosexuality, do we just discount the remark as homophobia, or do we think about how we're presenting different sexual orientations? If a colleague comments on the fact that the authors of the books we use in our classes are not diverse or appropriately representative, do we immediately claim that we can't cover books by everyone, or do we ask for recommendations? We do not need to accept what people say as the unadulterated truth, but we can use their feedback as an opportunity for reflection.

We can also notice the events, discussions, or workshops that we make time to attend and those that we never seem to fit in. We can consider how these choices reflect what we consider more or less important or issues we want to avoid. If we pride ourselves on being more sensitive and socially conscious than others or on being committed to equity and fairness, we can find it more difficult to acknowledge the ways in which we do not live up to these ideals. Yet to truly achieve these goals, we need to explore the places where we fall short.

In general, we need to know our triggers. Although there is always the chance that we can be surprised, we can pay serious attention to the people or situations that push our buttons. We can explore when we feel most vulnerable and what gets us most angry. We can reflect on why we have certain reactions to certain people. As we become more conscious of our triggers, we can find ways to manage and eliminate them; we can look to address their source. This may mean working on healing some of our own pain and wounds or overcoming conditioned responses.

One way to do this is through self-talk. Before a class or in the moment when a triggering event occurs, we can silently talk to ourselves to get through the situation. We might think things like, "Remember, they're speaking out of pain or ignorance," "I can handle this calmly and rationally," "Just keep breathing," "He's just trying to get my goat, and I'm not going to fall for it," or "She's just showing off for her friends, but she's probably scared underneath." If we know in advance the kinds of things that tend to push our buttons, we can develop and practice in advance what we could say to ourselves to keep us centered.

Another strategy that more broadly helps us to be present and to deal with our triggers and prejudices is to practice mindfulness. Mindfulness is the "art of conscious living." It means "paying attention in a particular way: on purpose, in the present moment, nonjudgmentally. This kind of attention nurtures greater awareness, clarity and acceptance of present-moment reality" (Kabat-Zinn, 1994, p. 4). Mindfulness is being awake and aware and able to "look deeply." In situations in which we feel we are not being conscious or are immersed in negative reactions, it can help us return to a more centered way of being and deepen our understanding of what is really going on. By developing mindfulness, we are less likely to be caught in conditioned responses and unproductive thoughts. During the times we do get stuck, it provides a way out. When we are able to be present and conscious in the moment, it expands our understanding and choices; it puts us in touch with our wisdom and creativity. Mindfulness helps us to develop awareness, calm, and joy in our lives and, by extension, in our educating. We can move away from dualistic thinking and better appreciate our interconnection. Kabat-Zinn suggests a way to check to see whether we are really awake—look at other people and ask yourself if you are really seeing them or just your thoughts about them.

Essentially, mindfulness practice is conscious breathing. You tune into and follow your breath. A helpful way to stay focused on your breathing is to say "In" as you breathe in and say "Out" as you breathe out. You do this silently without trying to control your breath. Mindfulness meditation is a way to systematically cultivate present-moment awareness and to connect your body and mind. Mindfulness meditation (as well as other forms of meditation) can be a "path for developing oneself, for refining one's perceptions, one's view, one's consciousness" (Kabat-Zinn, p. 264). In many ways, mindfulness is similar to other meditative practices. For these purposes, I will not go into a comparison or explain in depth the philosophy and practice of mindfulness. There are currently many helpful and accessible books about mindfulness meditation available. (See, for example, Braza, 1997; Goldstein & Kornfield, 1987; Hanh, 1991; Kabat-Zinn, 1994.) Although mindfulness grows out of Buddhism, it is not a religious practice and can be done alone or along with other spiritual traditions.

Developing and Maintaining Respect and Compassion

Engaging in the process of self-development and reflection tends to expand our capacity for being open-hearted and non-judgmental. Nevertheless, developing and maintaining respect and compassion for people from privileged groups can still be highly challenging. When people act resistant, treat others (or us) in hurtful ways, express offensive views, or presume entitlement, it generally strains our ability to be empathic. Dealing with deep levels of ignorance or defensiveness can be frustrating. However, if we seek to create "the teaching presence" and relationships that support growth and change, we need to be able to sustain feelings of respect and compassion.

Writing from a Buddhist perspective, Sharon Salzberg (1995) defines compassion as,

> The strength that arises out of seeing the true nature of suffering in the world. Compassion allows us to bear witness to that suffering, whether it is in ourselves or others, without fear; it allows us to name injustice without hesitation, and to act strongly, with all the skill at our disposal. To develop this mind state of compassion . . . is to learn to live with sympathy for all living beings, without exception. (p. 103)

Her description contains several important components that I will address in more detail. First, compassion encourages us to have sympathy. Her use of sympathy is akin to my use of empathy in that it requires us to be able to sense what another's experience is like. It enhances our sense of interconnection. One thing that blocks these feelings is our inability to see the full humanity or human dignity within each person. As I noted earlier, when we objectify or demonize individuals, we undermine our ability to be empathic and accepting. "Process can be destructive when we lose sight of the person's potential for learning, growth and change" (Romney, Tatum, & Jones, 1992, p. 98). When we deepen our understanding, we deepen our capacity to really see others and, thus, to care about them. There are several ways we can try to gain or recapture this sense of human connection.

We can draw upon our own experiences of being a member of a privileged group to understand the feelings and behaviors of others from dominant groups. Whenever I feel angry or frustrated with men who are unable to see their privilege, are oblivious to common acts of sexism, behave in condescending ways, or belittle the concerns of women, I think of all the times I've heard people of color accuse White people of these same things. When I see men being defensive, feeling self-conscious about how to act and what to say, or tired of being made aware of all the things they do as men that perpetuate male dominance, I can see my own struggles in unlearning racism. It is humbling for me to think about how difficult it has been for me to look at parts of myself that I wish did not exist (and some that I still avoid), how painful it has been to acknowledge the ways in which I and other White people have systematically oppressed others, and how hard it is to try to rid myself of ingrained and sometimes unconscious attitudes, beliefs, and behaviors. Yet it is by drawing on these similar feelings that I can develop more compassion for others in privileged groups. As described in Chapter 2, there are common social forces that produce some shared characteristics of dominant groups. I realize that my consciousness and responses are not so different from theirs. I can appreciate the difficulty and effort involved in grappling with issues of oppression as someone from a privileged group.

When I am having difficulty feeling patient and compassionate, I've started to do a version of a Buddhist meditation, Metta, which is used to help cultivate compassion for oneself and others. (This is described in detail in Salzberg, 1995). I will repeat to myself, "May I be happy, may I be healthy, may I be safe, may I be at ease." Depending on the time I have, I will do this several times. I will then think of someone that I like and repeat the phrases directed at her or him, "May you be happy, may you be healthy, may you be safe, may you be at ease." I'll continue doing this as I think about someone I have neutral feelings for and, finally, about someone whom I'm having difficulty liking or accepting. I've been amazed at how this meditation has allowed me to be more calm and open. I will also do it silently, while looking around at the students, as I sit waiting for a session to begin. I tried it one day with a class that was experiencing a lot of tension and conflict. I felt that they were getting into rigid positions and conceptions of each other, and I wanted to do something before we engaged in further hard conversation. At the beginning of class, I invited the students to close their eyes and go through this process with me: thinking first about themselves, then someone in the class they had a good relationship with, then someone they felt neutral about, and then someone they were having difficulty with. Although it didn't completely change the class dynamics, it did seem to soften some of the animosity, and it certainly allowed me to be more present.

Another strategy to develop a sense of connection is to try to look for something good in the person. As trite as this may sound, it is not uncommon for educators to get fixated on the ways in which an individual is unpleasant or difficult and to lose sight of all else. As long as we perceive the individual only in these terms, we are unable to see the complete person and will be unable to feel openly toward her or him. Intentionally look for admirable characteristics and behaviors. I have yet to be unable to identify some redeeming quality. This can provide an opening to expand our view of the person, develop some positive feelings, and begin to see him or her more fully as a human being.

Another related approach is to separate the humanness of the person from their actions. Regardless of what people do or who they are, we need to remember that they are human beings with innate human dignity. It can be helpful to remember that they are someone's son or daughter or to imagine them as young children, before they became so damaged. Nonviolent activists have this perspective at the core of their philosophy and practice.

As Martin Luther King, Jr. (1981), advised,

When we look beneath the surface . . . we see within our enemy-neighbor a measure of goodness and know that the viciousness and evilness of his acts are not quite representative of all that he is. We see him in a new light. We recognize that his hate grows out of fear, pride, ignorance, prejudice and misunderstanding, but in spite of this, we know God's image is effably etched in his being. Then we love our enemies by realizing that they are not totally bad. (p. 51)

A second component of Salzberg's definition states that to be compassionate means to recognize the pain and suffering in ourselves and others and to bear witness to it. As Henry Wadsworth Longfellow said, "If we could read the secret history of our enemies we should find in each man's life sorrow and suffering enough to disarm all hostility" (as quoted in Salzberg, 1995, p. 125). If we can truly acknowledge someone's suffering, it can profoundly shift our perspective and feelings. We can see them as wounded individuals, not just as destructive or "evil" people. Often the pain is not apparent, especially when people have material comforts or positions of social power. As I discussed earlier in the context of resistance, people who have not dealt with their own pain are the ones most likely to be resistant to acknowledging or addressing someone else's suffering; they are more likely to mistreat others. In social justice education, we often need to help people heal from their pain, especially that caused by systems of domination. This requires that we ourselves are able to be an "enlightened witness" in their process. Bearing witness means accepting people where they are and being with them as they struggle through unlearning and relearning. We may need to work through some of our own issues to have the emotional capacity and understanding to do this.

Last, as Salzberg states in her definition, compassion enables us to take action and change the things that cause suffering and injustice. This is a critical point because being compassionate is often misinterpreted as being passive and inactive. We can accept individuals as people with human dignity and acknowledge their suffering while working to change their behaviors and the conditions that create suffering. King reminds us that we can oppose the unjust system while at the same time loving the perpetrator of that system. Compassion does not mean condoning harmful action, denying injustice, accepting abuse, or allowing inequity. Salzberg asserts that to develop compassion, it is important to consider the human condition on every level—personal, social, and political—and then to try to change the conditions that create the social problems and cause suffering (p. 114). When we act with compassion, we are able to act with clarity, centeredness, and love, rather than out of anger, fear, and pain. We can make better choices and implement them more effectively. Martin Luther King, Jr. proposed that "Love is the only force capable of transforming an enemy into a friend" (1981, p. 54). He was referring not to sentimental, affectionate love but to "understanding, redemptive, creative good will for all men" (p. 52).

Terms like *evil* and *enemy* might seem harsh or extreme when thinking about students and workshop participants or even about others we encounter in our social change efforts. And although I hope that we don't see the people we work with in this way, I have heard (and have said) things that reflect this type of thinking and feeling. When we are derisive, dismissive, insulting, or disdainful about individuals because of what they have done, their social identity, or their social position, I think we begin to take on this negative view. And although the term *love* may seem a bit overblown, it is this spirit that I think is crucial to our work. It encompasses the respect, nonjudgmentalness, presence, and empathy deemed central to creating relationships that foster change.

I believe this orientation toward others is beneficial in all aspects of our lives. Especially when we are in an educational role, it is incumbent upon us to act in a responsible manner. In the rest of our lives, we may choose not to associate with certain individuals, avoid engaging in certain types of conversations, or treat people less thoughtfully. (Sometimes I feel like I just want to be "off duty.") Yet when I'm in an educational capacity, I am accountable to all the students or participants. I need to do my best to do whatever I can to help facilitate each person's learning and growth. Although I cannot make some people think critically or change, neither can I just ignore them or write them off.

In a discussion about diversity training, a former student and colleague exclaimed, "How can anyone do this work without a sense of spirituality?" I know that many people do so, drawing on other moral or philosophical frameworks. However, various spiritual traditions provide philosophies and practices that aid us in cultivating love, compassion, and mindfulness as we work for social justice. (See Ingram, 1990, as one of many examples.) In this chapter, I have described what I personally have found most helpful. I encourage readers to draw upon whatever frameworks and practices are most meaningful and useful to them. We need all the strength, wisdom, and inspiration we can get.

Note

1. I learned this expression several years ago and have found it very helpful, as have the people I've shared it with. So, at the risk of offending some readers, I wanted to share it here.

10

Hope and Possibilities

Our obedience to the demands of justice can bring us the possibility of a far deeper happiness, security and sense of integrity than can any commitment to individual wealth or personal comfort.

—David Hilfiker

It is easy to look around and feel some despair at the state of the world. We can see the pervasive problems and formidable forces that impede our goal of creating a just and caring world. Yet we probably also know that this is not the full reality. If we are to do social justice education, I assume that each of us has our own experiences, theories, and beliefs that allow us to maintain our faith that things can be different.

A sense of hope and possibility is critical for both educators and students. As an educator, I find that I often need to hold out to others the possibility that change does and can occur, that there are more healthy and productive ways to structure our social, political, and economic systems. Social justice educators also need to sustain the belief that people can change and that people from privileged groups can accept and actively support efforts toward greater equity.

It is important that people learning about diversity and oppression realize how our sense of reality is socially constructed and can be transformed. If people accept the dominant worldview and our current system as the way things are, have been, and will always be, there is little reason to imagine or work for significant change. If they assume that efforts to promote equity will diminish their lives, they will resist altering the status quo. We need to help individuals develop positive alternative visions and a sense of hopefulness that they can be achieved. In this chapter, I will consider how our students and we can retain a sense of optimism in creating a different future. I'll suggest some models and signs to nurture our sense of hope and possibility. Throughout this discussion, I will return to some of the themes I have raised earlier in the book.

Shifting the Paradigm

As I discussed in Chapters 2 and 4, the dominant ideology and supporting social structures shape our attitudes, opinions, behaviors, and openness to change. The dominant paradigm is the thoughts, perceptions, values, and beliefs that form a particular vision of reality. It influences what people assume to be true about themselves, others, and social relations. People tend to see reality the way the dominant paradigm portrays it. In turn, ideology becomes the perceived reality. What people assume to be normal and natural affects what they can envision or believe can be achieved. As long as people accept systems of domination as inevitable and assume that it is human nature to want to control others, there is little hope for creating a just society. As long as people are conditioned to accept that personal value is gained by a sense of superiority, they will be reluctant to stop striving to be better than others or to transform unjust social structures. We need to help people understand how our social structures and ideology shape our sense of reality. And just as important, we need to provide alternatives to our present system.

Although there are many ways to describe our current reality and alternative ways of organizing society, I'll focus on two frameworks described by Riane Eisler (Eisler, 1987, 1996; Eisler & Loye, 1990/1998). By identifying underlying social patterns, Eisler has depicted two different types of social organization. She describes a dominator model and a partnership model that make very different assumptions about human beings, social relationships, and social structures. Her descriptions of these models are based on extensive cross-cultural and historical evidence from anthropology, archaeology, religion, history, art, and the social sciences. I find these constructs helpful in educational contexts for several reasons. First, they are based on actual human societies, not imagined realities. Second, they present models of social organization in a fairly neutral and accessible way. Third, they help people look at the connections between social structures and underlying cultural and personal patterns. Rather than just describing particular elements of more egalitarian societies or human relationships, they illustrate a comprehensive social system with interrelated aspects.

According to Eisler (1987), the main characteristics of a dominator model include the following:

- Ranking and inequality, in which differences are systematically converted into superior and inferior (beginning with men and women)
- Hierarchical and authoritarian social structures
- Institutionalized social violence
- Widespread infliction of or threat of pain

Because the dominator model relies on fear and force to maintain the system, trust is systematically undermined. Power is often used to dominate and destroy—people as well as nature. A sense of scarcity is created to justify exploitive economic policies and a politics of fear. Planning is for the short term, with little thought for future generations.

Our current social organization, with its various forms of oppression, resembles the dominator model in many ways. This is reflected in our high rates of incarceration (especially of the poor and of men of color), the grossly unequal distribution of wealth, widespread incidents of rape and domestic violence, the exploitation of human and natural resources, the competitive individualism within our institutions, and the threat of job loss or physical harm if one is too much of a threat to the status quo.

In contrast, the partnership model highlights the following:

- Linking, in which differences (beginning with males and females) are valued and respected

- A low degree of social violence where violence is not a structural component of the system
- Generally egalitarian social structures
- Interactions based on mutual respect and empowerment

In the partnership system, human relations are held together more by trust and pleasure than by fear and pain. Equality is actively nourished. Power is generally used to give, nurture, and illuminate life. A sense of abundance is created, with a value placed on ensuring that people are taken care of. Planning includes long-term concern for present and future generations.

Eisler cautions that these models are not mutually exclusive. She maintains that history is shaped by the tensions between these alternative systems. Both models operate within a given society, within a given institution, and within a given individual. Yet societies tend to orient more toward one than the other. Some differences between the models are due to differences in emphasis or degree. For example, although there may be cooperation in both models, in the dominator model, cooperation is generally based on fear and aggression toward an out-group (consider war, team sports, business). In the partnership model, cooperation is based on trust and reciprocity with the other group or other individuals (consider cooperative learning).

Moreover, hierarchies exist in both models, but they are conceptualized very differently. In a dominator mode, hierarchies are based on power over others and are used for the purpose of domination. These types of hierarchies separate people, suppress empathy, and stifle creativity. In contrast, in a partnership mode, there are hierarchies of actualization. These help bring forth our human potentials. They support our growth and development (such as in the cases of parents with children or mentors with mentees).

A partnership pattern of social relations is not a utopian model. According to Eisler, it is unrealistic to assume that there would be no violence, pain, or cruelty in such a model because these seem to be part of the human condition (Eisler & Koegel, 1996). However, in partnership societies, these modes of relating are neither idealized nor institutionalized. Domination, fear, and force are not needed to maintain rigid and coercive systems of ranking. In a dominator system, there tends to be a high degree of conflict, with a win-lose orientation. Conflict is violently suppressed when it threatens the dominant group and is encouraged when it benefits the status quo (such as within and between oppressed groups). In contrast, a partnership system openly recognizes conflict, sees it as potentially creative, and tries to make it nonviolent. A win-win orientation is promoted.

Extending the work of Eisler, Koegel (1997) suggests that these paradigms of social relations lead to different ways of thinking and acting. The dominator model encourages people to assume that people are inherently selfish, insatiable, and violent; that social life is a zero-sum, win-lose conflict; that relational inequality is inevitable; and that structural inequality is desirable. On the other hand, partnership patterns lead people to assume that people are or can be caring, benevolent, and respectful; that social structures can foster institutional dynamics that are more win-win; that relational equality is possible; and that increasing structural equality is beneficial (p. 49). Unless the dominator paradigm is challenged, there is a mutually reinforcing cycle. People will continue to reproduce the ways of thinking and acting that allow systems of domination to exist.

Certainly, the concepts presented in the dominator and partnership models are not new. In the past few decades, psychologists and social scientists have been illuminating aspects of a partnership model in interpersonal relationships and institutional structures. Feminists, in particular, have been critiquing patriarchal systems, redefining power, and creating alternative personal and organizational dynamics (see Miller, 1976, 1991; Starhawk, 1982, 1987). Western, patriarchal societies have predominantly conceptualized power as *power over*, as relationships of domination that involve force, exploitation, coercion, and manipulation. Consistent with a dominator model, power is seen as the ability to get one's own needs met by being able to control others. An alternative conception of power is *power with*. In this view, power is seen as "being able" or having the "capacity to produce a change" (Miller, 1991, p. 198). In power-with relationships, "all participants in the relationship interact in ways that build connection and enhance everyone's personal power" (Surrey, 1991, p. 165). The work of the Stone Center at Wellesley College has focused on developing theories that validate and explicate these types of relationships (Jordan et al., 1991; Jordan, 1997). They talk about "mutual empowerment" and "agency-in-community." Power with emphasizes interdependence and developing the capacity to act and do together. In synergistic communities where power with flourishes, "self and community work toward the common good while seeking to fulfill their own perceived needs" (Katz, 1986, p. 22, as cited in Kreisberg, 1992).[1] Other social scientists and activists have been advancing in theory and practice more egalitarian, collaborative, and democratic organizations and policies—worker-owned and cooperatively structured workplaces, economic policies that don't value profits over people, and political processes that are truly participatory.[2]

I have asked students to identify how they have experienced partnership and dominator types of relations in their own lives—in personal and institutional contexts. People have little difficulty describing examples of dominator relations, whether with a controlling parent, an authoritarian teacher, an arrogant and dismissive doctor, a possessive and abusive lover, or a boss who expected obedience and conformity. They easily remember experiences with social service agencies, the police, judicial systems, and government bureaucracies in which they were threatened, intimidated, and denied a voice. Identifying partnership patterns is more challenging for some, especially in organizational settings. Most people can identify interpersonal relationships with family and friends that were supportive and mutually fulfilling. Some people can think of work situations in which they were treated respectfully, involved in decision making, and encouraged to contribute. Others describe classroom environments that fostered equitable participation, an appreciation of differences, creativity, and support for each other's learning. People also discuss religious/spiritual groups where there is a loving and supportive atmosphere and shared efforts to attend to individual and community needs.

It is important to provide real illustrations of partnership patterns. Doing so allows people to imagine and experience different ways of thinking, feeling, and relating. Specific examples help make the concepts of partnership come alive. People can better understand the difference between ranking and linking by having the opportunity to work effectively on a group project in which various abilities and talents are valued and people are not being pitted against each other for recognition and personal gain. By learning nonviolent conflict resolution skills, people can appreciate how conflict can be an opportunity for learning and growth; that it is not necessarily a destructive process.

However, the partnership model is more than just the sum of its parts; these elements are not isolated events. In a partnership paradigm, they are part of a larger integrated system that has very different underlying values and assumptions. They are aspects of an interlocking pattern that fosters a different way of organizing social relations on a societal level. As many of us know, it is often difficult to create and sustain partnership structures and patterns of interaction when they are embedded in a social context that operates according to dominator norms and values. In fact, the larger system can be hostile to such efforts and usually is. Both the ideology and social structures need to change in order to advance real social justice. In sum, it is not possible to create true equity and systemic partnership relations within a dominator paradigm.

Clearly, the dominator and partnership models have implications for how social, political, and economic relations are organized. It is not my intent to prescribe how these should be structured. I offer these models as tools to expand people's frame of reference, as suggestions about new ways to conceptualize reality, and as challenges to the assumption that human nature or innate differences alone are responsible for inequities. These frameworks can help individuals see how patterns of social organization foster oppression and social injustice. The dominant ideology and social structures encourage personal and material gain at the expense of others (and the environment), assume that there is not enough for everyone, and institutionalize force and fear (explicit or implicit) to maintain compliance.

These paradigms also help people to evaluate current systems and envision alternatives. *Partnership literacy* is the ability to use the dominator and partnership models to analyze individual, interpersonal, institutional, and cultural dynamics. It allows us to examine the ways in which we have become conditioned to accept patterns of domination and subordination and how these dominator patterns operate in our own lives. Partnership literacy also enables us to develop ways to foster partnership patterns of relating and transform systems of domination. It can help us move from a dominator to a partnership way of life. Educators can help promote partnership literacy.

To have greater social justice, we need to shift the current paradigm. We need to provide visions and alternatives that change people's ways of thinking, acting, and behaving. As long as we operate within our current paradigm, people from either the dominant group or the subordinate group will seek dominance and superiority. Regardless of which group or individual is in power, the same oppressive, unequal, and unfair dynamics will be in place. In this sense, the aim is not to change roles or change who has power but to change the very nature of the system.

The Appeal of Partnership Relations and Social Justice to People from Privileged Groups

Although more equitable, partnership-oriented dynamics may sound appealing, is it likely that people from privileged groups will trade in their power over for power with? It is clearly naive to assume that any fundamental progressive social change is simple, quick, or easy. I can just as easily argue that the glass is half empty (that significant social change is unlikely) as that it is half full (that there are hopeful signs of social transformation). What I'll offer here are ways in which social justice does and can attract people from dominant groups. In Chapters 7 and 8, I described specific ways to motivate people from privileged groups to support social justice efforts. In this chapter, I approach the issue less strategically and more philosophically. I'll explore the broader appeal of equity to advantaged groups and some reasons why they would embrace it.

In Chapter 6, we saw that one of the general costs of oppression to people from privileged groups was the loss of humanity and authenticity. Systemic social injustice compromises their ability to live with integrity, meaning, and honesty. It impedes their ability to lead lives that that are fulfilling and that nurture their full human potential. Oppression interferes with the human needs for recognition and interconnectedness.

Wineman (1984) discusses why people would seek to change a system in which they are advantaged. He suggests that superiority and domination are self-limiting experiences:

> Exercising power over others does not oppress the oppressor, it is simply a less attractive, less gratifying, less human way of life than treating people as equals and respecting their full humanity. Negative consciousness or rejecting access to the privilege and power of the oppressor is based on the notion that equal relations can be experienced as more rewarding than top-down relations. (p. 187)

All people's basic humanity and integrity are better nurtured when they can experience mutuality, sensitivity, connectedness, and shared power. According to Wineman (1984), people are more likely to make sacrifices or changes when these changes are connected to the quality of their everyday lives rather than when they are just based on ideological beliefs. When people can recognize how their personal relations are enhanced by rejecting or dismantling superiority and domination, they can see the personal reward of greater equality.

Preference for Partnership Relationships

In his work with graduate and undergraduate students, Koegel (1998) found support for the view that people preferred relationships based on the partnership model. He asked hundreds of individuals to describe their best and worst relationships. These relationships could be in the private realm—with a friend, lover, parent, or sibling—or in the public realm—with a boss, teacher, or co-worker. Koegel consistently found similarities in how people described their best and worst relationships. Time and again, despite differences in the context of the relationships, students characterized their worst relationships as unequal and unfair. These types of relationships made people feel diminished, inferior, weak, and violated.

Summarizing the common characteristics of the worst relationships, Koegel (1998) notes that these relationships routinely do the following:

> a) use intimidation, domination, and manipulation to maintain an unequal, unjust relationship and to resolve conflicts; b) convert differences into right and wrong, good and bad, better and worse; c) make one person feel more competent and complete and the other feel more incompetent and incomplete; d) generate what Abraham Maslow (1968) calls "deficit motivations" for the subordinate parties (such as fear, insecurity, shame, distrust of self, and mistrust of others) and the dominant parties (such as selfishness, intolerance, anger, arrogance); and e) draw on the widespread cultural belief that supports dominance. (p. 29)

On the other hand, most of the best relationships were described as mutually empowering and mutually beneficial. They were win-win; both people gained and grew. The relationships were seen as basically fair and equal with a high degree of reciprocity and responsiveness. People in these relationships generally felt stronger, more complete, more connected, valued, and happier. In these relationships, individuals

> a) work to promote relational mutuality and to reduce inequality within the relationship; b) value the process of meeting the needs and enhancing the growth of each other; c) strive to maximize productive conflict, to minimize destructive conflict, and to honor differences within the relationship; d) engage in mutual caring, responsibility, and respect; e) cultivate empathy, compassion, understanding; and f) reflect an established cultural belief that supports partnership. (p. 30)

For obvious reasons, people prefer the more egalitarian, mutually enriching relationships that resemble partnership dynamics rather than the unequal and unfair ones based on dominator dynamics. To be sure, some individuals acknowledge that they have enjoyed being in the dominant role in an unequal relationship. However, few, if any, spontaneously cite such an instance as an example of their best relationship. Koegel uses this exercise as a way to explore issues of social dominance and privilege systems by making the link between people's own personal experiences and societal dynamics. This also provides the opportunity to discuss why some people prefer being in power-over relationships. We can explore how this is linked to the way that people are conditioned to feel important and successful, again challenging the notion that people inherently want to oppress others.

Benefits of Social Justice

As previously discussed, people from dominant groups are able to recognize numerous psychological, moral/spiritual, social, intellectual, and material costs of oppression to themselves and others from privileged groups. In a myriad of ways, they realize the loss of mental health and an authentic sense of self; the loss and diminishment of relationships; the loss of moral integrity and spiritual center; the loss of a full range of knowledge; and the loss of safety, resources, and quality of life. Yet eliminating the costs does not clearly indicate what it might be like if there was true equality.

I have also found that people from privileged groups can readily identify the benefits of social justice. Many people realize their personal stake in fostering equity. Imagining a different future reduces the tendency for people from dominant groups to become attached to victim status when they realize the costs. We can encourage people from privileged groups to see that creating "liberty and justice for all" can, in fact, have positive results for them as well as others. Enabling them to identify and envision the benefits of greater equity offers an invitation for change. It encourages people to consider ways to create a better society for everyone. When people from dominant groups recognize what they stand to gain, they are more motivated to change.

Below, I present some of the benefits of social justice that people from privileged groups have discussed. The positive effects of equality that I briefly describe are based more on conjecture than my discussion of the costs. Because we have yet to live in a truly just society, the benefits suggested below are based on what people imagine life would be like. They also reflect our experiences when we do have moments of freedom, authenticity, and equity (in relationships, personal pursuits, workplaces, social/religious organizations). Exactly how the benefits would look or be experienced would depend in part on the larger social system. My intent is not to portray a full alternative reality. Rather, it is to point to possibilities and to suggest how justice could lead to greater humanity, connection, and fulfillment for people from privileged groups.

Psychologically, people could have the freedom to explore their interests and abilities without the interference of rigid, externally imposed norms and expectations. There could be greater opportunity for creativity and experimentation. Individuals could have greater trust and confidence in their accomplishments without feeling they were somehow ill-gotten or fraudulent. Real choice about how one wanted to live one's life—in terms of work, partner, or lifestyle—could be available. Psychological and emotional development would be nurtured and enhanced.

Many fears and worries would also diminish. People would be able to walk the streets, interact with others, and explore new areas and interests with a greater sense of ease. The fear of offending someone from a dominated group or of retaliation and violence from the have-nots would fade. People could spend less energy on protecting and worrying about themselves, their loved ones, and their possessions and would have more time for productive and enjoyable pursuits.

Socially, if the dominant-subordinate structure and other barriers that block equal relationships between people were removed, meaningful connections with different kinds of people could be established. Relationships that were previously prevented or distorted could be allowed to flourish on the basis of mutual interests and respect. Differences in social identities would not tear families or communities apart. Individuals would not have to choose between living their conscience and their heart and maintaining important relationships. People would no longer be isolated from other human beings. There would be greater potential for honesty and depth in relationships.

Morally, because the conditions that give rise to many moral contradictions and pangs of conscience would be eliminated, people could more easily create lives that would be consonant with their morality and spirituality. They could experience a sense of liberation as a result of acting in ways consistent with their beliefs and of knowing that others can live with dignity as well. People could feel pride in their identity and life choices, not shame, guilt, or envy. There would be greater freedom to explore the world, not a need to rationalize or hide from it for fear of moral discomfort.

Intellectually, people's minds and worlds could be expanded and enriched by the exposure to and knowledge of other ways of being and doing (e.g., solving problems, setting priorities, relating to nature). Intellectual and personal development could flourish. People could more readily enjoy the foods, music, and arts from other cultural traditions. The diversity of worldviews could contribute to our understanding of the universe and to a more complete and accurate view of reality. We also could have access to the creativity, wisdom, and insights from all those who could help illuminate and alleviate social concerns. Our potential as human beings and a planet would have the greatest opportunity to develop and thrive.

Materially and physically, people would experience less stress and economic insecurity. For most people, their standard of living would rise if wealth were distributed more equitably. Without the intergroup conflicts that are promoted to prevent people from uniting to change an unjust system, we would be able to have more effective and collaborative working relationships in workplaces that did not exploit employees. Because individual and cultural differences would exist, conflict itself would not disappear, but it would not be fueled by social, political, and economic inequities. The ways of addressing conflict would also be significantly different and far more productive, as discussed earlier. Morale would improve, and the barriers between people that were based on social identities and hierarchical positions would be eliminated. Organizations would be better able to attract and retain desired employees and better able to allow them to maximize their talents and contributions.

Because housing would no longer be (de facto) segregated, people would have more options for where to live, at more reasonable prices. Overall, public schools would be improved, and sending children to private schools to get a good and safe education would not be necessary. Neighborhoods could reflect the diversity of our society and allow for the development of relationships across differences.

Violence would be significantly reduced. Because all people would have their basic needs met and their human rights respected, there would be less need to engage in personally and socially destructive actions. The resources and energy used to maintain inequalities and to address the results of social injustice could be used to address issues that affect us all. There would be more money available to devote to things like health, education, and the environment. There would be more time and energy available to develop broad-based efforts on other common concerns because people would not be fighting for their basic rights, exhausted from just trying to survive, or disenfranchised from society.

A better-educated, productive, and engaged populace could allow us to better realize our national democratic goals. If people really believe that a democracy is the best form of government and way of life, this could provide us with a closer model of what it might truly look like. Our political system and other organizations could be more reflective of and responsive to the needs of (all) the people. Without such compelling self-interests, fostered by social and economic inequities, there could be greater opportunity for institutions to function more effectively and efficiently.

These benefits are also interconnected. Psychological well-being is one aspect that can underlie or affect other benefits. If individuals have good mental health, including a strong sense of self-esteem and personal authenticity, they are more likely to desire and be able to have meaningful relationships with different people and to feel a sense of connection and responsibility to other human beings. They will be able to create effective collaborative relationships and organizations that value their members and will be able to support social systems that foster the empowerment and dignity of all people.

After doing this exercise with a group in which they identified the costs of oppression and the benefits of social justice for dominant-group members, the participants reminded me that it wasn't simply that there would be less fear, better relationships, or improved quality of life. There also would be more joy and fun. This is a wonderful example of how health is not simply the absence of illness, that wellness transcends just the removal of the sickness. They spoke about how people could more fully experience life and truly enjoy themselves and others. There is a freedom and exuberance that is captured by the word *joy* that more accurately reflects the liberation that a just and caring world could offer us.

The above examples provide a broad outline of how life could be improved for people from privileged groups if there was greater social justice. These illustrations do not ignore the fact that there would be some losses as well. However, they highlight that diversity and equity hold benefits and promote the liberation of all people. We all have something to gain.

Desire for Meaning

Another reason why people from privileged groups may be willing to challenge the dominant paradigm and support social justice is their desire for greater connection, purpose, and meaning in their lives. This is another manifestation of people seeking greater authenticity and a fuller sense of their humanity. As previously noted, Lerner (1996) describes our current system as based on an ethos of selfishness, greed, materialism, and cynicism. The dominant culture promotes a materialist and reductionist view of human beings—that we are isolated individuals motivated by material self-interest. This pervasive perspective is rooted in the economic and political structures of the competitive marketplace. Many others have voiced concerns about how the dominance of corporations and free market capitalism has promoted a preoccupation with self and money and has eroded a sense of morality, social responsibility, and community (Daly & Cobb, 1994; Derber, 1997; Handy, 1998; Korten, 1995). We are expected to look out for ourselves, view others in terms of what they can do for us, and pursue our own short-term gains. Many believe that if they don't push for their own interests first, they will be taken advantage of. The more people try to live up to these societal norms, the more alone and vulnerable they feel. Economic dislocation (downsizing, sending jobs to other countries) intensifies the feeling that no one is there for them and that they need to look out for themselves. Given these social dynamics, it is hard to develop caring and trusting relationships. People are surrounded by others who are self-absorbed and indifferent to their well-being. As a result, they feel unrecognized, disconnected from others, and lacking a sense of meaning in their lives.

Lerner's (1996) perspective initially grew out of his work with thousands of middle-income people at the Institute for Labor and Mental Health. Beginning in 1976, he and his colleagues wanted to understand the psychodynamics of working people and why so many were moving to the political Right. In the context of "stress clinics," they met with individuals over many weeks. After some initial defensiveness and the desire to present themselves as "together," participants revealed a hunger for community, recognition, and higher purpose. Even those who seemed most unconcerned about connections to others ultimately expressed a deep frustration about and yearning for meaningful relationships, a pessimism about one's ability to ever get one's needs met, and a deep shame about one's own imagined failures (p. 7). Overall, they found that people wanted to have their fundamental value as a human being recognized, to feel connected to a community, and to experience a higher purpose to their lives. However, escalating levels of selfishness and cynicism diminish the possibility of the kinds of lives people want.

Lerner is certainly not alone in claiming that people are seeking more meaning and spirituality in their lives. The lack of purpose and connection has been cited as a source for a variety of social problems, including gangs, school dropouts, early pregnancy, and addictions. This has devastating effects not only on these individuals and their communities but also on the larger society and on efforts for social justice. It also has some direct implications for working with people from dominant groups. For example, in his book *The Racist Mind*, Raphael Ezekiel (1996) explores the psychological foundations of neo-Nazis and Klansmen. He found that many of the youth who join Nazi movements are poor and are high school dropouts.

Meaning, not ideology, was the most compelling reason they joined these right-wing groups. They longed to be truly seen by an adult and to feel a sense of purpose and importance. (After spending many evenings talking with them, Ezekiel felt he easily could have led over half of them away from Nazism if he had had somewhere else to take them.) Even though they come from an oppressed group (the poor), they identified with their dominant identity, White (and male). They then acted against certain dominated groups—people of color, gays and lesbians, Jews. Many became involved in attacks or supported public policies that limited the rights and resources of oppressed groups.

According to Lerner, the rise of the Right is due to its ability to speak to the spiritual and ethical crisis people are experiencing and to address some of their longing for recognition. They understand that people are angry, frustrated, and confused about the lack of meaning in their lives and the range of social problems they encounter (crime, violence, homelessness, the breakdown of families). However, instead of blaming the impact of the competitive marketplace for these problems, it blames the traditionally demeaned Others—feminists, people of color, gays and lesbians, immigrants, and so on. They divert the attention away from corporate greed and concern for the bottom line and focus the scorn on groups struggling for full participation in society (Pharr, 1996). Although the Right may address the needs for care, community, and meaning in the private realm, they fail to address these needs in the public realm. Instead, they reinforce conservative politics and antidemocratic agendas that limit access to social and economic justice for marginalized groups.

Lerner cautions that there are limits to how long people will respond to the pain of others when no one seems to care about their own pain: "Unless we can provide the American Majority with a deep sense of being recognized, it will never respond to the pain of the most oppressed" (p. 174). Moreover, when people (especially White men) are repeatedly told that they are the oppressors, they will start to identify with that position and not with the oppressed.

Lerner claims that the Left has not been successful because it has failed to acknowledge and speak to these meaning needs and instead has focused primarily on the economic interests and political rights of oppressed groups. Social movements that have most successfully motivated people have framed the issues in a broader moral and meaning context (e.g., the New Deal, civil rights and Martin Luther King, Jr.), not narrow individual rights. The question is not whether economic issues need to be addressed but how to include an ethical and spiritual dimension in the analysis. Lerner sees the economic and meaning crises as two aspects of the same issue. Economic realities are, in part, shaped by our framework of meaning. He suggests that if people had a different framework of meaning, they would demand different economic arrangements. If people came to see their own needs as best served by a society with a concern for the common good, they would be more open to economic policies that better provided for more people (e.g., redistributing work over a shorter workweek). They would also be more likely to collectively challenge policies that unfairly disadvantaged people (e.g., transferring jobs abroad).

Unlike some others who talk about an ethical and spiritual crisis, Lerner shows how it is a result of our social, political, and economic structures and suggests a progressive alternative. His critique of the dominant culture links the public and the private. He advocates more than just individual solutions and changes in people's personal situations. A progressive politics of meaning challenges the ethos of the competitive marketplace and the economic and political arrangements that undermine human relationships. The central goal is to build a society that encourages mutual recognition, caring, ethical and spiritual sensitivity, and ecologically attuned social practices.

Lerner's recognition of meaning needs in conjunction with economic and social concerns is an important perspective.[3] It is especially relevant when working with people from privileged groups. After all, most people from dominant groups are not part of the very wealthy and powerful elite. Many people who choose to participate in and support policies that systematically disadvantage others do so to increase their own sense of self-worth and self-protection, yet they often do this at a large personal and spiritual cost. If people can see how their needs are better met by challenging the dominant ethos rather than by accepting it and blaming the disadvantaged, there is the potential to create allies for change.

The Need for Both Individual and Societal Change

Even when people believe in fairness and equity, they are less likely to support practices and changes they feel pose a threat to

their well-being. Therefore, along with educating for critical consciousness, we need to create the social and economic conditions
that allow people to more easily make choices that move us toward
social justice. Changes in the policies and structures of the dominant
culture can make it safer for people to support greater meaning and
equity in our world. People need opportunities to act according to
their highest ideals and not feel as if they are being fools or self-
destructive. Underlying social and economic institutions are needed
that foster, nurture, and sustain the experience of community, mutual interdependence, and social responsibility (Alperovitz, 1996).
We need to work with the ongoing dialectic between the dominant
ideology and people's belief systems, between social conditions and
people's attitudes and behavior. Because oppression operates on individual, institutional, and cultural levels and because these different dimensions interact and support each other, all aspects need to
be targeted.

An ethos of selfishness and materialism, a culture of competitive individualism, and policies that create a sense of scarcity fuel
people's narrow self-interest. With a zero-sum mentality, people feel
that there's not enough for everyone, that others are getting something at their expense. Many people assume that immigrants are
taking jobs away from Americans, that White women and people of
color are taking opportunities away from White men, and that gays
and lesbians are demanding special rights beyond the equal rights
afforded everyone else. Middle-class people fear that using their tax
dollars to improve the quality of poor schools will compromise the
quality of their own children's education. Money from one social
service program is often taken to support another.

It is undeniable that people are facing real choices and losses.
However, it is highly questionable whether the problem is that there
is not enough to go around. The sense of scarcity and a zero-sum
mentality is promulgated by our economic and social policies. In
dominator models, as Eisler (1987) pointed out, dominant groups
foster a sense of scarcity to maintain the status quo.

Economic inequality and the inequitable distribution of wealth
is a pivotal factor in perpetuating social injustice and eroding social
relations. The gap between the rich and poor is the largest it has ever
been and is rapidly growing; it is also the largest of any industrialized nation. The 10% wealthiest own 73% of all the wealth in the
United States (the top 1% own about 39%; Wolff, 1998). Between

1979 and 1994, family income fell 14% for those in the lowest quintile (20%) and rose 83% for the top 1%. In contrast, between 1947 and 1979, all quintiles grew between 86% and 116%, with the bottom quintile growing the most and the top quintile growing the least. In 1965, the average chief executive officer's income was 44 times that of the average U.S. worker's income; in 1995, that was up to 212 times as much—a ratio higher than that of any other industrialized nation. Between 1990 and 1995, corporate profits rose 50%, and CEO pay rose 65%. During the same time period, worker layoffs were up 39%, and worker pay was down 1%.[4] Such disparities undermine democracy because fewer people have access to full and equitable participation and decision making in our society.

To challenge the systems that create the sense of scarcity, we need to direct the attention toward those who are responsible for people not having what they need. (This is not to say we don't also need to look at our overuse of natural resources and excessive consumption of material goods.) Economic priorities and issues such as tax laws, corporate welfare, wage scales, and campaign finance need to be examined. Instead of having people fighting over the crumbs, we can look at how the whole pie is being divided. We can question systems and policies that set up a zero-sum game, demand more accountability from those who create situations of unnecessary scarcity, and challenge practices that put people in "us or them" situations. We can explore how to expand the "pie" and utilize resources in ways that do not pit people against each other. We can highlight shared goals, collective well-being, and mutual responsibility. For example, a recent controversy arose in New York City as to whether wealthy parents should be able to raise money to fund teachers' salaries and school programs. The chancellor of the New York City Schools was concerned that this would just further disparities in a public education system. Through letters to the editor in the local newspaper, I followed some of the discussion and the proposed solutions. Some parents, taking a very individual-rights orientation, argued that it was their right to support their child's education. Other parents offered a more collaborative, interdependent approach. I read few letters that recognized that it was in everyone's best interest for all of the children in their city to have a decent education. There was the suggestion that half of the money raised by the economically advantaged parents be shared with poorer schools. A couple of people suggested that the parents could be using this energy and skill to be lobbying together to demand more adequate educational funding that would benefit all the schools.

Even when there is scarcity, people can respond in ways that are not selfish. There have certainly been other times when in situations of need, people have pulled together to provide for each other. The policies during the Depression were more reflective of this orientation. However, without a sense of community and mutual responsibility and with a heightened sense of cynicism, people are more likely to look out for themselves, regardless of the effect on others.

Significant social change inevitably meets with resistance and backlash. In fact, this is often how people can tell whether they are really having an impact. The power elite will try to protect their power. Historically, they have never been the ones to initiate change. Nevertheless, the subordinate group has always had allies from the dominant group. Although we should never overlook anyone as a potential ally, we can focus our energy on the majority of people (including those from privileged groups) who are not the main beneficiaries of oppression or who are initially most responsive to and see the benefits of equity. A general rule is that a minority of people will clearly be supportive of our goals, another minority will actively oppose them, and the large majority in the middle will be open to persuasion. In both organizational and societal change, we can work on developing a critical mass and not assume that we need to win over every person.

For all the signs I see of hope and possibility, there are as many barriers. Yet when we become pessimistic about people from privileged groups and the possibility of change, we fall prey to the culture of cynicism that undermines social change. *Surplus powerlessness* (Lerner, 1986) is our tendency to see ourselves as more powerless than we really are. It makes us feel that it is impossible or unrealistic in the face of real power inequities to try to create fundamental change. Surplus powerlessness is not based on a realistic assessment of the political situation but on the internalization of messages from the dominant culture that tell us that nothing can really change and that we had better do what we can to protect ourselves. However, we have a history rich with examples of people who had the courage to expect and demand change and who, in the process, inspired and empowered others to join them.

I often think of the words of Elie Wiesel, Holocaust survivor, writer, peace activist. He had just finished speaking about his trips to various places in the world that were beset with war, conflict, and human cruelty and his efforts to promote peace and healing. An audience member asked, "In light of all that you've seen, how do you keep going?" He responded, "What choice do I have?" For those of us who carry a commitment to a caring and just world in our hearts and souls, what choice do we really have but to continue the struggle? For ultimately, justice frees us all.

Notes

1. See Kreisberg (1992) for an excellent review and discussion of power over and power with.

2. The Center for Partnership Studies documents the workings of the partnership model in contemporary family, economic, spiritual, and political life. See also other organizations listed in the appendix.

3. For a more comprehensive and in-depth presentation of his views and a politics of meaning, see *Tikkun Magazine* and *The Politics of Meaning* by Lerner (1996).

4. All statistics were taken from United for a Fair Economy. (1997, March). *The Growing Divide: Inequality and the Roots of Economic Insecurity*. Boston, MA.

Appendix

There are innumerable organizations and educational materials on different aspects of diversity and social justice. These are a few suggested resources that focus on curriculum, training activities, and workshop designs.

Training Manuals and Books on General Diversity and Multiple Forms of Oppression

Beyond Heroes and Holidays: A Practical Guide to K-12 Anti-Racist, Multicultural Education and Staff Development. Enid Lee, Deborah Menkart, & Margo Okazawa-Rey. (Eds.). (1998). Washington, DC: Network of Educators on the Americas. Primarily focuses on antiracism but also addresses multiculturalism in general and other forms of oppression.

Dealing with Differences: Taking Action on Class, Race, Gender, and Disability. Angeles Ellis & Marilyn Llewellyn. (1997). Thousand Oaks, CA: Corwin. Has training designs on class and classism; race, racism, and xenophobia; gender, sexism, and heterosexism; and disability and ableism. Geared for young adults but also useful for adults.

Diversity at Work Training Series. Available from Diversity at Work, A Division of Lambert and Associates, 1945 Morningview Dr., Hoffman Estates, IL 60192, (847) 429-9764. Offers a variety of training materials geared for the workplace, including diversity ice-breakers, managing cultural diversity, and gender issues.

Managing Diversity Survival Guide. Lee Gardenswartz & Anita Rowe. (1994). New York: Irwin. Training activities oriented toward the workplace.

Multicultural Teaching in the University. David Schoem, Linda Frankel, Ximena Zuniga, & Edith Lewis (Eds.). (1995). Westport, CT: Praeger. See especially the book's Part VIII.

Teaching for Diversity and Social Justice: A Sourcebook. Maurianne Adams, Lee Anne Bell, & Pat Griffin. (Eds.). (1997). New York: Routledge. Has curriculum designs for racism, sexism, hetero-sexism, anti-Semitism, ableism, and classism as well as multi-issue courses.

Training and Educational Materials on Specific Forms of Oppression

Racism

Uprooting Racism: How White People Can Work for Racial Justice. Paul Kivel. (1996). Philadelphia: New Society Press.

Teaching/Learning Anti-Racism: A Developmental Approach. Louise Derman-Sparks & Carol Brunson Phillips. (1997). New York: Teachers College Press.

White Awareness: Handbook for Anti-Racism Training. Judith Katz. (1978). Norman: University of Oklahoma Press.

Classism

The Growing Divide: Inequality and the Roots of Economic Insecurity: Trainers Manual. United for a Fair Economy. (1997). Boston, MA: Author. Available from United for a Fair Economy, 37 Temple Pl., 5th Floor, Boston, MA 02111; (617) 423-2148. This organization regularly publishes new materials on addressing income inequality and organizing around economic and class issues.

The New Field Guide to the U.S. Economy. Center for Popular Economics. (1995). New York: New Press.

Sexism

Men's Work. Paul Kivel. (1998). Center City, MN: Hazelden.

When the Topic Is Race: White Male Denial. Cooper Thompson. (1996). Available from Cooper Thompson, 25 Whitney Ave., Cambridge, MA 02139; (617) 868-8280. Article on how to address White men's resistance to dealing with racism.

Heterosexism and Homophobia

Guide to Leading Introductory Workshops on Homophobia. Campaign to End Homophobia. Available from CRC, 521 Broadway, Nyack, NY 10960; (914) 353-1796.

Opening Doors to Understanding and Acceptance. Kathy O'Bear. Also available from CRC, 521 Broadway, Nyack, NY 10960; (914) 353-1796.

Homophobia: How We All Pay the Price. Warren Blumenfeld. (Ed.). (1992). Boston: Beacon. Contains an appendix titled, "Conducting Antiheterosexism Workshops: A Sample."

Homophobia 101: Introductory Staff Training and Homophobia 201: Advanced Teacher Training. Both are available from the Gay, Lesbian and Straight Education Network (GLSEN), National Office, 121 West 27th St., Suite 804, New York, NY 01001; (212) 727-0135. GLSEN also has many other materials for addressing homophobia in schools.

Overcoming Heterosexism and Homophobia: Strategies That Work. James T. Sears & Walter L Williams. (Eds.). (1997). New York: Columbia University Press.

Road Blocks and Responses in Addressing Lesbian, Gay, Bisexual, and Transgender (LGBT) Issues: Responding to Resistance From Teachers, Administrators, Students, and the Community. Warren J. Blumenfeld & Laurie Lindop. Available from Warren Blumenfeld, P.O. Box 929, Northampton, MA 10161; (413) 585-9121.

Ableism

I was unable to find published training or workshop materials that focused on ableism other than those that educated about a particular type of disability.

Perspectives on Disabilities. Mark Nagler. (1993). Palo Alto, CA: Health Market Research. A collection of short articles useful to inform training.

Organizations That Publish Educational and Training Materials on Diversity and Social Justice

Griggs Productions
2046 Clement St.
San Francisco, CA 94121-2118
(800) 210-4200; (415) 668-4200
Materials for the workplace and for organizations.

Jossey-Bass/Pfeiffer
350 Sansome St., 5th Floor
San Francisco, CA 94104
(800) 274-4434
Materials for the workplace and for organizations.

ODT, Inc.
P.O. Box 134
Amherst, MA 01004
(413) 549-1293
Materials for the workplace and for organizations.

Teaching for Change
Network of Educators on the Americas
P.O. Box 73038
Washington, DC 20056-3038
(202) 238-2379

Most materials are oriented toward K-12 education, but there are also some for school and community.

Journals and Magazines With
Training and Educational Ideas

On Diversity

Cultural Diversity at Work
The GilDeane Group
13751 Lake City Way N.E., Suite 106
Seattle, WA 98125-8612
(206) 362-0336

Democracy & Education
313 McCracken Hall
Ohio University
Athens, OH 45701
(614) 593-45331

Multicultural Education
Caddo Gap Press
317 S. Division St., Suite 2
Ann Arbor, MI 48104
Tel: (313) 662-0886

Multicultural Perspectives: An Official Publication of the
    National Association for Multicultural Education (NAME)
Lawrence Erlbaum, Inc.
10 Industrial Ave.
Mahwah, NJ 07430-2262
(201) 236-9500

*Tranformations: A Resource for Curriculum Transformation
    and Scholarship*
The New Jersey Project
William Paterson University
300 Pompton Rd.
Wayne, NJ 07470
(973) 720-2296

Organizations That Offer Progressive
Social, Political, and Economic Alternatives

Center for a Living Democracy
RR #1 Black Fox Rd.
Brattleboro, VT 05301
(802) 254-4331

Center for Ethics and Economic Policy
2512 9th St., No. 3
Berkeley, CA 94710-2542
(510) 549-9931

Center for Partnership Studies
P.O. Box 51936
Pacific Grove, CA 93950

Co-op America
2100 M St. NW, Suite 403
Washington, DC 20037
(800) 424-2667; (202) 872-5307

Institute for Democracy and Education
119 McCracken Hall
Ohio University
Athens, OH 45701-2979
(614) 593-4531

Rethinking Schools
1001 East Keefe Ave.
Milwaukee, WI 53212
(414) 964-9646

References for Responding to the Religious Right

Eyes Right: Challenging the Right-Wing Backlash. C. Berlett. (1995).
Boston: South End.

Facing the Wrath: Confronting the Right in Dangerous Times. S. Diamond. (1996). Monroe, ME: Common Courage Press.

The Bible Tells Me So: Uses and Misuses of the Holy Scripture. J. Hill & R. Cheadle. (1996). New York: Anchor.

References

Adair, M. (1993). *From leadership to empowerment: Creating collaborative contexts.* San Francisco: Tools for Change.

Adair, M., & Howell, S. (1988). *The subjective side of politics.* San Francisco: Tools for Change.

Adams, M., Bell, L., & Griffin, P. (1997). *Teaching for diversity and social justice: A sourcebook.* New York: Routledge.

Allsup, C. (1995). What's all this White male bashing. In R. Martin (Ed.), *Practicing what we teach: Confronting diversity in teacher education.* Albany: State University of New York Press.

Alperovitz, G. (1996). The reconstruction of community meaning. *Tikkun Magazine, 11*(3), 13-16, 79.

Andrzejewski, J. (1995). Teaching controversial issues in higher education: Pedagogical techniques and analytical framework. In R. Martin (Ed.), *Practicing what we teach: Confronting diversity in teacher education.* Albany: State University of New York Press.

Apple, M. (1982). *Education and power.* London: Routledge & Kegan Paul.

Ayvazian, A. (1995, January/February). Interrupting the cycle of oppression: The role of allies as agents of change. *Fellowship,* pp. 6-9.

Banks, J. (1991). *Teaching strategies for ethnic studies.* Boston: Allyn & Bacon.

Batson, C. (1989). Prosocial values, moral principles and a three-path model of prosocial motivation. In N. Eisenberg, J. Reykowski, & E. Staub (Eds.), *Social and moral values: Individual and societal perspectives* (pp. 2-28). Hillsdale, NJ: Lawrence Erlbaum.

Batson, C., Polyarpou, M., Harmon-Jones, E., Imhoff, H., Mitchner, E., Bednar, L., Klein, T., & Highberger, L. (1997). Empathy and attitudes: Can feeling for a member of a stigmatized group improve feelings toward the group? *Journal of Personality and Social Psychology, 71*(1), 105-118.

Baxter, M. M. (1992). *Knowing and reasoning in college: Gender-related patterns in student development.* San Francisco: Jossey-Bass.

Belenky, M., Clinchy, B., Goldberger, N., & Tarule, J. (1986). *Women's ways of knowing: The development of self, voice and mind.* New York: Basic Books.

Bell, L., Washington, S., Weinstein, G., & Love, B. (1997). Knowing ourselves as instructors. In M. Adams, L. Bell, & P. Griffin (Eds.), *Teaching for diversity and social justice: A sourcebook* (pp. 299-310). New York: Routledge.

Bellah, R. N., Madsen, R., Sullivan, W. M., Swidler, A., & Tipton, S. M. (1985). *Habits of the heart: Individualism and commitment in American life.* New York: Harper & Row.

Bennett, M., & Bennett, J. (1992). "Defensiveness"—A stage of development. *Cultural Diversity at Work, 5*(1), 4-5.

Berman, S. (1997). *Children's social consciousness and the development of social responsibility.* Albany, NY: State University of New York Press.

Bingham, S. (1986). The truth about growing up rich. *Ms. Magazine, 14,* 48-50.

Blumenfeld, W. (Ed.). (1992). *Homophobia: How we all pay the price.* Boston: Beacon.

Bohmer, S., & Briggs, J. (1991). Teaching privileged students about gender, race and class oppression. *Teaching Sociology, 19,* 154-163.

Bole, W. (1987, April 10). To learn about inner-city plight, walk in their shoes. *Poughkeepsie Journal,* A 11.

Bowser, B., & Hunt, R. (Eds.). (1981/1996). *Impacts of racism of White Americans.* Thousand Oaks, CA: Sage.

Braza, J. (1997). *Moment by moment: The art and practice of mindfulness.* Boston: Charles E. Tuttle.

Brookfield, S. (1987). *Developing critical thinkers: Challenging adults to explore alternative ways of thinking and acting.* San Francisco: Jossey-Bass.

Brookfield, S. (1990). *The skillful teacher.* San Francisco: Jossey-Bass.

Broverman, I., Broverman, D., Clarkson, F., Rosencrantz, P., & Vogel, S. (1970). Sex role stereotypes and clinical judgements of mental health. *Journal of Consulting and Clinical Psychology, 34,* 1-7.

Capossela, T. (1993). *The critical writing workshop: Designing writing assignments to foster critical thinking.* Portsmouth, NH: Boynton/Cook.

Chan, C., & Treacy, M. J. (1996). Resistance in multicultural courses: Student, faculty and classroom dynamics. *American Behavioral Scientist, 40*(2), 212-221.

Chavez, R., & O'Donnell, J. (1998). *Speaking the unpleasant: The politics of (non)engagement in the multicultural terrain.* Albany: State University of New York Press.

Clark, A. (1991). The identification and modification of defense mechanisms in counseling. *Journal of Counseling and Development, 69,* 231-236.

Colby, A., & Damon, W. (1992). *Some do care.* New York: Free Press.

Cose, E. (1995). *A man's world.* New York: HarperCollins.

Crowfoot, J., & Chesler, M. (1996). White men's roles in multicultural coalitions. In B. Bowser & R. Hunt (Eds.), *Impacts of racism on White Americans* (pp. 202-244). Thousand Oaks, CA: Sage.

Crum, T. (1987). *The magic of conflict.* New York: Touchstone.

Cruz, N. (1990). A challenge to the notion of service. In J. C. Kendall (Ed.), *Combining service and learning: A resource book for community and public service* (Vol. 1, pp. 321-323). Raleigh, NC: National Society for Internships and Experiential Education.

Daloz, L. P., Keen, C., Keen, J., & Parks, S. D. (1996). *Common fire: Leading lives of commitment in a complex world.* Boston: Beacon.

Daly, H., & Cobb, J. (1994). *For the common good.* Boston: Beacon.

Delpit, L. (1995). *Other people's children: Cultural conflict in the classroom.* New York: New Press.

Derber, C. (1979). *The pursuit of attention: Power and individualism in everyday life.* Boston: G. K. Hall.

Derber, C. (1996). *The wilding of America: How greed and violence are eroding our nation's character.* New York: St. Martin's.

Domhoff, G. W., & Zweigenhaft, R. (1988a). The new power elite: Women, Jews, African-Americans, Asian-Americans, Latinos, Gays and Lesbians. *Mother Jones, 22*(2), 44-47.

Domhoff, G. W., & Zweigenhaft, R. (1998b). *Diversity in the power elite: Have women and minorities reached the top?* New Haven, CT: Yale University Press.

Duke, L. (1992, June 8). Blacks, Whites define "racism" differently. *Washington Post,* A 1.

Eisler, R. (1987). *The chalice and the blade: Our history, our future.* New York: Harper and Row.

Eisler, R. (1996). *Sacred pleasure: Sex, myth, and the politics of the body.* New York: HarperCollins.

Eisler, R., & Koegel, R. (1996). The partnership model: A signpost of hope. *Holistic Education Review, 9*(1), 5-15.

Eisler, R., & Loye, D. (1990/1998). *The partnership way.* New York: HarperCollins.

Elliot, A., & Devine, P. (1994). On the motivational nature of cognitive dissonance: Dissonance as psychological discomfort. *Journal of Personality and Social Psychology, 67*(3), 382-394.

Ezekiel, R. (1996). *The racist mind: Portraits of American neo-Nazis and Klansmen.* New York: Penguin.

Feagin, J., & Vera H. (1995). *White racism.* New York: Routledge.

Fernandez, J. (1996). The impact of racism on Whites in corporate America. In B. Bowser & R. Hunt (Eds.), *Impacts of racism on White Americans* (2nd ed., pp. 157-178). Thousand Oaks, CA: Sage.

Fine, M. (1997). Witnessing Whiteness. In M. Fine, L. Weis, L. Powell, & L. Mun Wong (Eds.), *Off White: Readings on race, power, and society* (pp. 57-65). New York: Routledge.

Fine, M., Weis, L., Powell, L., & Mun Wong, L. (1997). *Off White: Readings on race, power, and society.* New York: Routledge.

Frankenberg, R. (1993). *White women, race matters: The social construction of Whiteness.* Minneapolis: University of Minnesota Press.

Freire, P. (1970). *Pedagogy of the oppressed.* New York: Herder & Herder.

Freire, P. (1994). *Pedagogy of hope: Reliving pedagogy of the oppressed.* New York: Continuum.

Friedman, V. J., & Lipshitz, R. (1992). Teaching people to shift cognitive gears: Overcoming resistance on the road to model II. *Journal of Applied Behavioral Science, 28*(1), 118-136.

Gaertner, S., & Dovidio, J. (1986). The aversive form of racism. In J. F. Dovidio & S. L. Gaertner (Eds.), *Prejudice, discrimination, and racism* (pp. 61-89). Orlando, FL: Academic Press.

Gaertner, S., Dovidio, J., Banker, B., Rust, M., Nier, J., Mottola, G., & Ward, C. (1997). Does White racism necessarily mean antiBlackness? Aversive racism and proWhiteness. In M. Fine, L. Weis, L. Powell, & L. Mun Wong (Eds.), *Off White: readings on race, power, and society* (pp. 167-178). New York: Routledge.

Gallagher, C. (1997). Redefining racial privilege in the United States. *Transformations, 8*(1), 28-39.

Gilligan, C. (1980/1993). *In a different voice.* Cambridge, MA: Harvard University Press.

Giroux, H. (1983). *Theory and resistance in education: A pedagogy for the opposition.* South Hadley, MA: Bergin & Garvey.

Glyn, A., & Miliband, D. (Eds.). (1994). *Paying for inequality: The economic cost of social injustice.* London: IPPR/River Oram Press.

Goldberger, N., Clinchy, B., Belenky, M., & Tarule, J. M. (1998). *Knowledge, difference and power: Essays inspired by women's ways of knowing.* New York: Basic Books.

Goldstein, J., & Kornfield, J. (1987). *Seeking the heart of wisdom: The path of insight meditation.* Boston: Shambala.

Greenfield, P. M., & Cocking, R. R. (1996). *Cross-cultural roots of minority child development.* Hillsdale, NJ: Lawrence Erlbaum.

Grossman, D. (1995). *On killing: The psychological cost of learning to kill in war and society.* Boston: Little, Brown.

Handy, C. (1998). *The hungry spirit: Beyond capitalism. A quest for purpose in the modern world.* New York: Broadway Books.

Hanh, T. N. (1991). *Peace is every step: The path of mindfulness in everyday life.* New York: Bantam.

Hardiman, R., & Jackson, B. (1992). Racial identity development: Understanding racial dynamics in college classrooms and on campus. In M. Adams (Ed.), *Promoting diversity in college classrooms: Innovative responses for the curriculum, faculty, and institutions* (pp. 21-37). San Francisco: Jossey-Bass.

Hardiman, R., & Jackson, B. (1997). Conceptual foundations for social justice courses. In M. Adams, L. Bell, & P. Griffin (Eds.), *Teaching for diversity and social justice: A sourcebook* (pp. 16-29). New York: Routledge.

Hawkesworth, M. E. (1993). *Beyond oppression: Feminist theory and political strategy.* New York: Continuum.

Helms, J. (1990). *Black and White racial identity: Theory, research, and practice.* Westport, CT: Greenwood.

Helms, J. (1992). *Race is a nice thing to have.* Topeka, KS: Content Communications.

Helms, J. (1995). An update on Helm's White and people of color racial identity models. In J. G. Ponterotto, J. M. Casa, L. A. Suzuki, and C. M. Alexander (Eds.), *Handbook of multicultural counseling.* Thousand Oaks, CA: Sage.

Higginbotham, E. (1996). Getting all students to listen: Analyzing and coping with student resistance. *American Behavioral Scientist, 40(2)*, 203-211.

Hilfiker, D. (1994). *Not all of us are saints: A doctor's journey with the poor.* New York: Hill & Wang.

Hoehn, R. A. (1983). *Up from apathy: A study of moral and social involvement.* Nashville, TN: Abington.

Hoffman, M. (1989). Empathy and prosocial activism. In N. Eisenberg, J. Reykowski, & E. Staub (Eds.), *Social and moral values: Individual and societal perspectives* (pp. 65-85). Hillsdale, NJ: Lawrence Erlbaum.

hooks, b. (1989). *Talking back.* Boston: South End.

Ignatiev, N. (1995). *How the Irish became White: Irish-Americans and African-Americans in nineteenth century Philadelphia.* New York: Verso.

Ingram, C. (1990). *In the footsteps of Ghandi: Conversations with spiritual social activists.* Berkeley, CA: Parallax.

Johnson, A. (1997). *The gender knot: Unraveling our patriarchal legacy.* Philadelphia: Temple University Press.

Jones, J., & Carter, R. (1996). Racism and White racial identity: Merging realities. In B. Bowser & R. Hunt (Eds.), *Impacts of racism on White Americans* (2nd ed., pp. 1-23). Thousand Oaks, CA: Sage.

Jordan, J. (1997). *Women's growth in diversity: More writings from the Stone Center.* New York: Guilford.

Jordan, J., Kaplan, A., Miller, J. B., Stiver, I., & Surrey, J. (1991). *Women's growth in connection: Writings from the Stone Center.* New York: Guilford.

Kabat-Zinn, J. (1994). *Wherever you go, there you are: Mindfulness meditation in everyday life.* New York: Hyperion.

Kaufman, M. (1993). *Cracking the armor: Power, pain, and lives of men.* New York: Penguin.

Kegan, R. (1982). *The evolving self: Problems and process in human development.* Cambridge, MA: Harvard University Press.

Kelman, H. D., & Hamilton, V. L. (1989). *Crimes of obedience.* New Haven, CT: Yale University Press.

Kendall, J. C. (1990). Combining service and learning: A resource book for community and public service (Vols. 1 & 2). Raleigh, NC: National Society for Internships and Experiential Education.

Kessler, S. (1991). The teaching presence. *Holistic Education Review, 4*, 4-15.

Kimmel, M. (1993). The struggle for gender equality: How men respond. *Thought and Action, 8(2)*, 49-76.

Kimmel, M., & Messner, M. (Eds.). (1989/1995). *Men's lives.* New York: Macmillan.

King, M. L., Jr. (1981). *Strength to love.* Philadelphia: Fortress.

King, P. M., & Kitchener, K. S. (1994). *Developing reflective judgment: Understanding and promoting intellectual growth and critical thinking in adolescents and adults.* San Francisco: Jossey-Bass.

Kivel, P. (1992/1998). *Men's work.* Center City, MN: Hazelden.

Kivel, P. (1996). *Uprooting racism: How White people can work for racial justice.* Philadelphia: New Society Press.

Kloss, R. (1994). A nudge is best: Helping students through the Perry scheme of intellectual development. *College Teaching, 42(4)*, 151-158.

Kochman, T. (1981). *Black and White styles in conflict.* Chicago: Chicago University Press.

Koegel, R. (1997). Partnership intelligence and dominator intelligence: Their social roots, patterns, and consequences. *World Futures, 49,* 39-63.

Koegel, R. (1998). Using our worst and best relationships to learn about social dominance and social justice. *Encounter: Education for Meaning and Social Justice, 11*(2), 28-35.

Kohn, A. (1990). *The brighter side of human nature: altruism and empathy in everyday life.* New York: Basic Books.

Korten, D. (1995). *When corporations rule the world.* San Francisco: Kumarian Press.

Kreisberg, S. (1992). *Transforming power: Domination, empowerment, and education.* Albany: State University of New York Press.

Kurfiss, J. (1988). *Critical thinking: Theory, research, practice, and possibilities.* (ASHE-ERIC Higher Education Reports, Vol. 17, No. 2). New York: John Wiley.

Landrine, H. (1992). Clinical implications of cultural differences: The referential versus the indexical self. *Clinical Psychology Review, 12,* 401.

Lappe, F., & Du Bois, M. (1994). *The quickening of America.* San Francisco: Jossey-Bass.

Larew, J. (1996). Why are droves of unqualified kids getting into our top colleges? Because their dads are alumni. In K. Rosenblum & T.-M. C. Travis (Eds.), *The meaning of difference: American constructions of race, sex and gender, social class, and sexual orientation* (pp. 208-213). New York: McGraw-Hill.

Lazarre, J. (1993). *Beyond the Whiteness of Whiteness: Memoir of a White mother of Black sons.* Durham, NC: Duke University Press.

Lerner, M. (1986). *Surplus powerlessness.* Oakland, CA: Institute for Labor and Mental Health.

Lerner, M. (1996). *The politics of meaning.* Reading, MA: Addison-Wesley.

Lorde, A. (1983). There is no hierarchy of oppressions. *Interracial Books for Children Bulletin, 14,* Council on Interracial Books for Children.

Lynch, J., Kaplan, G., Pamuk, E., Cohen, R., Heck, K., Balfour, J., & Yen, I. (1998). Income inequality and mortality in metropolitan areas in the United States. *American Journal of Public Health, 88*(7), 1074-1080.

Lyons, N. (1988). Two perspectives: On self, relationships and morality. In C. Gilligan, J. V. Ward, & J. M. Taylor (Eds.), *Mapping the moral domain* (pp. 21-48). Cambridge, MA: Harvard University Press.

MacKinnon, C. (1989). *Feminism unmodified.* Cambridge, MA: Harvard University Press.

Mandela, N. (1994). *Long walk to freedom.* New York: Little, Brown.

Martin, R. (Ed.). (1995). *Practicing what we teach: Confronting diversity in teacher education.* Albany, NY: State University of New York Press.

McIntosh, P. (1985). *Feeling like a fraud* (Working Paper No. 18, Stone Center Work in Progress Papers). Wellesley, MA: Center for Research on Women.

McIntosh, P. (1988). *White privilege and male privilege: A personal account of coming to see correspondences through work in women's studies* (Working

Paper No. 189, Stone Center Work in Progress Papers). Wellesley, MA: Center for Research on Women.

Miller, A. (1984). *For your own good: Hidden cruelty in childrearing and the roots of violence*. New York: Farrar, Straus & Giroux.

Miller, A. (1990). *For your own good: Hidden cruelty in childrearing and the roots of violence*. New York: Farrar, Straus & Giroux.

Miller, J. B. (1976). *Towards a new psychology of women*. Boston: Beacon.

Miller, J. B. (1991). Women and power. In J. Jordan, A. Kaplan, J. B. Miller, I. Stiver, & J. Surrey (Eds.), *Women's growth in connection: Writings from the Stone Center* (pp. 197-205). New York: Guilford.

Minuchen, S., & Fishman, C. H. (1981). *Family therapy techniques*. Cambridge, MA: Harvard University Press.

Mogil, C., & Slepian, A. (1992). *We gave away a fortune*. Philadelphia: New Society Press.

Oliner, S., & Oliner, P. (1988). *The altruistic personality*. New York: Free Press.

Opotow, W. (1990). Moral exclusion and injustice: An introduction. *Journal of Social Issues, 46*(1), 1-20.

Orren, G. R. (1988). Beyond self-interest. In R. Reich (Ed.), *The power of public ideas*. Cambridge, MA: Ballinger.

Pear, R. (1996, July 19). House approves shift on welfare. *New York Times*, p. 28.

Perry, W. (1968). *Forms of intellectual and ethical development in the college years: A scheme*. New York: Holt, Rinehart & Winston.

Peters, W. (1971). *A class divided*. New York: Doubleday.

Pettigrew, T. F. (1981). The mental health impact. In B. P. Bowser & R. G. Hunt (Eds.), *Impacts of racism on White Americans* (1st ed., pp. 97-118). Beverly Hills, CA: Sage.

Pharr, S. (1996). *In the time of the right: Reflections on liberation*. Berkeley, CA: Chardon.

Reardon, K. (1994). Undergraduate research in distressed urban communities: An undervalued form of service-learning. *Michigan Journal of Community Service Learning, 1*, 44-54.

Reimer, J., Paolitto, D., & Hersh, R. (1983). *Promoting moral growth*. New York: Longman.

Roediger, D. (1991). *The wages of Whiteness*. New York: Verso.

Rogers, C. (1980). *A way of being*. Boston: Houghton Mifflin.

Romney, P., Tatum, B., & Jones, J. (1992). Feminist strategies for teaching about oppression: The importance of process. *Women's Studies Quarterly*, 1&2, 95-110.

Rose, L. (1996). White identity and counseling White allies about racism. In B. Bowser & R. Hunt (Eds.), *Impacts of racism of White Americans* (2nd ed., pp. 24-47). Thousand Oaks, CA: Sage.

Rosenblum, K., & Travis, T. (1996). *The meaning of difference: American constructions of race, sex and gender, social class, and sexual orientation*. New York: McGraw-Hill.

Rubin, Z., & Peplau, L. A. (1975). Who believes in a just world? *Journal of Personality and Social Psychology, 31*(3), 65-89.

Ryan, W. (1970). *Blaming the victim*. New York: Random House.

Sadker, M., & Sadker, D. (1994). *Failing at fairness: How America's schools cheat girls.* New York: Scribner.

Salzberg, S. (1995). *Loving kindness: The revolutionary art of happiness.* Boston: Shambala.

Sampson, E. (1988). The debate on individualism: Indigenous psychologies of the individual and their role in personal and societal functioning. *American Psychologist, 43,* 15-22.

Sampson, E. (1991). *Social worlds, personal lives.* New York: Harcourt Brace Jovanovich.

Sears, D., & Funk, C. (1990). Self-interest in Americans' political opinions. In J. Mansbridge (Ed.), *Beyond self-interest* (pp. 147-170). Chicago: Chicago University Press.

Shipler, D. (1997). *A country of strangers.* New York: Knopf.

Shirts, G. (1969). *Star power.* La Jolla, CA: Western Behavioral Sciences Institute.

Simon, L., Greenberg, J., & Brehm, J. (1995). Trivialization: The forgotten mode of dissonance reduction. *Journal of Personality and Social Psychology, 68*(2), 247-260.

Sleeter, C. (1992). Resisting racial awareness: How teachers understand the social order from their racial, gender, and social class locations. *Educational Foundations, 6*(2), 7-32.

Smith, R. E., & Tyler, T. R. (1996). Justice and power. *European Journal of Social Psychology, 26,* 171-200.

Spelman, E. V. (1995). Changing the subject: Studies in the appropriation of pain. In L. A. Bell & D. Blumenfeld (Eds.), *Overcoming racism and sexism* (pp. 181-196). Lanham, MD: Rowman & Littlefield.

Starhawk. (1982). *Dreaming the dark.* Boston: Beacon.

Starhawk. (1987). *Truth or dare.* San Francisco: Harper & Row.

Staub, E. (1978). *Positive social behavior and morality: Social and personal influences.* New York: Academic Press.

Staub, E. (1989). Individual and societal (group) values in a motivational perspective and their role in benevolence and harmdoing. In N. Eisenberg, J. Reykowski, & E. Staub (Eds.), *Social and moral values: Individual and societal perspectives* (pp. 45-61). Hillsdale, NJ: Lawrence Erlbaum.

Steele, C., Spencer, S., & Lynch, M. (1993). Self-image resilience and dissonance: The role of affirmational resources. *Journal of Personality and Social Psychology, 64*(3), 885-896.

Surrey, J. (1991). Relationship and empowerment. In J. Jordan, A. Kaplan, J. B. Miller, I. Stiver, & J. Surrey (Eds.), *Women's growth in connection: Writings from the Stone Center* (pp. 162-180). New York: Guilford.

Tannen, D. (1990). *You just don't understand.* New York: Ballantine.

Tatum, B. D. (1992). Talking about race, learning about racism: The application of racial identity development theory in the classroom. *Harvard Educational Review, 62*(1), 1-24.

Tatum, B. D. (1994). Teaching White students about racism: The search for White allies and the restoration of hope. *Teachers College Record, 95*(4), 462-476.

Tatum, B. D. (1997). *"Why are all the Black kids sitting together in the cafeteria?"*
and other conversations about race. New York: Basic Books.

Terry, R. (1978). White belief, moral reasoning, self-interest and racism. In
W. W. Schroeder & F. Winter (Eds.), *Belief and ethics* (pp. 349-374). Chicago: Center for the Scientific Study of Religion.

Terry, R. (1981). The negative impact on White values. In B. Bowser & R.
Hunt (Eds.), *Impacts of racism of White Americans* (1st ed., pp. 119-151).
Beverly Hills, CA: Sage.

Thompson, C. (1992). On being heterosexual in a homophobic world. In W.
Blumenfeld (Ed.), *Homophobia: How we all pay the price* (pp. 235-248).
Boston: Beacon.

Thompson, C., & Campaign to End Homophobia. (1990). *A guide to leading*
introductory workshops on homophobia. Cambridge, MA: Campaign to
End Homophobia.

Tyler, T. R., Boeckmann, R. J., Smith, H. J., & Huo, Y. J. (1997). *Social justice in*
a diverse society. Boulder, CO: Westview.

Viadro, D. (1996, April 10). Culture clash. *Education Week,* pp. 39-42.

Wachtel, P. (1989). *The poverty of affluence: A psychological portrait of American*
way of life. Philadelphia: New Society.

Wellman, D. (1977). *Portraits of White racism.* New York: Cambridge
University Press.

Wildman, S. (1996). *Privilege revealed.* New York: New York University Press.

Williams, M. K., Dunlap, M. R., & McCandies, T. (1999). Keepin' it real:
Three Black women educators discuss how we deal with student resis-
tance to multicultural inclusion in the curriculum. *Transformations: The*
New Jersey Project Journal, 10(2), 11-23.

Wineman, S. (1984). *The politics of human services.* Boston: South End.

Wolff, E. (1998). Recent trends in the size distribution of household wealth.
Journal of Economic Perspectives, 12(3), 131-150.

Wright, S. D., Taylor, D. M., & Moghaddam, F. M. (1990). The relationship of
perceptions and emotions to behavior in the face of collective inequality. *Social Justice Research, 4,* 229-250.

Young, I. (1990). *Justice and the politics of difference.* Princeton, NJ: Princeton
University Press.

Author Index

Subject Index

Able-bodied people:
 privileges, 22, 26-27
 See also Privileged group members
Ableism, 10, 62
 See also Oppression
Acceptance stage of social identity
  development, 54-55, 72, 172-173
Achebe, Chinua, 126
Activism. *See* Prosocial activism
Advertising, 92
Affirmative action, 156, 159
African Americans. *See* Blacks; Racism
Ageism, 10
 See also Oppression
Allies:
 motives and qualities, 164
 See also Prosocial activism
Altruism:
 as motive for action, 130
 distinction from social activism, 128
Americans with Disabilities Act, 7
Anti-Semitism, 10, 89
Appropriation, paradox of, 146
Authenticity, 122-123

Beauty, 14
Bias. *See* Prejudices
Blacks:
 middle- and upper-class, 23, 31-32
 See also Racism; Subordinate groups
Breathing, conscious, 183
Buddhist meditation, 185-186
Business:
 dominant culture in, 17
 mission statements and goals, 93

Care. *See* Morality of care
Change:
 fear of, 74-75
 need for, 205-209
 resistance to, 208
Christianity, 18
Class privileges, 21-22, 31
Classism, 10
 costs of, 105
 reactions to education about, 11, 62
 See also Oppression
Cognitive dissonance, 73-74

About the Author

Diane J. Goodman, EdD, has taught at several universities in the areas of education, psychology, and women's studies. As a trainer and consultant, she has worked with a range of organizations and schools on diversity and social justice issues, sexual harassment, conflict resolution, and intergroup relations. She currently lives in Nyack, New York.